University of Michigan Museum of Anthropology
Technical Report 22

Two Terminal Archaic/Early Woodland Sites in Central Michigan

by

Scott G. Beld

Ann Arbor
1991

Printed in the
United States of America

ISBN 0-915703-27-0

The paper used in this publication meets the requirements of the
ANSI Standard Z39.48-1984 (Permanence of Paper)

CONTENTS

TABLES

FIGURES

ACKNOWLEDGMENTS

The excavations and analysis of 20GR176 and 20GR33 were funded, in part, through a grant from the U.S. Department of the Interior, National Park Service (under provisions of the National Historic Preservation Act of 1966, as amended) through the Michigan Department of State. However, the contents and opinions herein do not necessarily reflect the views or policies of the Department of the Interior. The excavations described here have been the subject of previous reports to the Bureau of History, Michigan Department of State.

We would like to express our gratitude to the landowners, Howard Mills (20GR176) and the City of Alma (20GR33). Their support and interest in the sites and our work is greatly appreciated.

The excavations were conducted as part of Alma College's local archaeology program. Those at 20GR33 were directed by J. Tracy Luke (1977-1985) and the author (co-director, 1983-1985) and were supervised by Caven Clark (1977-1978) and the author (1979-1981). The excavations at 20GR176 were co-directed by Tracy Luke and the author.

The late Ronald O. Kapp (Alma College), William Lovis (Michigan State University), Michael Shott (University of Northern Iowa), and Henry Wright (University of Michigan) read earlier drafts of this report and offered many useful comments.

The contributions of Donald Simons (Michigan Archaeological Society) are perhaps apparent from the references to his unpublished manuscript in the text. Less apparent is the benefit the author derived from the sometimes lively discussions while working on his Paleo-Indian Gainey site project.

Finally, Tracy Luke (Alma College) deserves special thanks. He is largely responsible for the existence of Alma College's local archaeology program and without his support and encouragement the present study would not have been possible.

Scott G. Beld
Alma College
August 30, 1991

PART 1

SITE 20GR176, GRATIOT COUNTY, MICHIGAN

Introduction

Site 20GR176 is located on the southwest end of a low beach ridge of pro-glacial Lake Warren (207 m above sea level) about three kilometers northeast of Ashley, Michigan (Figure 1). The ridge on which the site is located extends about eight kilometers to the northeast. Government land surveyor records indicate an alder and tamarack swamp around this ridge in the early nineteenth century. The site is currently located in a woods which has never been plowed. A pond was excavated about 30 m north of the site in the mid-1970s and the sand removed was used for road construction.

The site consists of two or three small clusters of cultural material spread over an area 36.5 m (SW/NE) by 9 m (NW/SE) (Figure 2). In 1981 and 1985, 100 m^2 were excavated by field crews from Alma College.

Stratigraphy

The stratigraphy consisted of a layer of black humus 6 to 12 cm thick which was usually sterile or contained very little cultural material. Below the humus was a discontinuous layer of gray sand (10YR-7/1) which extended to about 30 cm below the surface and contained most of the cultural material. Below this was a layer of orange sand (10YR5/8) often with areas of iron cemented sand.

Features

Three features were noted in the course of excavations. All three were located in Cluster 1.

Feature 1 was a black and gray (7.5YR2/0 and 10YR4/3) organic stain 73 cm by 82 cm and 12 cm deep in unit 485N790E. This feature contained 40 flakes (31 of Bayport chert and 9 of pebble cherts) but no fire-cracked rock. Charcoal from the feature yielded a C-13 corrected C-14 date of 2330 ± 80 b.p. (Beta-13467, 380 b.c., calibrated 399 B.C.).

Feature 2 was a concentration of fire-cracked rock to the southeast of and adjacent to Feature 1 in unit 485N790E measuring 55 cm in diameter and 6 cm deep. This feature contained 15.4 kg of fire-cracked rock. The feature contained no charcoal.

Feature 3 was a concentration of fire-cracked rock at the corner of units 470N795E, 470N800E, 475N-795E, and 475N800E measuring 46 cm in diameter and 12 cm deep. It contained 16.8 kg of fire-cracked rock. The feature contained no charcoal.

Waste Flakes

During excavation waste flakes were recovered from both 1/4" and 1/8" screens. Eighth-inch screens were used on 32.5 m^2 in an effort to recover small retouch flakes of exotic chert and 67.5 m^2 were sifted through a 1/4" screen. During analysis all of the flakes from the site were placed on a 1/4" screen and separated.

A total of 454 flakes weighing 216.55 grams was recovered from the 1/4" screen. All of this was local cherts (Bayport, Charity Island/Norwood, and locally available pebble cherts).

A total of 2,513 flakes weighing 109.2 grams fell through the 1/4" screen. Of this, 97.5% was local cherts and 2.5% was exotic cherts.

Raw Materials. Bayport chert accounts for 74.7% of the flakes from the 1/4" screen and 74.0% of the flakes which fell through the 1/4" screen. This chert occurs in outcrops on either side of Saginaw Bay and on islands in Saginaw Bay (Figure 1). However, Bayport chert without cultural associations also occurs in the glacial till in Gratiot County. Because of the small size of most of the flakes from the site and the similarity between some of the local pebble cherts and Bayport chert, the distinction between them is somewhat arbitrary for the flakes from 20GR176.

Pebble cherts account for 24.0% of the flakes from the 1/4" screen and 23.0% of the flakes which fell through the 1/4" screen.

Charity Island/Norwood chert accounts for 1.3% of the flakes from the 1/4" screen and 0.5% of the flakes which fell through the 1/4" screen. Both of these cherts are banded and some varieties can be distinguished from each other. A source of Charity Island chert occurs on Charity Island in Saginaw Bay (information and samples supplied by Don Simons).

Onondaga chert accounts for 0.3% of the flakes from the 1/8" screen. Outcrops of this chert occur in eastern Ontario and western New York, though it is also found in glacial deposits south of Lake Erie.

Flint Ridge chert accounts for 1.2% of the flakes from the 1/8" screen. Sources of this chert are located in southern Ohio.

A glossy light brown exotic chert accounts for 0.8% of the flakes from the 1/8" screen. The source of this chert is unknown.

Other unidentified exotic cherts account for 0.2% of the flakes from the 1/8" screen.

In addition to the chert flakes, 56 quartzite flakes were recovered from the 1/4" screen in Cluster 1.

Description. Counts and weights of the flakes from the site are given in Tables 1-5. Figure 3 shows the distribution of the flakes on the site. The categories used in the flake analysis are those defined by Krakker (1984:98). While flakes from all stages of manufacture except cortex striking platforms are represented, small ridged striking platform flakes, indicating bifacial retouch, dominate the sample: 28.2% (or 59.6% if flake fragments are excluded).

Lithic Artifacts

Projectile Points (Descriptions follow Binford 1963c).

Dustin Points (Figure 4, Table 6). This projectile point type has been discussed by a number of authors (including Harrison 1966; Ozker 1976; Wright and Morlan 1964). These points have been defined as narrow-blade expanding stem or side-notched points with characteristic lamellar and contracting flake scars which form a ridge on one face. They generally have triangular or diamond shaped transverse sections and often have unifacial flaking and unfinished bases.

Six Dustin points were recovered from 20GR176 (3 from Cluster 1 and 3 from Cluster 2) and form the most numerous point type on the site. Unmodified bases occur on 60% (3 of 5) and 66.7% (4 of 6) are "unifacial" with the original surface of the flake preserved and only edge retouch on one face. All are made of Bayport chert or local pebble cherts.

Corner-notched or Expanding Stem Point (Figure 5A, Table 6). This category is represented by one point blade made of Bayport chert from Cluster 2. It has a broad, ovate blade with lens shaped cross sections.

Meadowood Point (Figure 5D, Table 6). This point type was defined by Ritchie (1971: 35-36 and Plate 17) and will be discussed in more detail in Part 2. One fragment of the base of a Meadowood point made of Onondaga chert was recovered from Cluster 1.

Side-notched Point (Figure 5C, Table 6). This point is made of a pebble (?) chert and is heavily patinated and iron stained. The base is irregular and ground and the blade is serrated and heavily reworked. This point is similar to small serrated side-notched points recovered from the Middle Archaic levels of the Weber I site near Frankenmuth. The levels from which these points were recovered have been C-14 dated from 6230 to 4560 b.p. (Robertson 1989:83). The heavy patination and iron staining of the 20GR176 specimen sets it apart from the rest of the assemblage and indicates a probable earlier date for this point.

Miscellaneous Points. One projectile point blade (#80) of Bayport chert broken in the hafting element (Figure 5B, Table 6) and a fragment of the base of a side-notched point made of Bayport chert were recovered from Cluster 1 (Figure 5E, Table 6).

Projectile Point Tip (Figure 5F). One projectile point tip made of Bayport chert was recovered from Cluster 1.

Miscellaneous Bifaces and Biface Fragments. Fifteen other bifaces and fragments were recovered from Cluster 1 (Figure 6). Eight are made of Bayport chert, six of pebble chert, and one of Charity Island/Norwood chert.

Three bifaces were recovered from Cluster 2. Two are made from pebble cherts and one from Bayport chert.

One biface fragment of Bayport chert was recovered from Cluster 3.

Unifaces/Utilized Flakes. Eight unifaces/utilized flakes were recovered on the site. One endscraper of Flint Ridge chert (Figure 7E) and two bit fragments of Bayport chert were recovered from Cluster 1. Two utilized flakes were recovered from Cluster 1 (1 of Bayport chert - retouch on lateral edge and 1 of pebble chert - retouch on distal end), two from Cluster 2 (1 of Bayport chert - retouch on lateral edge and one of pebble chert - retouch on distal end), and one from Cluster 3 (Bayport chert with outer cortex - retouch on lateral edge and distal end).

Bipolar Cores (Figure 7A-D, Table 7). Four bipolar cores were recovered from Cluster 1. Three are made of pebble cherts and one is made of Bayport chert.

Quartzite Artifacts. In addition to the quartzite flakage described above, three quartzite tools were recovered. Two "choppers," one from Cluster 1 and one from Cluster 2, and one "scraper" from Cluster 1.

Gorget. One slate gorget fragment was recovered in Cluster 1.

Bead. One reddish-brown polished cylindrical stone bead (not catlinite) with a hole drilled from both ends was recovered from Cluster 1. Metrics: 1.08 cm by 1.16 cm, 0.70 cm thick, diameter of hole 0.64 cm.

Ceramics

No pottery was recovered from the site.

Radiocarbon Date

One sample of wood charcoal weighing 5.0 grams from Feature #1 was submitted for radiocarbon dating. This sample yielded a C-13 corrected C-14 date of 2330 ± 80 b.p. (Beta-13467, 380 b.c.). This date calibrates to 399 B.C., one sigma range 481-364 B.C., two sigma range 762-210 B.C. (Stuiver and Becker 1986).

Discussion

20GR176 is a small site measuring about 36.5 m by 9 m which is divided into two or three small clusters of cultural material. The complete lack of faunal and floral remains does not allow the identification of the season of occupation. However, the dominance of projectile points and resharpening flakes in the assemblage indicate that 20GR176 was probably a briefly occupied hunting camp where projectiles were refurbished and other camp activities performed.

When viewed within existing typologies and chronological reconstructions developed for the Saginaw Valley of Michigan, the cultural affiliation of this site presents some problems. Dustin points are the dominant projectile point type on the site (6 examples). These points together with Feeheley points have been considered to date to the Late Archaic period (c. 2000-1500 B.C.) (Harrison 1966; Keene 1979; Ozker 1976; Taggart 1967; Wright and Morlan 1964). One Meadowood point of Onondaga chert was also recovered. Meadowood points have been firmly dated to the middle of the first millennium B.C. at three sites in Michigan, i.e. 20GR33 (see below), Schultz (Speth 1972:61; Ozker 1982), and Green Point (Wright 1964), and to the first half of the first millennium B.C. in New York state (Granger 1978) and Ontario (Spence and Fox 1986).

While the occurrence of "Late Archaic" Dustin points and Terminal Archaic/Early Woodland Meadowood points may indicate two occupations, Dustin points have never been firmly dated and questions have been raised as to their use as chronological markers (Fitting 1975:71-72). The chronological placement of Dustin points was based on the dating and stratigraphy of the Schmidt and Feeheley sites. Recently, Lovis and Robertson (1989) have reevaluated Late Archaic chronology and the dating of the Schmidt site and found that the beach ridge on which the site is located is actually three feet lower than previously described (i.e. Harrison 1966; Fairchild 1977). They argue that the site was primarily post-Nipissing as opposed to Nipissing. They also suggest comparison with Merom and Trimble types from Illinois (Winters 1969) and consider Dustin points "... the Michigan representatives of a pan-regional small point horizon dating between 3000 b.p. and 3500 b.p. in the Midwest and Ontario" though they note later dates from Weber I (near Frankenmuth, Michigan) and Preston Rockshelter (Wisconsin) for similar forms (Lovis and Robertson 1989:13; cf. Spence and Fox 1986:6-11).

In western Michigan, Garland (1986:73, 75) has noted the predominance of notched and expanding stem points (as opposed to stemmed points) within the Terminal Archaic to Middle Woodland time span.

In northwestern Ohio, Stothers (1975) has reported a date of 2730 ± 150 b.p. (calibrated 895/867/839 B.C., Stuiver and Becker 1986) for points with a distinct medial ridge which closely resemble Dustin points (Stothers 1975:Plate 1, Fig. 1 and 2). It may be noted that a point which falls within the range of metrics for Meadowood points also occurs with them (Stothers 1975: Plate 1, Fig. 3) and what appear to be two bifacial trianguloid end scrapers (Stothers 1975: Plate 1, Fig. 4 and 5, described as "bulbous based drills or borers" in the text p. 6) were recovered.

In New York Granger (1978:117, 274) has shown that Lamoka, subtype B, points (i.e. Dustin points) "...were directly associated with Meadowood points in a homogeneous cultural context" at the Sinking Ponds site.

This recent research is showing that narrow-blade, notched and expanding-stem points span a rather long period of time and should not be used as phase / period markers in central Michigan without further C-14 dates from other sites. It is likely that the C-14 date from 20GR176 would fall within a series of dates for this point style.

TABLE 1

20GR176, CLUSTER 1, WASTE FLAKES (1/4" SCREEN)

Chert Type	Cortex# Wt.	Flat #	Flat Wt.	Ridged #	Ridged Wt.	Battered #	Battered Wt.	Fragments #	Fragments Wt.	Shatter #	Shatter Wt.	TOTAL #	TOTAL Wt.
Bayport	-- --	23	13.1g	56	9.8g	18	5.2g	84	20.7g	3	2.0g	179	50.8g
w/ outer cortex	-- --	6	11.5g	--	--	1	1.7g	7	9.8g	1	8.1g	15	31.1g
w/ cortex	-- --	20	8.3g	8	2.2g	2	1.9g	18	4.6g	1	0.2g	49	17.2g
cortex	-- --	6	3.0g	6	1.7g	1	1.5g	7	1.4g	--	--	20	7.6g
HM (pink)	-- --	2	2.6g	--	--	--	--	2	0.3g	--	--	4	2.9g
w/ cortex	-- --	--	--	2	0.2g	--	--	--	--	--	--	2	0.2g
cortex	-- --	--	--	--	--	--	--	1	0.1g	--	--	1	0.1g
HM (potlid)	-- --	2	2.7g	--	--	--	--	--	--	--	--	2	2.7g
Dark (HM)	-- --	4	0.7g	5	0.5g	--	--	8	2.0g	--	--	17	3.2g
w/ cortex	-- --	1	0.8g	--	--	--	--	1	0.2g	--	--	2	1.0g
Total - Bpt.	-- --	64	42.7g	79	14.4g	22	10.3g	128	39.1g	5	10.3g	298	116.8g
Charity Island	-- --	2	2.6g	--	--	--	--	2	0.8g	1	2.1g	5	5.5g
Pebble	-- --	29	12.7g	10	1.8g	7	1.8g	40	11.8g	21	20.5g	107	48.6g
Quartzite	-- --	1	0.3g	--	--	1	0.2g	40	36.6g	14	22.1g	56	39.2g
TOTAL*	-- --	95	58.0g	89	16.2g	29	12.1g	170	51.7g	27	32.9g	410	170.9g

*Not including Quartzite.

TABLE 2

20GR176, CLUSTER 1, WASTE FLAKES (1/8" SCREEN)

Chert Type	Cortex #	Cortex Wt.	Flat #	Flat Wt.	Ridged #	Ridged Wt.	Battered #	Battered Wt.	Fragment #	Fragment Wt.	Shatter #	Shatter Wt.	TOTAL #	TOTAL Wt.
Bayport	--	--	54	2.8g	319	14.9g	31	1.3g	560	18.3g	6	0.9g	985	38.2g
w/ outer cortex	--	--	--	--	--	--	--	--	1	0.2g	--	--	1	0.2g
w/ cortex	--	--	11	0.9g	73	3.9g	7	0.3g	131	5.0g	2	0.4g	224	10.5g
cortex	--	--	13	1.0g	28	1.1g	5	0.4g	114	4.4g	2	0.2g	162	7.1g
HM (pink)	--	--	1	0.2g	8	0.6g	1	0.1g	16	1.0g	--	--	26	1.9g
w/ cortex	--	--	1	0.1g	1	0.1g	1	0.1g	1	0.1g	--	--	4	0.4g
cortex	--	--	1	0.1g	--	--	--	--	2	0.2g	--	--	3	0.3g
HM (potlid)	--	--	--	--	--	--	--	--	13	0.9g	--	--	13	0.9g
Dark (HM)	--	--	17	1.3g	116	5.4g	10	0.6g	155	5.3g	--	--	298	12.6g
w/ cortex	--	--	3	0.2g	11	0.8g	1	0.1g	33	1.6g	--	--	48	2.7g
Total - Bpt.			101	6.6g	556	26.8g	71	2.9g	1026	37.0g	10	1.5g	1764	74.8g
Charity Island	--	--	2	0.2g	8	0.5g	--	--	3	0.3g	--	--	13	1.0g
Pebble	--	--	59	3.2g	101	5.4g	32	1.6g	367	12.2g	19	2.1g	578	24.5g
Onondaga	--	--	1	0.1g	5	0.3g	1	0.1g	--	--	--	--	7	0.5g
Flint Ridge	--	--	1	0.1g	12	0.7g	--	--	17	1.7g	--	--	30	2.5g
Exotic - glossy brown	--	--	4	0.2g	7	0.3g	--	--	9	0.6g	--	--	20	1.1g

TABLE 2 (CONTINUED)

Chert Type	Cortex #	Cortex Wt.	Flat #	Flat Wt.	Ridged #	Ridged Wt.	Battered #	Battered Wt.	Fragment #	Fragment Wt.	Shatter #	Shatter Wt.	TOTAL #	TOTAL Wt.
Exotic - unident.	--	--	--	--	4	0.2g	--	--	1	0.1g	--	--	5	0.3g
TOTAL			168	10.4g	693	34.2g	104	4.6g	1352	51.9g	29	3.6g	2417	104.7g

TABLE 3

20GR176, CLUSTER 2, WASTE FLAKES (1/4" SCREEN)

Chert Type	Cortex #	Cortex Wt.	Flat #	Flat Wt.	Ridged #	Ridged Wt.	Battered #	Battered Wt.	Fragment #	Fragment Wt.	Shatter #	Shatter Wt.	TOTAL #	TOTAL Wt.
Bayport	--	--	2	0.4g	6	0.9g	4	1.6g	7	5.6g	2	8.2g	21	16.7g
w/ cortex	--	--	3	1.4g	3	0.4g	3	1.9g	--	--	--	--	9	3.7g
cortex	--	--	1	0.2g	--	--	--	--	1	0.1g	1	0.3g	3	0.6g
Dark (HM)	--	--	--	--	--	--	--	--	1	0.2g	--	--	1	0.2g
Total - Bpt.			6	2.0g	9	1.3g	7	3.5g	9	5.9g	3	8.5g	34	21.2g
Pebble	--	--	1	7.7	--	--	--	--	--	--	--	--	1	7.7g
TOTAL			7	9.2g	9	1.3g	7	3.5g	9	5.9g	3	8.5g	35	28.9g

TABLE 4

20GR176, CLUSTER 2, WASTE FLAKES (1/8" SCREEN)

Chert Type	Cortex		Flat		Ridged		Battered		Fragment		Shatter		TOTAL	
	#	Wt.	#	Wt.	#	Wt.	#	Wt.	#	Wt.	#	Wt.	#	Wt.
Bayport	--	--	1	0.1g	36	1.6g	7	0.4g	37	1.4g	--	--	81	3.5g
w/ cortex	--	--	4	0.3g	2	0.2g	--	--	3	0.2g	--	--	9	0.7g
cortex	--	--	--	--	5	0.3g	1	0.1g	--	--	--	--	6	0.4g
TOTAL			5	0.4g	43	2.1g	8	0.5g	40	1.6g			96	4.6g

TABLE 5

20GR176, CLUSTER 3, WASTE FLAKES (1/4" SCREEN)

Chert Type	Cortex #	Cortex Wt.	Flat #	Flat Wt.	Ridged #	Ridged Wt.	Battered #	Battered Wt.	Fragment #	Fragment Wt.	Shatter #	Shatter Wt.	TOTAL #	TOTAL Wt.
Bayport	--	--	--	--	2	4.2g	--	--	1	0.6g	--	--	3	4.8g
w/ outer cortex	--	--	1	7.2g	--	--	--	--	--	--	--	--	1	7.2g
w/ cortex	--	--	--	--	--	--	--	--	1	0.3g	1	1.9g	2	2.2g
HM (potlid)	--	--	--	--	--	--	--	--	1	0.3g	--	--	1	0.3g
Total - Bpt.			1	7.2g	2	4.2g			3	1.2g	1	1.9g	7	14.5g
Charity Island	--	--	--	--	--	--	--	--	1	0.9g	--	--	1	0.9g
Pebble	--	--	--	--	--	--	--	--	--	--	1	1.2g	1	1.2g
TOTAL			1	7.2g	2	4.2g			4	2.1g	2	3.1g	9	16.6g

TABLE 6

20GR176 PROJECTILE POINT METRICS

(in Centimeters)

#	Width: Base	Width: Tang	Width: Shoulder	Length: Axis	Length: Tang	Length: Notch	Thickness	Chert
Dustin Points								
30	1.44	1.29	1.86	(3.31)	1.11	0.69/0.69	0.75	Pebble
33	1.23	0.98	1.58	3.33	0.99	0.64/0.71	0.67	Bayport
34	1.21	0.87	1.66	3.07	1.15	0.55/0.65	0.54	Bayport
52	--	--	1.67	(3.94)	--	--	0.75	Bayport
75	1.15	0.87	1.35	2.98	1.08	0.76/0.55	0.64	Peeble
76	--	0.90	1.46	(3.14)	--	--	0.67	Bayport
Corner-notched / Expanding Stem								
32	--	1.24	2.95	(3.88)	--	--	0.73	Bayport
Meadowood Point								
79	(1.60)	--	--	(0.67)	--	--	(0.41)	Onondaga
Side-Notched Point								
	1.82	1.10	1.77	2.69	1.02	0.92/0.83	0.63	Bayport

TABLE 6 (CONTINUED)

	Width			Length				
#	Base	Tang	Shoulder	Axis	Tang	Notch	Thickness	Chert
Miscellaneous Points								
80	--	1.43	2.27	(3.35)	--	--	0.65	Bayport
	(0.92)	--	--	(0.90)	--	--	(0.37)	Bayport

() Broken Attribute.

TABLE 7

20GR176 BIPOLAR CORE METRICS

(in Centimeters)

#	Length	Width	Thickness	Chert Type
81	2.57	1.86	0.76	Pebble
82	2.22	1.98	0.98	Pebble
83	2.05	1.67	0.87	Pebble
--	2.46	1.34	0.68	Bayport

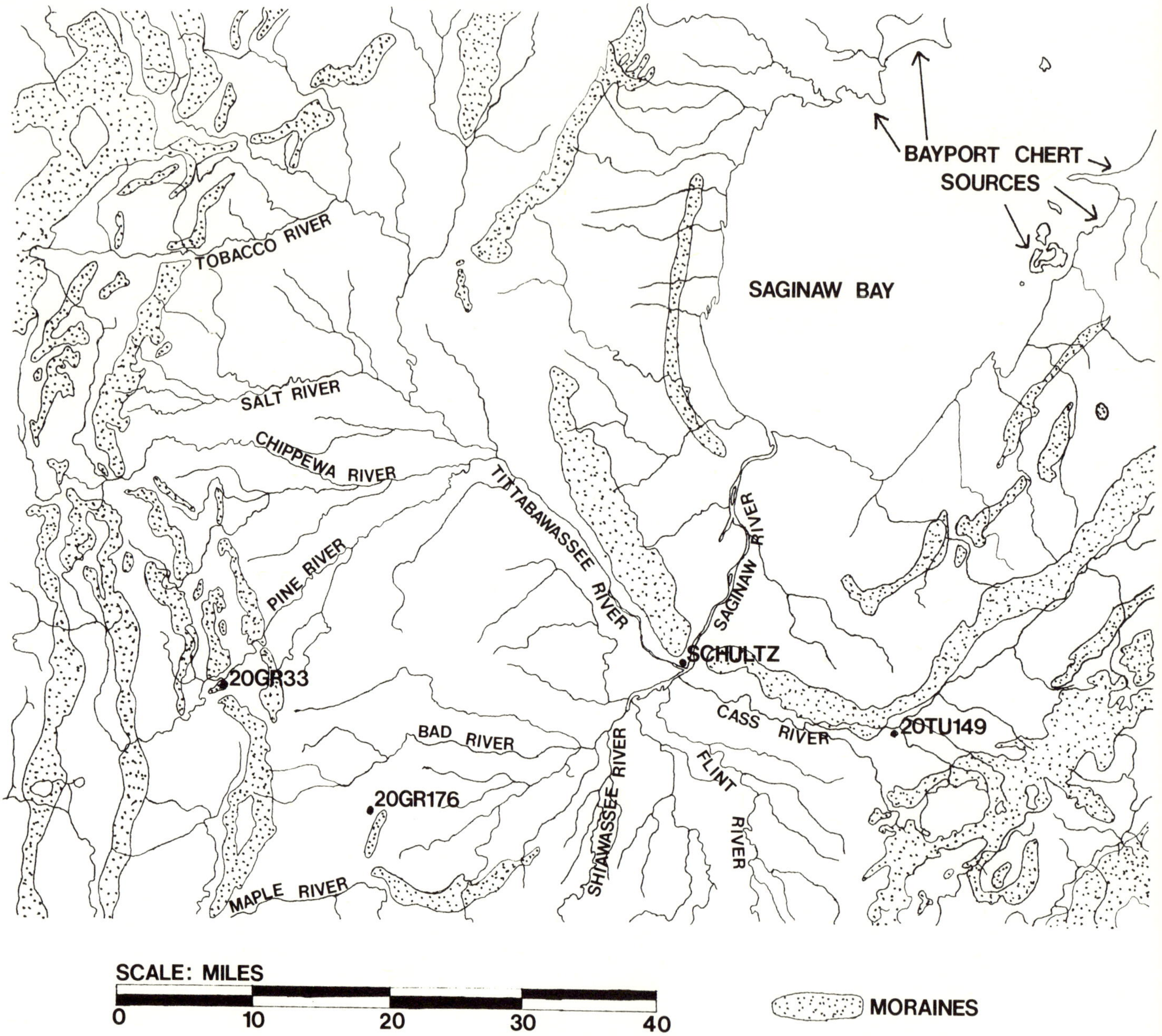

NORTHERN AND CENTRAL
SAGINAW RIVER DRAINAGE

FIGURE 1

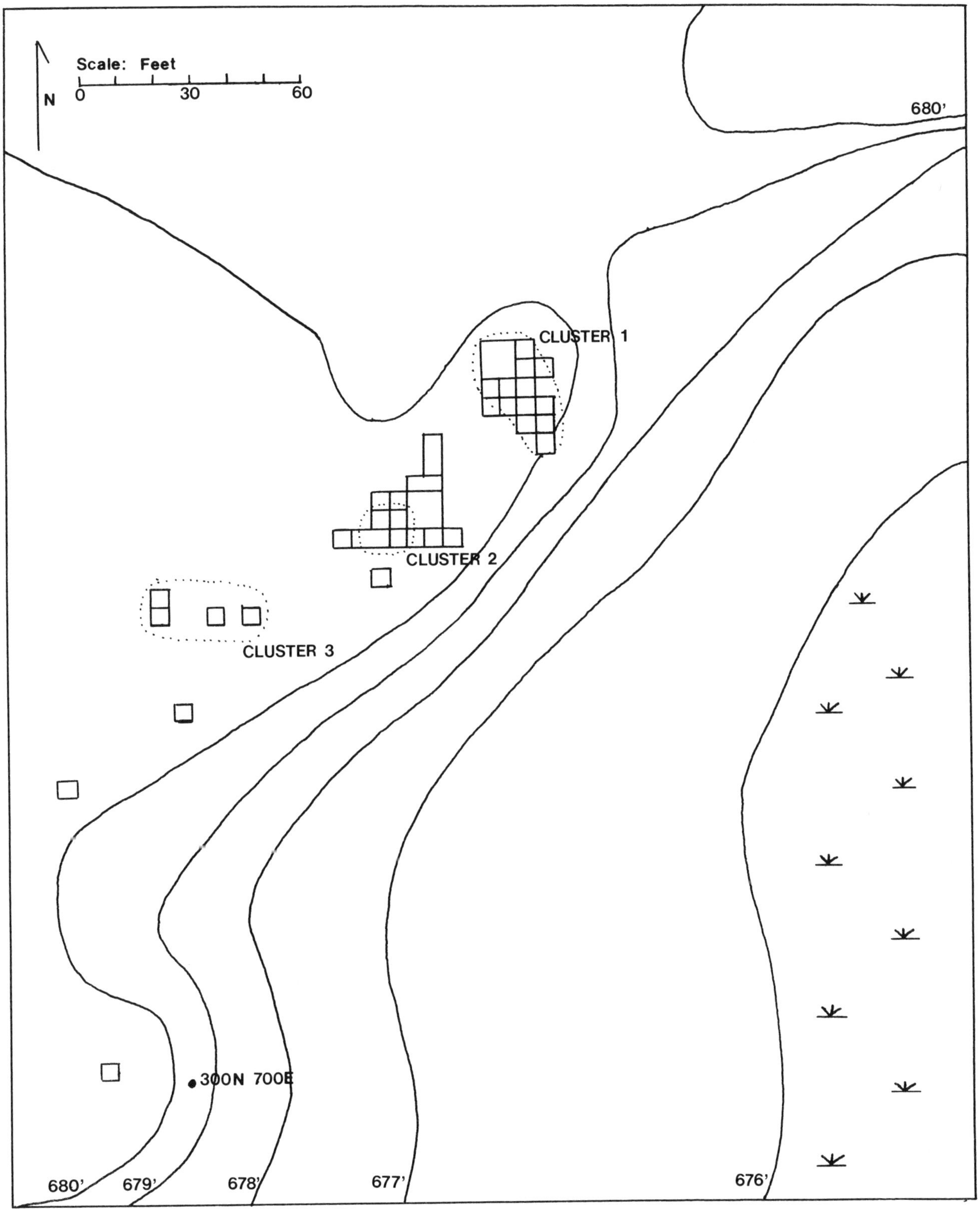

20 GR 176, MILLS 2

FIGURE 2

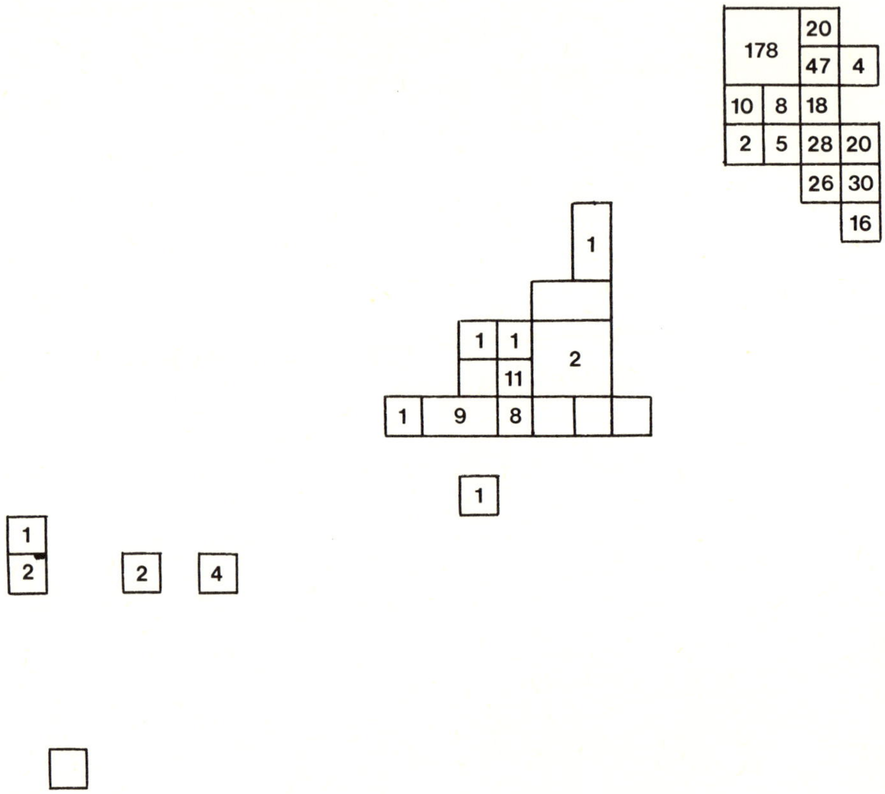

20 GR 176
Flakes/Unit
1/4" Screen

FIGURE 3

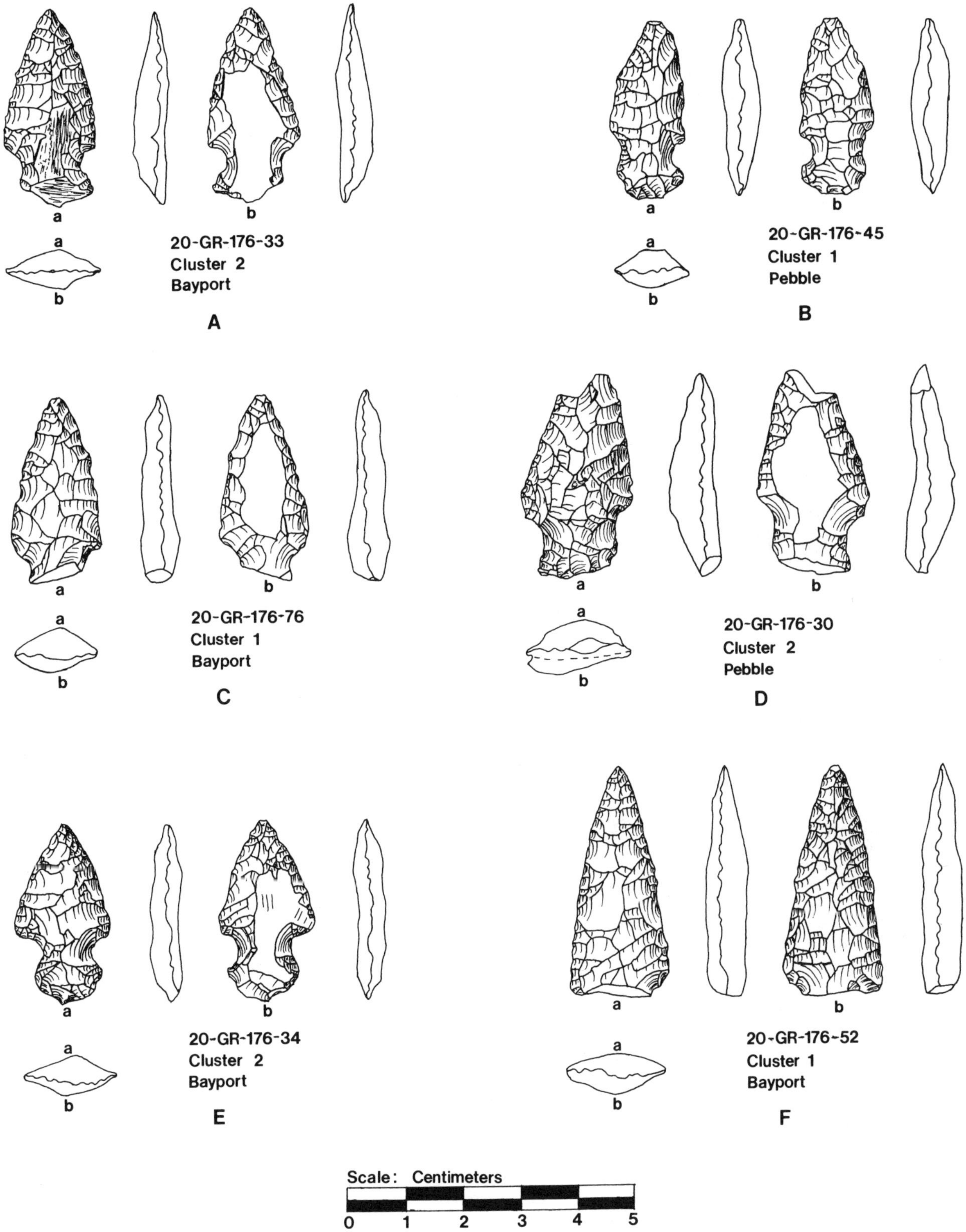

DUSTIN POINTS

FIGURE 4

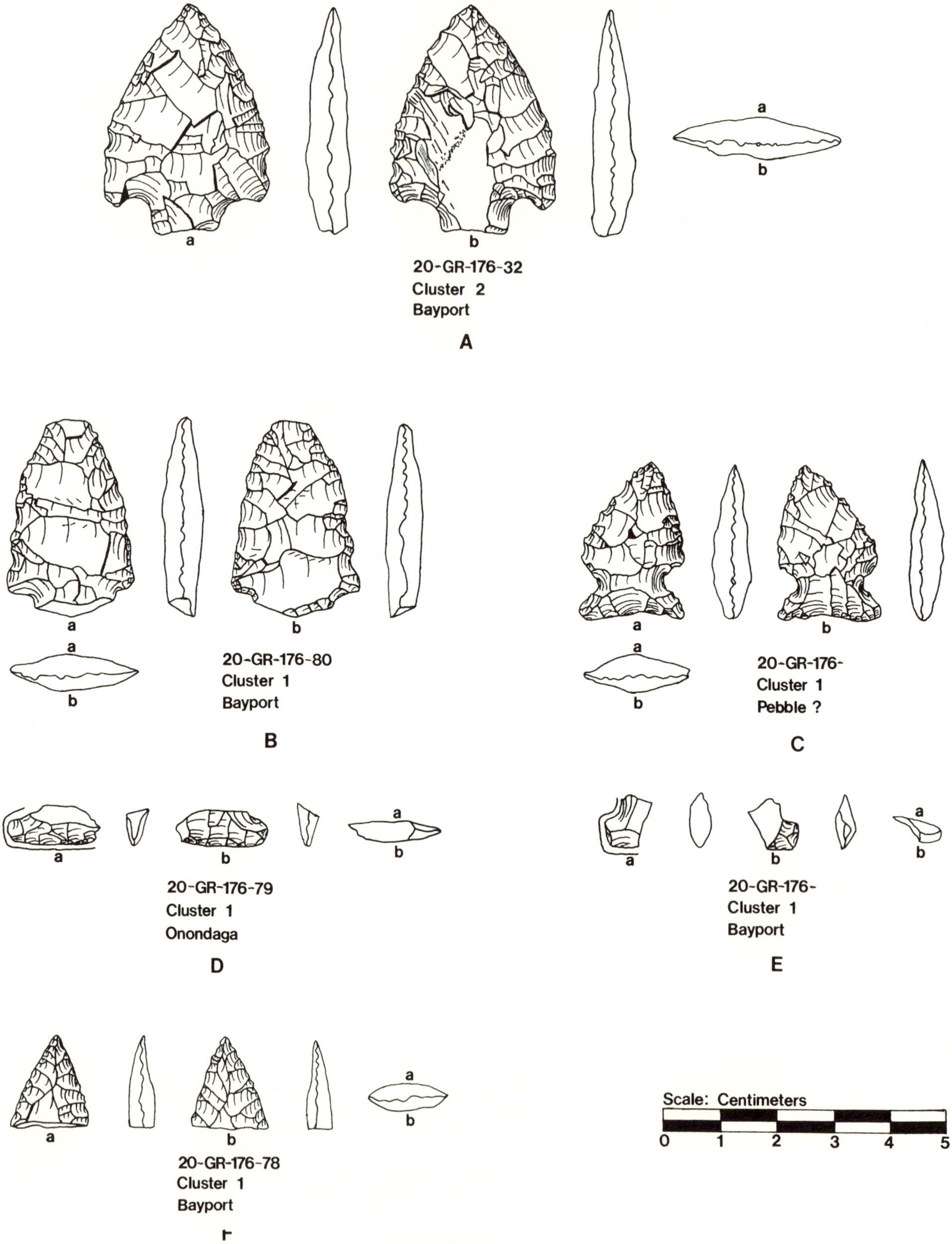

MISCELLANEOUS POINTS

FIGURE 5

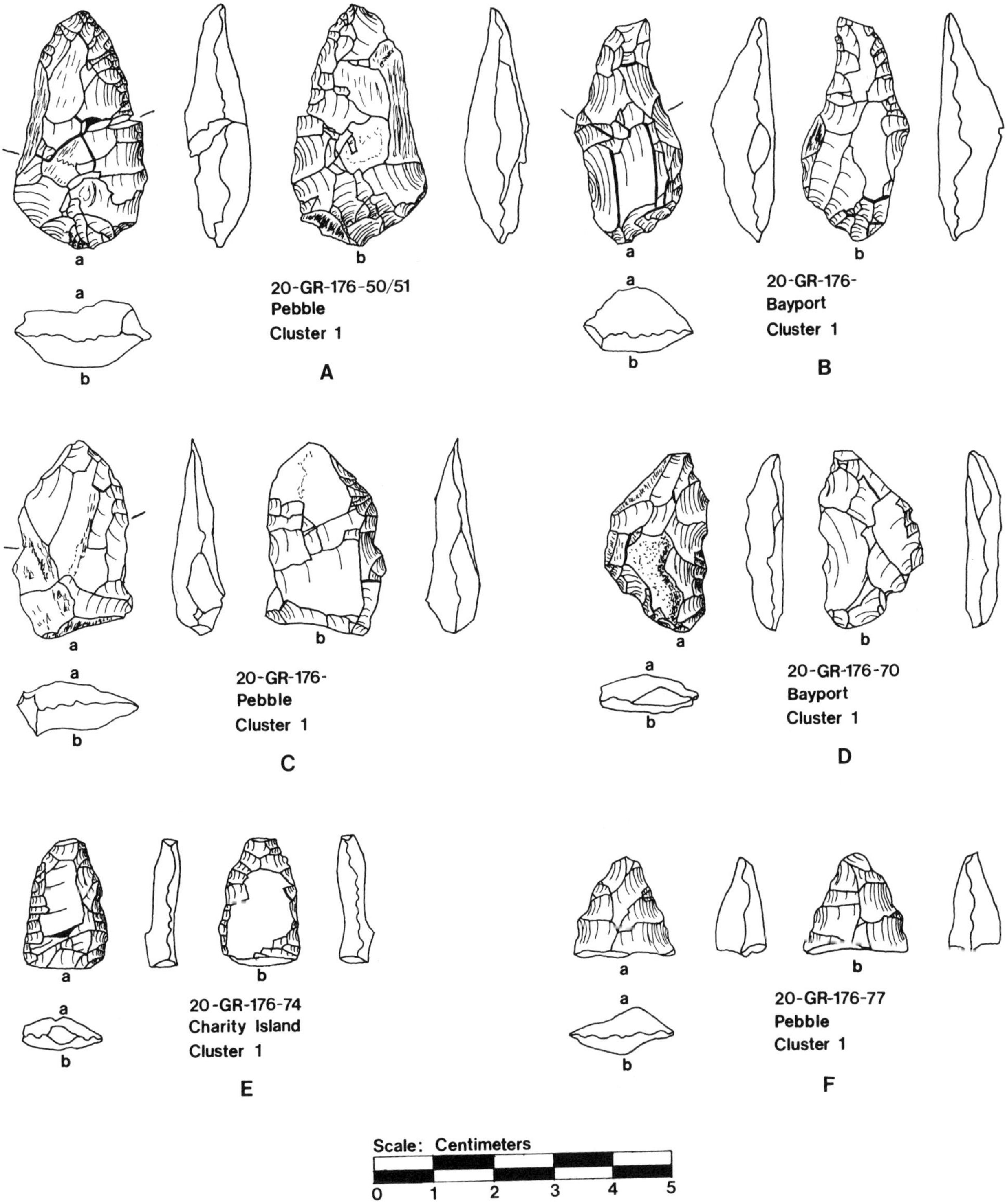

BIFACES

FIGURE 6

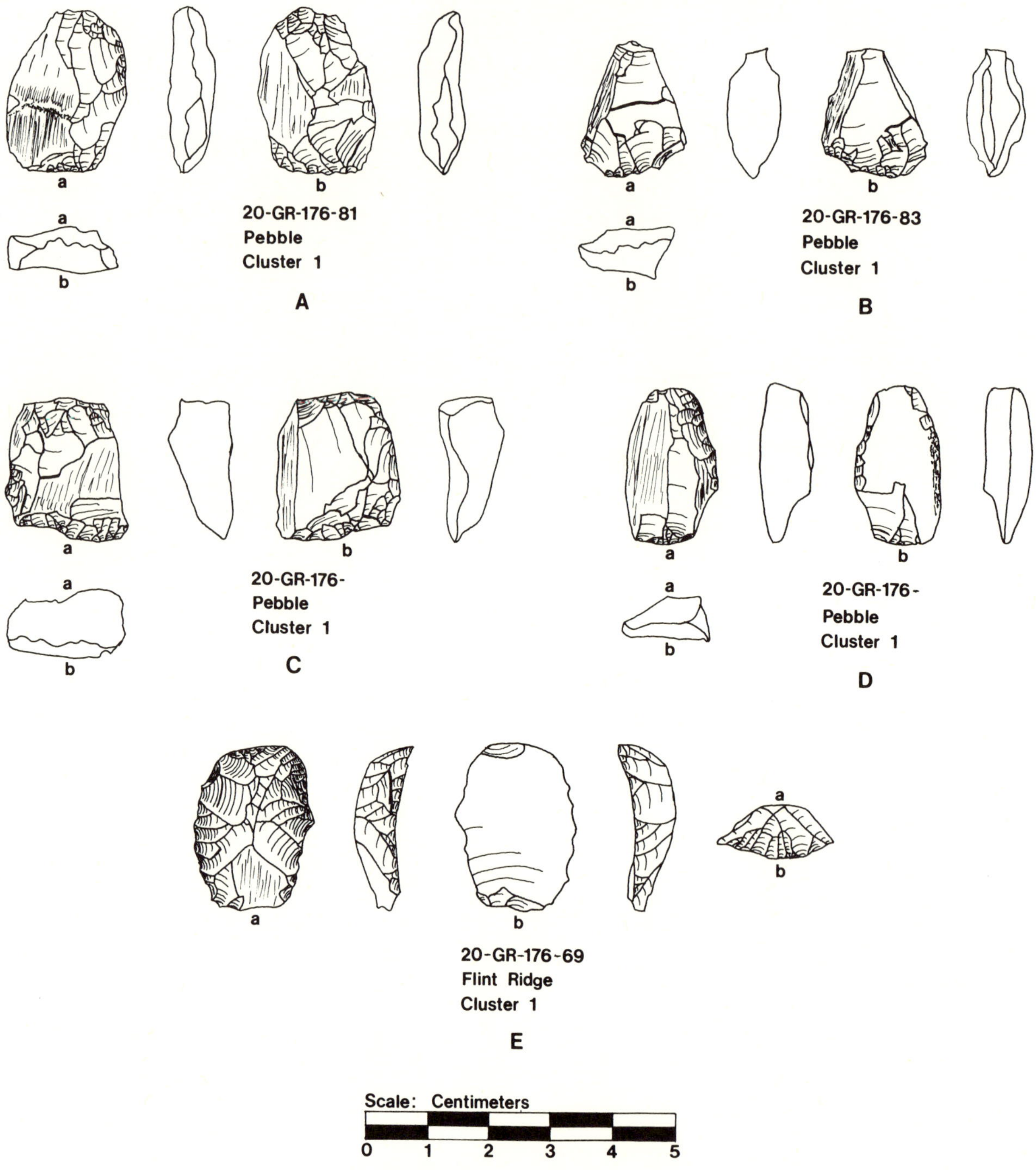

BIPOLAR CORES AND UNIFACES

FIGURE 7

PART 2

SITE 20GR33, GRATIOT COUNTY, MICHIGAN

Introduction

Site 20GR33 lies on well drained sandy soil along the Pine River in the City of Alma, Michigan (Figures 1, 8). The site was discovered in the summer of 1976 by archaeologists from Alma College who found fire-cracked rock in road construction at the south end of the site and fire-cracked rock and chippage eroding from the bank of the Pine River. A total of 441.8 square meters was excavated by field crews from Alma College between 1977-1981 and 1983-1985 (Figures 2, 3-5) and Terminal Archaic/Early Woodland material was recovered from an area of about 0.6 hectares.

The site is bounded on the north by the Pine River and on the east by a small swamp with an intermittent stream. The site is located on a terrace about 2 to 3 m above the Pine River Mill Pond at a point where the river cuts through a glacial moraine. The western edge of pro-glacial Lake Saginaw was located about 7.5 km east of the site. The glacial features east of this are lake plain and beach ridges formed by the various stages of the pro-glacial Great Lakes. The glacial features around and to the west of the site are moraines, till and outwash plains and channels formed by the Saginaw Lobe of the Laurentide Ice Sheet (see Figure 1).

Examination of Government Land Survey records for Gratiot County indicates beech-mixed hardwoods and beech-sugar maple forests in the immediate site area with nearby areas of swamp forest during the nineteenth century. Areas of beech-pine-hardwood forest with abundant pine were located within 15 km to the west of the site and areas of sugar maple-basswood-birch forest were located within 15 km to the east (see Kapp 1978).

Stratigraphy

The soil on the site is designated as Plainfield loamy sand by the *Soil Survey of Gratiot County* (Feenstra 1979: plate 24). Figure 12 illustrates a typical unit profile. The first soil zone (A) is a dark grayish brown (10YR4/3) plow zone which usually extends about 30 cm below the surface but can be as shallow as 18 cm or as deep as 42 cm. The second zone (B1) is yellowish brown (10YR5/8). Most of the cultural material was found in the plow zone (A) or the top 6-9 cm of the B1 zone. Below the B1 zone are a zone (B2) of brownish yellow sand (10YR6/6) and a zone (C) of pale brown sand (10YR7/4). These two zones (B2 and C) were sterile except for an occasional small retouch flake apparently the result of animal burrowing.

Procedures

Excavation units were laid out in a grid measured

in feet (most units were 5' by 5'). Units were labeled by the distance from a datum point on the bank of the river to the southeast corner of the unit (i.e. 50S45E = 50' south and 45' east of datum). All excavation was conducted using shovels or trowels. The plow zone was removed as a unit and floors trowelled to identify features. Below the plow zone units were excavated in two tenths of a foot (0.2' = 6 cm) arbitrary levels. All dirt removed from units was sifted through 1/8" or 1/4" hardware cloth (see Figure 8). Cultural material was bagged, labeled, and returned to Alma College for cleaning and analysis.

Features were drawn and/or photographed and most were excavated. During excavation, one half of the feature was excavated and the profile drawn, then the second half of the feature was excavated. Soil from the features was placed in plastic bags for floatation and charcoal fragments were placed in aluminum foil for C-14 dating. Floatation samples were processed in 1984.

In the summer of 1978 a proton magnetometer was used on the site in an unsuccessful effort to locate fire-cracked rock features (Summerlee 1981).

Features

Forty-three features were noted during excavations. Data on the features is given in Tables 8-10 and the locations of the features are shown in Figures 9-11. All features were disturbed by rodent activity.

Features from Area I (Table 8; Figures 9, 10). Fourteen features were noted in Area I. Data from the first four features excavated (A-D) was inadequately recorded so only a very rough description is given in the table.

Two features (NN and QQ) were large pits. Both of these features were first noted by the presence of large numbers of flakes which continued to occur well into the B1 soil zone (cf. Figure 12). At the transition between the B1 and B2 zones, a soil stain (10YR6/4) was noted as Feature NN with numerous flakes coming from the stain. The soil stain and flakes continued to a depth of 90 cm below the surface. Only a small corner of Feature NN was excavated so its dimensions are uncertain. Feature QQ was only recognized by the numerous flakes which extended to a depth of about 80 cm below the surface and no soil stain was observed. The heavy flakage was distributed throughout two 5' by 5' units and the feature had a diameter of more than three meters.

One other pit (Feature H) was a gray soil stain which was sterile except for two fire-cracked rocks and seven small retouch flakes.

Feature O was a gray stain noted at the base of the plow zone and could possibly be a historic feature (the feature fill was the same color as the plow zone).

The rest of the features from Area I were fire-cracked rock features (A-G, P-R). With the exception of Feature R which was a concentration of fire-cracked rock without a soil stain, these were black and gray stains with variable amounts of fire-cracked rock (from a few pieces to 60 pounds) and measuring between 45 cm and 1.2 m in diameter and 10-35 cm deep.

In Area I the highest concentrations of cultural material were recovered in an area about 3-5 m around the features. Units beyond this distance were usually sterile.

Features from Area II (Table 9; Figure 10). Four features were noted in Area II and differed somewhat from those in Area I. These features had smaller quantities of fire-cracked rock than the features in Area I and with the exception of Feature I, were smaller. As in Area I, the largest concentrations of cultural material occurred in units with features.

Features from Area III (Table 10; Figure 11). Twenty-four features were noted in Area III. They were arranged in two rows forming a rough oval about 18 m long (NW-SE) by 7.5-9 m wide (NE-SW) (see Figure 11). It is possible that this patterning reflects the distribution of features within or around a structure, though no post molds were noted. A possible explanation for the lack of post molds may be that any holes for posts were not dug below (deeper than) the B1 soil zone (see Figure 12, i.e. c. 45 cm below the present surface). A situation similar to this was noted with features which had not had a fire in them or were not dug into the yellow sand (C zone). These features were leached out and were not identifiable in the B zone. Thus in the B1 zone (10YR5/8), Features NN and QQ could only be defined on the basis of the flakes in the feature fill. A similar situation was noted at site (20GR91) where similar soil conditions occur (Beld 1990:59-60).

Eleven of the features (J, K, S, T, V-X, Z, AA, CC, FF) were similar to the fire-cracked rock features of Area I though they generally did not contain as much F.C.R. Four features (U, Y, BB, DD) were similar to the features from Area II in their smaller size and lack of F.C.R. One feature (HH) was a deep pit similar to Feature H in Area I. Six features were not excavated due to time constraints and the redundant nature of the data expected from them.

Two features were noted outside the oval cluster. One (OO) was apparently a small Late Woodland feature which contained one sherd in the fill and the other (PP) was apparently a tree fall.

Features from the Exploratory Units. Feature MM was a black (7.5YR2/0) and brown (10YR4/6) stain along the east wall of unit 185S90E measuring 70 cm (NS) by 45+ cm (EW) and 21 cm deep. This feature was heavily disturbed by rodent activity and was first noted at the base of the plow zone. It contained 1.4 kg of fire-cracked rock.

Waste Flakes

During the excavation of 20GR33, waste flakes were recovered from 1/4" and 1/8" screens. 150.25 m^2 were excavated with a 1/8" screen in an attempt to recover small retouch flakes of exotic chert and 293.8 m^2 were sifted through a 1/4" screen. During analysis the flakes from units excavated with a 1/8" screen were placed on a 1/4" screen and separated. The categories used in the flake analysis were those defined by Krakker (1984:98).

A total of 9,900 flakes weighing 4,914.25 grams were recovered from the 1/4" screens. Of this, 99.4% was of local cherts (Bayport, Charity Island, and pebble cherts) and 0.6% was of exotic cherts (half of this, 0.3% was Onondaga chert).

A total of 5,441 flakes weighing 263.4 grams were recovered from the 1/8" screens. Of this, 95.6% was of local cherts and 4.4% was of exotic cherts (4.0% was Onondaga chert).

Raw Materials. The raw material types of the flakes include most of those described above for 20GR176 (i.e. Bayport, pebble, Charity Island/Norwood, Onondaga, Flint Ridge, and unidentified exotic cherts). Two additional chert types were recovered at 20GR33: 1) Indiana Hornstone/Wyandotte chert, sources of which are located in southern Indiana and Illinois, and 2) Pipe Creek chert, sources of which are located near Sandusky, Ohio (information and samples supplied by Don Simons, see Simons n.d.). Table 11 gives percentages of the various raw materials of the flakes.

Description. Counts and weights of the waste flakes are presented in Tables 12-19 and Figures 16-21 show the distribution of flakes on the site. The main excavations of the site have been divided into three areas (I-III, Figure 8). Area I includes most of the northern part of the site (Tables 12, 13), Area II the middle part (Table 14), and Area III the southern part (Tables 15, 16). Tables 17 and 18 present the flakes from exploratory units on the west and south edges of the site. And Table 19 presents flakes recovered from a unit and surface collected from the trail on the northern part of the site.

There is a relatively low density of waste flakes at 20GR33: 21.8 flakes/m^2 (38.6 in Area I, 24.7 in Area II, and 7.2 in Area III), though this is not as low as a number of small sites in the area (3.3 flakes/100 m^2 at Chodolak [Middle Woodland], 2.6 at Brown [early Late Woodland], and 0.9 at Holiday Park [Late Woodland - c. A.D. 1300]). This low density of chert on the site may be the result of short term occupations and/or the lack of dependable chert sources in the area (Bayport chert is the nearest dependable source, 110 km as the crow flies or 165-185 km by river and the shore of Saginaw Bay).

Bayport chert has the largest amount of flakes represented at the site (74.5%) followed by pebble cherts (24.8%). However, these figures are skewed by the relatively large amount of Bayport flakes from Area I. Area I had 84.7% Bayport chert (6410 flakes) and 12.0% pebble cherts (883 flakes), while Area II had 30.4% Bayport (249 flakes) and 69.1% pebble

(566 flakes) and Area III had 38.0% Bayport (525 flakes) and 60.8% pebble (840 flakes).

235 Bayport flakes with outer cortex were recovered from the site. While these flakes are scattered lightly throughout Areas I-III, there was a concentration in Area I (215 from Area I, 7 from Area II, and 13 from Area III), particularly in the units around Features A-F (195 flakes). This distribution is paralleled by cortex flakes (i.e. "decortication flakes") of Bayport chert (46 from Area I of which 44 come from the units around Features A-F, 2 from Area II, and 1 from Area III) and ridged flakes with heavily ground striking platforms of Bayport chert (281 throughout Area I, 1 from Area II, and 1 from Area III) resulting from bifacial core and biface reduction (see Figures 22-27). These flakage patterns indicate that Bayport nodules were brought to and worked on the site, particularly in Area I. The 3,174.8 grams of Bayport chert from Area I is approximately the amount of waste flakage which would be derived from three or four medium sized Bayport nodules (see Ozker 1982:117-118 for quantities of waste flakes derived from working of a Bayport nodule).

Lithic Artifacts

Projectile Points (Descriptions are according to Binford 1963c).

Meadowood Points (Figures 35-39; Table 20). This projectile point type was defined in New York by Ritchie (1971:35-36, Plate 17) and data, including metrics, is provided for points of this type from a number of New York sites by Granger (1978:301-306, Appendix A, Table A.1b). These points are *thin* medium breadth points with small side notches (sometimes double-notched) and flat flake scars (i.e. ill-defined bulbs of percussion and ridges).

Thirty-three points and fragments from 20GR33 were classified as Meadowood points and represent the largest point type recovered. Most of these are made from exotic cherts: 60.5% Onondaga chert, 6.1% of Pipe Creek chert, 12.1% unidentified exotic cherts, and only 21.2% Bayport chert. All are broken and/or extensively reworked. In addition to the points and point fragments, three Meadowood points from the site were reworked into other forms: one narrow side-notched point (Figure 40A), one double-notched hafted end scraper (Figure 44B), and one bifacial trianguloid end scraper (Figure 44D).

It should be noted that several of the points from 20GR33 do not have the "characteristic" small side-notches of "classic" Meadowood points from New York and as such might not be grouped with Meadowood points by other researchers. However, at 20GR-33, this lack of small side-notches is due in part to the extensive use and reworking to which the points were subjected. As classified here the notching was of secondary importance for classifying a point as Meadowood (cf. the discussion of stylistic variation below pages 35-37). Of primary importance for the classification of the 20GR33 specimens was the thickness (all but one, #264, are less than 0.7 mm. thick - see Table 13 and compare Granger 1978:Table A.1b, p. 305) and flaking pattern (i.e. ill-defined bulbs of percussion and ridges). Chert type also played an important role in classification and it should be noted that 60% of the 20GR33 sample is made of Onondaga chert which is the chert from which Meadowood points are generally made in New York and Ontario.

Unlike mortuary sites where complete and unused specimens are often recovered, length and width metrics were of no use in classifying the 20GR33 specimens due to the highly curated nature of the assemblage. The length of the specimens (2.48-4.03 cm., mean - 3.3 cm.) probably represents the size at which the points were considered too small for further reworking and discarded. A similar size range was noted for the points recovered at 20GR176, 2.69-3.94 cm., mean - 3.3 cm. The width of most of the 20GR33 specimens has been modified by reworking and breakage.

In reduction sequences developed for New York assemblages, Meadowood points are notched forms of Meadowood blanks or "cache blades" (see Granger 1978:17, Figure 1.2 for a reduction sequence). In Michigan these cache blades have been referred to as Pomranky points which were defined because of perceived differences in the size of cache blades from the Great Lakes region (Binford 1963b:166). Three varieties of Pomranky points (Midland, Swan Creek, and Saginaw) were defined at the Pomranky site on the basis of differences in raw material correlated with differences in size, shape, orientation of the blank, and grinding of the base (*ibid.*:172-176). However, in a subsequent study it was noted that Pomranky points made of different materials at the same site have more similarities than ones made of the same material at different sites (Binford 1963d). The definition of varieties on the basis of chert types is further complicated because the eight chert types distinguished in the Pomranky site report for the cache blades (Binford 1963b:155-157) have subsequently been identified as variants of only two chert types - Ten Mile Creek/Dundee/Stony Creek and Pipe Creek (see Simons n.d.).

Occasionally notched points from habitation sites are still referred to as being made on one of the Pomranky site varieties (most recently Ozker 1982:-98). In addition to the problems with the definition of these varieties just noted, there is a further complication in attempting to correlate Meadowood points from habitation sites to varieties of "cache blades" from mortuary sites because use and reworking can alter the "original" form significantly as has been noted above. This is particularly evident with the sample of Meadowood points from 20GR33. Only one point had an unreworked blade and a hafting element which was not broken (#138, Figure 35A).

In the past, Meadowood points found on Michigan sites have been given a number of names: Davis points (Binford and Papworth 1963:102-104; Binford 1963a:133), Hodges points (Binford 1963a:129-132), Hunt points (Binford 1963a:132-133), and Green Point Side-notched points (Ozker 1982:97-98). These were considered to be different point types made from "Pomranky points."

Binford defined his types (Davis, Hodges, and Hunt) on the basis of differences in form and chipping. This differentiation was apparently (it is not explicitly stated) in the secondary chipping of the blade. Hodges points had serrated edges and continuous expanding and conchoidal secondary chipping of the blade with no signs of use. Hunt points had unserrated edges and continuous ovate and conchoidal secondary chipping of the blade with evidence of use in the form of crushing and nibbling along one edge. In addition to the secondary chipping of the blade, Hodges and Hunt points were also differentiated by the grinding of the base and hafting element: Hodges points had ground bases but unground hafting elements while Hunt points had both ground bases and hafting elements. Davis points had unserrated edges and continuous short lamellar secondary chipping of the blade with or without ground bases. These point "types" apparently differentiated on the basis of the secondary chipping of the blade, are most likely the results of stylistic choices by individual knappers and the uses to which the points were (or were not) put in the particular site assemblages. As such these three "types" should be viewed as stylistic and/or functional varieties within a larger point type.

Ozker (1982:98) defined her type (Green Point Side-notched) by contrasting the presumed date and the contexts of her type with Binford's "types" (i.e. "Early Woodland" versus "Late Archaic" date and habitation versus mortuary context). This definition on the basis of sixth century B.C. dates and campsite contexts implies certain assumptions about the distinction between "Terminal Archaic" and "Early Woodland" assemblages which can not be maintained. In view of the C-14 dates from 20GR33 (presented below pages 31-32), which are contemporary with the Schultz Early Woodland dates, the distinction between what are termed "Terminal Archaic" and "Early Woodland" assemblages in the Saginaw Valley cannot be maintained.

This proliferation of types, all based on small samples (Davis - 5, Hodges - 2, Hunt - 2, and Green Point Side-notched - 5) from one or two sites, has emphasized certain aspects of the individual assemblages while de-emphasizing larger cultural, geographical, and temporal aspects of these same assemblages. One of the characteristics of Michigan Meadowood points is the frequency with which they are made from exotic cherts (79% of the 20GR33 examples and all of the Hodges, Schultz and Green Point site examples, see also Simons n.d.). In his definition of Meadowood points, Ritchie (1971:36) noted that they are generally made of Onondaga chert and the data provided by Granger (1978:301) from ten New York sites indicates that 95% are made of Onondaga chert. It should be noted that the two points used to define Binford's "Hodges points" and about 58% of the examples from 20GR33 are made of Onondaga chert. With the exception of occasional Bayport examples and rare Kettlepoint examples, Meadowood points are made from circum-Lake Erie cherts (Simons n.d.:15). Because these points are made with the same technology and often with the same raw material (i.e. Onondaga chert) as the New York type, we have dispensed with the profusion of "type" names and refer to these points as Meadowood points.

A distinctive feature of several of the Meadowood points from 20GR33 is double-notching (Figures 36B-E, 37A, C). Double-notching is rather characteristic for this period and was noted by Ritchie (1961:35) in his definition of Meadowood points (see also Johnston 1984:26, Figure 12i). Of the 14 Meadowood points from 20GR33 which have hafting elements sufficiently preserved to determine if they are double or single notched, half (6) are double-notched. Two of these points could be single notched (#87 - Figure 36E and #259 - Figure 37A). However, they have been classified as double-notched here because of the reworked incurvate blades which do not occur on clearly single notched examples in the 20GR33 assemblage but are present on double-notched examples.

While the reason for this double-notching is unknown, it is likely that it is associated with certain uses of these tools and the assemblage from 20GR33 may offer some evidence concerning one of these uses. While single-notching would have been suitable for use of these points as projectiles, we would suggest that double-notching by lengthening the hafting element made the hafting securer for use of the lateral edges as knives. One feature of the double-notched points from 20GR33 which may be evidence for their use as knives is reworking to incurvate blades (three of the seven specimens exhibit this feature). A somewhat similar form of reworking and use as knives has been suggested for Late Paleo-Indian/Early Archaic Dalton "points" (Goodyear 1974:19-33) which have incurvate or indented blades in advanced stages of reworking. The fracturing and splintering of the hafting elements of many of the double-notched specimens in the 20GR33 assemblage (#12/24, 87, 255, 259, 263) would appear to indicate that the hafting element was under considerable stress.

The following sequence is suggested for the use-life of Meadowood points at 20GR33.

1) Meadowood preform (or "cache biface"). This stage corresponds to the Quaternary Blank of Granger's (1978:18) sequence. One Meadowood "quaternary blank" of Bayport chert (Figure 49C) was recovered in Area I associated with the workshop debris around Features A-F. The lack of Onondaga and other exotic chert manufacturing debris and rejects suggests that the points on exotic cherts were brought to the site at this stage or the next. Note, however, the unifacial (primary) blank of Onondaga chert (Figure 57A) which is suitable for manufacture into a Meadowood point.

2) Meadowood (projectile) points with single notching. This stage is represented by one unreworked point fragment (#138, Figure 35A). Some of the base fragments might be from this stage.

3) Unreworked double-notched Meadowood "points" (knives). These would have been manufactured from either stage 2 points by adding a second notch or from stage 1 preforms by double-notching. The closest point to this stage from the site is #12/24 (Figure 36B), though it has been slightly used/reworked.

4) Reworked double-notched Meadowood "points" (knives). While this stage could be subdivided, the small sample of points suggests a rather even progression of reworking from #12/24 (Figure 36B) which exhibits slight use/reworking to #264 (Figure 36C) which has a very slightly incurvate blade, to #189 (Figure 36D) and #259 (Figure 37A) which have pronounced incurvate blades and #87 (Figure 36E) which is completely expended.

The tips of broken points of stages 2-4 were reworked if large enough (#194, Figure 35C). A number of the points have badly battered "ears" (Figure 35B, E) which is paralleled by point bases broken through the middle and "ears" in the assemblage (Figure 38A-E).

Miscellaneous Narrow Side-notched and Expanding-Stem Points.

With the exception of point #1, which was found eroded from the river bank, these points were found together with Terminal Archaic/Early Woodland material and features. Metrics are given in Table 21.

A) This point, #139 (Figure 40A), is a heavily reworked tip of a Meadowood point made from Onondaga chert. The base is irregular and unprepared and the point has the small side-notches characteristic of Meadowood points.

B) This group of three points, #1, 174, 295 (Figure 40B-D), has similarities to Dustin points. #174 and 295 have lamellar flaking which produces a ridge on one face. The transverse sections are biconvex or convex-triangular. However, the bases are thinned and none are unifacial. #1 is made of a pebble chert with large cortical areas, #174 is made of a pebble chert, and #295 is made of a Ten Mile Creek/Dundee chert which outcrops in southeastern Michigan (Monroe County) and around Toledo, Ohio.

C) These two expanding stem points (Figure 40E, F) are grouped together on the basis of the chert from which they were manufactured. They are made of the same Bayport chert variant as the Meadowood base #257 (Figure 39C) and the hafted scraper #265 (Figure 44C). Other artifacts made with this chert are #224 (triangular biface - Figure 45D), 254 (point tip - Figure 43B), and 276 (preform - Figure 49A).

D) This side-notched point, #97 (Figure 41A) has a serrated edge and is made of Bayport chert.

E) Expedient Points. These two points are marked by their apparently quick manufacture. Both, #173 (Bayport) and 175 (pebble?), are unifacial points (Figure 41B, C). #175 could be placed with the stemmed points but has been placed here because of the lack of careful flaking.

F) Asymmetrical Hafting Elements. Point #241 (Figure 41E) is made of Onondaga chert with cortex and #209 (Figure 41D) is made of cortex which is identical to the cortex of #241. Both points are crudely worked with irregular blade edges, asymmetrical hafting elements (side-notched on one side and stemmed on the other), and straight ground bases. The hafting element of these two points may fall within the range of variation of the stemmed points from the Schultz site (Ozker 1982:Figure 37, 69437 and 69454; Figure 38, 68803 and 65779).

Stemmed Point (Figure 41F; Table 21).

One lobate stemmed point, #168, of Onondaga chert was recovered in Area II. In outline this point resembles Belknap/Dickson/Waubesa points from Illinois and Wisconsin which are associated with Black Sand ceramics and dated c. 500-150 B.C. (Salkin 1986; Conrad *et al.* 1986; Farnsworth and Asch 1986). The point from 20GR33 was recovered in Area II and it, the Meadowood primary flake blank (#167), and the expedient point (#209) are the only diagnostic Early Woodland material from this area. The one radiocarbon date from Area II (2690 ± 150 b.p., 740 b.c.) suggests a date earlier than similar forms in Illinois and Wisconsin.

Similar lobate-stemmed points made from Onondaga chert are fairly common in collections from south-central and eastern Michigan. Eight of these points which come from a site on the Cass River in Tuscola County near Tuscola (20TU149, Don Simons Collection) are illustrated in Figures 60-62. Seven are made from Onondaga chert and one from fossiliferous Bayport or pebble chert . Several primary, secondary, and tertiary blanks of Onondaga chert were also recovered from this site.

These points are frequently found with primary flake blanks from which they are apparently made and they often have part of the original flake surface preserved on one face. In the assemblages studied, they are always thicker than 7-8 mm whereas Meadowood points, which are also frequently made from Onondaga chert, are almost always thinner than 7 mm. These points appear to be locally made (expedient?) points made from Meadowood primary and secondary blanks.

Corner-notched Points (Figure 42A-C; Table 21). Three corner-notched points were recovered. #62 was found in Area I in association with Terminal Archaic/Early Woodland material while the other two points (#99 and 284) were found in exploratory units.

Late Woodland Triangular Points (Figure 42D-E; Table 21). Two triangular points were recovered (#216 and 271). Both were associated with Late

Woodland ceramics.

Miscellaneous Point Blades and Tips (Figure 43; Table 21). Six point blades and tips, all associated with Terminal Archaic/Early Woodland material, were recovered.

Turkey Tail Fragment (Figure 44A). One Turkey Tail blade fragment made of Indiana Hornstone/Wyandotte chert was recovered from Area I. The primary chipping is massive and flat with expanding flake scars. The edge is reworked with secondary chipping of continuous lamellar and expanding flake scars. This fragment exhibits extensive heat damage. Metrics: width - (3.07 cm) (original width c. 3.5 cm), length - (3.10 cm), thickness - (0.37 cm).

Turkey Tails form one of the nuclear traits of the "Red Ocher burial complex" (Ritzenthaler and Quimby 1962; Fitting 1975:81) and frequently occur in Terminal Archaic burials (cf. Binford 1963b:176-180) and caches (Green and Fitting 1964) from Michigan. When found on habitation sites they can have a combination stemmed and notched hafting element and are frequently used/reworked as knives (Simons n.d.:12-13). The example from 20GR33 has a retouched edge and may have been used as a knife.

Hafted Scrapers (Table 22). Two hafted end scrapers were recovered from Area III. Artifact #219 (Figure 44B) is a reworked double-notched Meadowood point made of Bayport chert. Artifact #265 (Figure 44C) closely resembles #235 (side-notched point) and is made of the same Bayport chert variant as it and #257 (Meadowood point base).

Bifacial Trianguloid End Scraper (Figure 44D). One of these end scrapers (#237), made of Pipe Creek chert, was recovered from Area III. This scraper is probably made from a broken Meadowood point tip. The longitudinal section is bi-plano and the primary chipping is massive, flat and bifacial with expanding(?) flake scars. Metrics: maximum width - 1.92 cm, length - 3.62 cm, and thickness - 0.60 cm.

These end scrapers are a characteristic artifact in Early Woodland Meadowood assemblages and are often made from the broken blades/tips of Meadowood points. In assemblages from central Michigan, they are usually made of Pipe Creek or Onondaga chert (see Simons n.d.:14, 39; Binford 1963a:134-135; Ozker 1982:105; Granger 1978:124-126, 216).

Hafted Knife (Figure 44E; Table 22). This large expanding stem knife (#286) was recovered in an exploratory unit and is made of a banded chert (probably Norwood chert).

Drill Blank (Figure 45A). This artifact (#158) is made of Bayport chert and was in the initial stage of manufacture. Most of the flaking is on the ventral face with lamellar and expanding flake scars. Large areas of the original flake surface are still present particularly on the dorsal face and the proximal end of the ventral face. The flake-blank had oblique orientation. Metrics: width - 1.71 cm, length - (3.48 cm), thickness - 0.67 cm.

Triangular Bifaces (Figure 45B-F; Table 23). While triangular bifaces are usually assigned to the Late Woodland, these particular examples are considered here to belong to the Terminal Archaic/Early Woodland occupation because of their lack of association with Late Woodland materials (i.e. ceramics), their association with Terminal Archaic/Early Woodland artifacts and features. The chert type of #171 and 224 is the same Bayport chert variant as #257 (Meadowood point base).

Large Bifacial Preforms (Table 23). Four large bifacial prefoms, all made of Bayport chert, were recovered from Area I.

Artifact #5/16 (Figure 46) is triangular with plano-convex transverse and longitudinal sections. The dorsal (plano) face is largely the unmodified face of the core from which the blade was struck and the "primary" flake scars are the result of trimming and removing previous flakes from the core. The primary chipping of the ventral (convex) face is massive with lamellar and expanding flake scars. The secondary chipping is bifacial and continuous along one lateral edge and unifacial and continuous along the opposite edge. The flake-blank orientation is distal with the striking platform preserved at the tip. One lateral edge (with bifacial secondary chipping) appears to have been a knife while the opposite edge (with unifacial secondary chipping) has steep (unifacial) retouch similar to tools classified as scrapers.

Artifact #148/150 (Figure 47A) is triangular with

a flat (unpointed) tip. The transverse and longitudinal sections are biplano. The primary chipping is massive and bifacial with lamellar and expanding flake scars. The secondary chipping is discontinuous and bifacial-bilateral with lamellar and triangular flake scars.

Artifact #151/152 (Figure 47B) is ovate (?) with biplano transverse and longitudinal sections. The primary chipping is massive and bifacial with expanding flake scars. The secondary chipping is continuous and bifacial-bilateral with lamellar flake scars.

Artifacts #192/193 and 202 (Figure 48) was found in three pieces, two of which fit together to form the distal half (#192/193) and one which represents the base (#202). This biface had an excurvate blade with a biconvex transverse section and a concavo-convex longitudinal section. The primary chipping is massive and bifacial with expanding and lamellar flake scars. The secondary chipping is bifacial-bilateral and discontinuous. The base is straight and unground. The primary chipping of the base is transverse and longitudinal with bifacial scars of mutually exclusive type. The secondary chipping is bifacial and discontinuous. The original length is estimated to have been 14-15 cm.

Medium/Small Bifacial Preforms (Table 23). Five medium/small bifacial preforms were recovered: three from Area I (#6, 67, 135, 232) and one from Area III (#276).

Artifact #135 (Figure 53A) is made of Bayport chert with cortex. It is made on a flake struck from the corner of a core with one face (dorsal) representing the original surface of the core and with part of the surface of the core on one lateral edge. The bifacial chipping results from an attempt to trim the flake with continuous alternating faces-bilateral retouch along the lateral edges.

Artifact #6 (Figure 46B) is made of Bayport chert. The blade, as far as preserved, is parallel with asymmetrically biconvex transverse and longitudinal sections. The primary chipping is unifacial and the secondary chipping is bifacial-bilateral. The base is straight and unground. The chipping of the base is bifacial and continuous. The flake-blank orientation is oblique with part of the striking platform at the corner of the base and one lateral edge.

Artifact #276 (Figure 49A) is made of a Bayport chert variant (same as #257 Meadowood point base). It is broken into several pieces from heat damage and some of the biface fragments from surrounding units may belong to it. It is ovate with a biconvex transverse section.

Artifact #232 (Figure 50B) is made of Charity Island/Norwood chert. It has an excurvate blade with biconvex transverse and longitudinal sections. The primary chipping is bifacial with expanding flake scars. The secondary chipping is discontinuous and bifacial-bilateral. The base is subconvex and unground. The flake-blank orientation was oblique.

Artifact #67 (Figure 50C) is a Meadowood "quaternary blank" made of Bayport chert. It has a slightly excurvate blade with a biconvex transverse section. The primary chipping is massive, flat, and bifacial with lamellar and expanding flake scars. The secondary chipping is discontinuous and bifacial-bilateral with smooth lamellar and triangular flake scars. The base is subconcave and unground. The chipping is bifacial and continuous obscuring laterally originating flake scars.

Bifacial Scrapers (?) (Table 23). Artifact #200 (Figure 52E) recovered from Area I is made of Bayport chert. It has a steep bevel on the end and may have functioned as an end scraper.

Artifact #117 (Figure 50A) recovered from Area I is made of Bayport chert with outer cortex and is heat modified. It has plano-convex transverse and longitudinal sections. One end has crushing and may have been used as an end scraper.

Artifact #159 (Figure 53B) recovered from Area I is made from a Bayport decortication flake.

Two possible bifacial scrapers, #221 (Figure 52A) and #287 were recovered in Area III. Both are made of Bayport chert.

Miscellaneous Bifaces (Table 23). Artifact #19 (Figure 50B) is made of a pebble chert and has asymmetrically biconvex transverse and longitudinal sections.

Artifact #166 (Figure 50C) is a triangular biface made of pebble chert. It has biconvex transverse and longitudinal (?) sections.

Biface Fragments (Figure 51, 52B-H, 53C, 54A).

Fifty-four biface fragments were recovered. Counts and chert types are given in Table 24.

Bipolar Cores (Figure 54B-G, 55A-F). Forty-seven bipolar "cores" were recovered. Data on them is given in Table 25.

Unifaces (Table 26).

Unifacial Blank (#167, Figure 57A). This artifact was recovered from Area II and is made of Onondaga chert. It is made from a flake which was struck from the corner of a core and has the original surface of the core at the striking platform and along one lateral edge. It may have been used as a side scraper. This unifacial blank fits the description of Meadowood primary blanks as defined by Granger (1978:16-18, 131, 345-346).

We have noted above (p. 25-26) that Meadowood points and their associated forms are very frequently made from exotic cherts derived from sources around Lake Erie (i.e. Onondaga, Pipe Creek, and Ten Mile Creek; see Simons n.d.). The questions of the form these raw materials took while moving through exchange networks has often been raised. Preforms/cache bifaces occur frequently in "red ocher" burials and caches from Michigan and could have been the form in which exotic raw materials where exchanged. On the other hand, a study of the variability between a number of caches indicated that Meadowood cache bifaces from Michigan were locally manufactured and not widely traded (Binford 1963d).

The unifacial blank from 20GR33 indicates that raw materials were moving through the exchange networks in early stages of manufacture. On the other hand, it must also be noted that primary blanks of Onondaga chert were not being reduced at 20GR33 and all Onondaga waste flakes can be attributed to the reworking and notching of Meadowood points. These unifacial blanks frequently occur with relatively thick lobate-stemmed points of Onondaga chert. It is probable that in central Michigan these lobate-stemmed points were manufactured from primary blanks while Meadowood points were manufactured from quaternary blanks.

Hafted End Scraper (#198, Figure 56D). This artifact was recovered in Area I and is made of a pebble chert.

End Scrapers (Figure 56A-C, E). Three end scrapers were recovered, two (#3 and 164) of Bayport chert from Area I and two (#213 and 234) of pebble chert from Area II.

Side Scrapers (Figure 55G, 56F). Three side scrapers were recovered from Area I, one of pebble chert and two of Bayport chert with outer cortex.

End/Side Scraper (#292). One scraper of Bayport chert with retouch on the end and sides was recovered from Area III.

Scraper Fragments. Three scraper fragments, one (#108) from Area I and two (#172 and 246) from Area III, were recovered.

Unifacial Blades (Figure 58). Four unifacial blades were recovered, all from Area I in units around Features E and F. They are all made from Bayport chert and three have outer surfaces of the nodule preserved.

Utilized Flakes (Figure 57B). Sixty-five utilized flakes were recovered during excavations. Table 27 gives counts by area of the site and position of retouch.

Plano-Convex Adze.

This artifact is pecked with a ground bit and ventral surface. It was recovered from Area I. Metrics: width - 4.65 cm, length - 10.44 cm, thickness - 2.30 cm. This adze is somewhat unusual by having a prepared hafting element which is thinner and narrower than the bit. Hafting element metrics: width - 3.47 cm, length - 5.37 cm, thickness - 2.04 cm. Plano-convex adzes have been found at a number of Terminal Archaic/Early Woodland sites (Binford 1963a:137; Wright 1964:19; Granger 1978:127, 218-219).

Sandstone Artifact.

This artifact was recovered from Area III. Metrics: maximum width - 5.54 cm, width at break - 4.40 cm, length - (4.37 cm), thickness - 2.26 cm. One other unmodified piece of sandstone was also recovered in Area III.

Slate Gorget Fragments (Plate 4).

Four fragments forming two fragments of one (?) gorget were recovered from Area III. Both are made of green slate and are similar to gorgets from the Hodges site (Binford 1963a:135-137). Fragment

#272/279 has part of one hole and is the rounded corner of a gorget. Fragment #280/282 has parts of two holes 3.73 cm apart. Both are split in half.

Ceramics

A total of 1,152 grams of pottery representing a minimum of eight vessels was recovered during excavations. Table 28 gives the weight of pottery and number of vessels per area and weight and vessels per square foot. Figures 28-30 show the distribution of pottery on the site. All pottery from the site is Late Woodland.

Vessel #1 (Surface of trail north of Area I). This vessel is represented by three decorated bodysherds. Decoration consists of horizontal rows of cord-wrapped stick impressions on two sherds and short vertical cord-wrapped stick impressions between horizontal rows of cord-wrapped stick impressions.

Vessel #2 (Area I, Unit 90S50E - E 1/2). This vessel is represented by one rimsherd. It has a slightly thickened lip with oblique cord-wrapped stick impressions (0.25 cm wide) across the lip. The surface treatment is cordmarking and oblique cord-wrapped stick impressions occur along the break in an undetermined pattern.

Vessel #3 (Area II, Units 140S190E, 150S190E). This vessel is represented by two rimsherds and two collared bodysherds. The vessel has a slightly thickened lip and a collar. The surface treatment is cordmarking.

Vessel #4 (Area II, Units 140S190E, 155S185E, 160S185E). This vessel is represented by four rimsherds. It has a square lip with oblique cordwrapped stick impressions. Exterior decoration consists of horizontal rows of cordwrapped stick impressions.

Vessel #5 (Area II, Unit 155S185E). This vessel is represented by one rimsherd. It has cordwrapped stick impressions oblique across the lip and vertical on the lip. The surface treatment is plain and exterior decoration consists of punctates.

Vessel #6 (Area III, Units 225S205E - NW 1/4, 235S195E - SE 1/4). This vessel is represented by two rimsherds. It has a slightly thickened lip with oblique cordwrapped stick impressions. The surface is fabric impressed and the vessel is collared.

Vessel #7 (Area III, Unit 225S195E - NW 1/4). This vessel is represented by one rimsherd. It is a miniature vessel with no decoration and a plain surface.

Vessel #8 (Exploratory Unit 340S340E). This vessel is represented by one small rimsherd. No decoration is preserved and the surface is plain.

Table 28 shows that most of the pottery was recovered in Area II and that there was only a light scatter of pottery over the rest of the site. The collared rimsherds are somewhat similar to the pottery from 20GR91 (dated c. A.D. 1300, Beld 1990), though none of the 20GR33 examples were large enough to determine if they have castellations. A C-14 date was obtained from one feature (I) in Area II which had much of the pottery around it. However, the date related to the Terminal Archaic/Early Woodland occupation and the pottery from 20GR33 remains undated.

Fire-Cracked Rock

A total of 619.5 kg of fire-cracked rock was recovered during excavations. Table 29 gives counts by area and kilograms per square meter. Figures 31-33 show the distribution on the site.

Radiocarbon Dates

Seven C-14 dates were obtained from wood charcoal recovered from the features. They average 2579 ± 102 b.p. (629 b.c.). All of the samples were from small pieces of wood charcoal scattered throughout the feature fill with the exception of the date for Feature T (Beta-9648) which was obtained from one piece of charcoal. As such the dates represent the average age of the charcoal sample within the features. Care was taken to collect charcoal fragments only from the feature fill with charcoal from rodent burrows being discarded.

Five of the dates standard deviations (1 sigma) -

three from Area I (Beta-9644, -9645, and GX-5746) and two from Area III (Beta-9649 and 10509) - overlap between 2505-2540 b.p. (555-590 b.c. uncorrected) and when calibrated produce an average age of 769/672/663 B.C. (1 sigma deviation 792-561 B.C., 2 sigma deviation 800-437 B.C., calibrated according to Stuiver and Becker 1986).

Two dates fall outside the range of these five dates. One date from Area III, Beta-9648 (Feature T), was on a single large piece of charcoal (10+ grams) and is about 300 years earlier than the average of the other dates. A piece of charcoal like this could easily come from the inner rings of a large tree. This date is inconsistent with the other dates from the site and should probably be discarded.

The second aberrant date, Beta-10508 (Feature I, Area II), came from a sample consisting of several small pieces of charcoal. The standard deviation of this date of 740 b.c. overlaps at the upper end of three of the other dates standard deviations.

Table 30 lists the dates by feature and Figure 34 shows the dates from 20GR33 in relation to dates from other Terminal Archaic/Early Woodland sites in Michigan, Ontario, and Northwest Ohio.

Other Data

Floral remains were recovered from several flotation samples taken from features and were analyzed by Tristine Smart of the University of Michigan Museum of Anthropology (Smart n.d.). Charred seeds consisted of *Carex* (3 seeds), *Chenopodium* (1 fragment), *Cornus* (1 seed), *Cyperaceae* (2 seeds), *Galium* (1 seed), *Rubus* (5 seeds), *Sambucus* (4 seeds and 1 fragment), and unidentifiable (6 seeds and 2 fragments). The largest group of seeds consists of berry seeds, i.e. blackberry/raspberry (*Rubus*) and elderberry (*Sambucus*), which indicate a summer (*Rubus/Sambucus*) and possibly early fall (*Sambucus*) occupation (Smart n.d.:273).

Faunal remains from the site were extremely sparse. Except for the remains of a young deer (historic) from the plow zone of Area III, only a few small calcined bone fragments were recovered. This almost total absence of faunal remains is rather surprising. The soil of the site is slightly acidic and faunal remains might not have been preserved, though the possibility that animals were butchered elsewhere and the bones were not brought back to the site or that bones were disposed of elsewhere on the site (perhaps the ravine to the east) should also be considered.

Conclusions

Site 20GR33 is a relatively large variable density site (Table 31). Terminal Archaic/Early Woodland material has been recovered from about 0.6 hectares. Late Woodland pottery was scattered very lightly over the site with a concentration in Area II (3 vessels), while outside of Area II Late Woodland material was negligible. The dating of the site is based on seven C-14 dates which range from 870 b.c. to 495 b.c., five of whose standard deviations overlap between 555-590 b.c. and indicate a date for the site around 560 ± 100 b.c (uncorrected, c. 750-650 B.C. corrected). Floral remains (berry seeds and lack of nut remains) recovered from the features indicate a possible summer occupation.

The artifacts from 20GR33 (Table 24) were used in a wide range of activities. These include weapons (projectile points), woodworking tools (adze), fabricating and processing tools (drill blank and abrader/sandstone artifact), general utility tools (bifaces, scrapers, and utilized flakes), chert working (flakage and preforms/blanks), and ceremonial/ornamental items (gorget). This wide range of activities agrees with models of foraging strategies of Late Archaic hunter-gatherers in the Saginaw Valley which suggest a broad range of subsistence activities during the summer (Keene 1979; 1981).

Indices of occupational intensity (Table 32) indicate that 20GR33 is a relatively low density site. This might be the result of a single or very few seasons of occupation. A single or few occupations is also indicated by the arrangement of features in patterns (clearest in Area III, somewhat less clear in Area I) which may indicate structures, by the complete lack of superimposition of features on one another, and by the distribution of cultural material around features and the lack of scattering of material (particularly flakes cf. Figures 16-18) all of which would be expected from multiple occupations. Comparison with the multi-component Feeheley and Schmidt sites which are recurrent camps with superimposed pits (Feeheley) and thick middens (Schmidt) and higher indices of occupational intensity supports the inference of relatively few occupations of 20GR33 (cf. Taggart 1967; Keene 1979).

It has been suggested that artifact ratios can be used to determine season of occupation (Taggart 1967; Fitting 1972:219). In these studies increased numbers of unifaces have been considered to be associated with fishing activities and spring/summer occupations, while increased numbers of bifaces have been considered to be associated with hunting activities and fall/winter occupations. While this may be valid for specific sites in a general way, such arguments do not take account of functional variation within artifact types or the use of different artifact types for similar functions. For example, at 20GR33 functional variation within a single artifact type was noted for Meadowood points which were likely used as projectiles, knives, and hafted endscrapers. The use of different artifact types for similar functions is illustrated by utilized flakes and hafted end scrapers. Utilized flakes used as end scrapers are common in Area I and while they occur in Area III (in much smaller quantities), hafted end scrapers and a bifacial trianguloid end scraper occur with them. This indicates the use of expedient tools in Area I as opposed to the use of both expedient and curated tools in Area III.

The use of curated tools, which are used for a number of tasks, are reworked and recycled, and are carried throughout the seasonal round, and expedient tools which are manufactured for and discarded after use in a particular task, has been discussed by Binford (1977; 1979) who relates the differences in curation to the organization of the subsistence-settlement system. Recently, Bamforth (1986) has emphasized the effect of the availability of raw materials on curation and suggests that maintenance and recycling varies with the availability of raw materials which results from both regional geology and patterns of human behavior. He has also noted that differing assemblages from behaviorally and ethnically identical sites can be the result of distance from sources of raw material.

These are factors which also affected the curation of the assemblage from 20GR33. Excluding small pieces of pebble cherts available in the local glacial till, the nearest dependable chert sources to 20GR33 are Bayport chert outcrops about 110 km east of the site (165-185 km by water). Because of the lack of easily accessible and dependable chert sources in the immediate area, chert had to be brought to the site from considerable distances. This has resulted in an extreme degree of reworking and re-use of tools at 20GR33 (i.e. curation). With the exception of the unifacial blank of Onondaga chert (Figure 57A) and possibly the adze (Plate 2, though this artifact has been heavily used) *all* of the artifacts from the site are broken and/or reworked to an extreme degree. Tools of exotic cherts (Onondaga, Pipe Creek, Ten Mile Creek and Flint Ridge) are reworked slightly more than Bayport chert. The larger artifacts of Bayport chert that are present on the site are found together with expedient tools (utilized flakes) in the chipping (nodule and bifacial reduction) scatters of Area I and were apparently broken at an early stage of manufacture.

A large portion of the artifacts from 20GR33 are made from exotic cherts. Two points concerning Terminal Archaic/Early Woodland use of exotic raw materials should be made. First, it is sometimes suggested that exotic raw materials were sought because of their high quality (cf. Granger 1980:119). While the exotic cherts can contain "higher" quality material than the local Bayport chert, there is variation in the quality of the imported cherts which includes poorer quality varieties than the locally available cherts. At 20GR33 this is illustrated by Onondaga chert which ranges from a poor quality grainy/silty indurated limestone to a high quality chert. Leaving aside the subjectivity of defining quality, it should be noted that archaeological assemblages in the Saginaw Valley of Michigan are dominated by Bayport chert which is completely adequate for the manufacture and uses of tools.

Second, it is sometimes suggested that the exotic raw materials, from sources up to 750 km away, and the artifacts made from them are luxury or status items. However, the assemblages being studied here are from habitation sites and the exotic raw materials are used as utilitarian items. While Meadowood points and preforms of various exotic cherts, Turkey Tails of Indiana Hornstone, and copper artifacts occur in social contexts ("sociotechnic," cf. Binford 1962) as grave offerings on mortuary sites from central Michigan (see Binford 1963a; 1963b), they also occur as utilitarian objects ("technomic," cf. Binford 1962) on habitation sites. Meadowood points of Onondaga chert (sources c. 500 km east of central Michigan), Pipe Creek chert (sources c. 275 km southeast) and Ten Mile Creek/Dundee cherts (sources c. 240 km southeast) occur at 20GR33, the Schultz site (Ozker 1982:97-98), the Green Point site (Wright 1964), and a number of sites studied by Simons (n.d.). Turkey Tails of Indiana Hornstone or Wyandotte chert (sources c. 700 km southwest) occur at 20GR33 and 20SA-642, -651, -653, and -721 (Simons n.d.), and 20SA14 (Thompson 1982, note the reworking of the blade). And copper artifacts (sources c. 630 km northwest) occur at the Schultz site (Ozker 1982: 131-133). All of these occur in clearly utilitarian contexts.

The occurrence of exotic cherts on Terminal Archaic/Early Woodland sites would be better explained by a model describing the social organization of these bands in gift-giving exchange networks (cf. Gregory 1982; Mauss 1967; Sahlins 1972:149-314 for discussions of gift exchange). However, before this is discussed, it is necessary to discuss the assemblage from 20GR33 in relation to other contemporary assemblages.

The artifact assemblage from 20GR33 falls within what has been termed "Terminal Archaic" and is closely related to the Hodges site (Binford 1963a), the Pomranky site (Binford 1963b), and the Green Point site (Wright 1964).

Recently the Green Point site has been reinterpreted by Doreen Ozker as Early Woodland, apparently on the basis of squash seeds, a sixth century B.C. C-14 date, and a "Green Point Side-Notched" point (Ozker 1982:40, 97-98; also Fitting 1975:90 where it is interpreted as a non-ceramic Early Woodland site). The Early Woodland as defined by Ozker is distinguished from the Late Archaic by the presence of cultigens, pottery, stemmed points, and burial mounds. She also defined a "Schultz Complex" as low floodplain sites for squash cultivation and mussel collecting with Kramer stemmed projectile points, Schultz Thick pottery associated with nut processing, and sixth century B.C. C-14 dates (*ibid.*:167). Early Woodland cultures were viewed as originating in the lower Illinois Valley and expanding into Michigan (*ibid.*:220-221) and not evolving out of the Saginaw Valley Late Archaic because of differences in burial practices (Red Ocher burials versus mounds) and the differences in projectile point forms (notched points of Feeheley, Schmidt, and Andrews versus Early Woodland stemmed) (*ibid.*:211-215).

The data presented in this paper does not allow this position to be maintained. Figure 34 shows the C-14 dates from 20GR33 in relation to dates from other sites in Michigan, Ontario, and northwest Ohio. It should be noted that five of the seven dates from 20GR33 together with their standard deviations fall within the standard deviations of the Schultz, Green Point, and Croton Dam Mounds dates, all of which are considered to be Early Woodland. This overlap of C-14 dates indicates that 20GR33 is contemporary with Early Woodland sites in Michigan. It should also be noted that Meadowood points which dominate the 20GR33 assemblage are Early Woodland artifacts and regularly occur with thick interior-exterior cordmarked ceramics in New York and Ontario.

If 20GR33 is a summer occupation, it adds another settlement type to the settlement system of the Terminal Archaic/Early Woodland in Michigan. Reconstructions of the settlement systems in Michigan during the Late Archaic and Early Woodland have indicated band level societies exploiting various resources in a seasonal round (Taggart 1967; Keene 1979, 1981; Ozker 1982:157-162). However, recent work in Illinois indicates a shift toward sedentism throughout the Archaic (Brown 1985; Brown and Vierra 1983; Phillips and Gladfelter 1983) and sedentary base locales at a period contemporary with the

Terminal Archaic/Early Woodland in Michigan (Emerson and McElrath 1983; McElrath and Fortier 1983).

While groups in west-central Illinois may have been sedentary by the first half of the first millennium B.C., the settlement data from the Saginaw Valley indicates small mobile populations occupying seasonal camps. Ozker (1982:especially 157-166) has shown that two distinct seasons of occupation, early summer (late May-early June) and fall (mid-October) with distinct assemblages and exploitation of different resources, are represented at the Schultz site. During the early summer occupations two to four households may have occupied the site possibly reaching a band size of twenty-five persons (*ibid.*:162). The fall occupations were generally of shorter duration, though two residential units indicate that some were of longer duration (*ibid.*:163). Site 20GR33 possibly represents a mid-late summer occupation (July-September). The low indices of occupational intensity indicate that the site was not repeatedly occupied and the relatively large size (0.6 hectares) indicates a base camp, possibly with as many as 50-100 persons. 20GR176, described above, represents an extractive settlement possibly associated with hunting and with an undetermined season of occupation.

Granger (1978:267-297) has noted a similar settlement pattern with seasonal movements for the Meadowood phase in New York. He reconstructs a settlement system with extractive settlements with populations of 25-50 persons exploiting resources in a 10 square mile (34.3 km^2) area, local bands with base settlements occupied during the autumn, winter, and early spring and populations of about 150 persons exploiting resources in a 400 square mile (1369 km^2) area, and regional bands consisting of two or more local bands and about 500 persons which share mortuary sites (*ibid.*:290-291).

If one compares 20GR33 with other "Terminal Archaic" sites and "Early Woodland" sites in central Michigan on the basis of artifact types alone one would conclude that two different cultures occupied the area at the same time (i.e. "Late Archaic" and "Early Woodland"). However, examination of the assemblages with regard to the function of artifacts and the season of occupation suggests some of the variation between these assemblages correlates with seasonal variation and confirms that these "Terminal Archaic" and "Early Woodland" assemblages are actually the product of one culture.

The lack of ceramics and cultigens at 20GR33 is not surprising. It has been reasonably suggested that thick interior-exterior cordmarked pottery was exclusively utilitarian and mainly associated with fall occupations and nut processing (Ozker 1982:77-79, 160-161). Cultigens would be expected on fall (and possibly winter/spring) sites. However, the fortuitous nature of the recovery of squash remains at Schultz where it was impressed on pottery (*ibid.*:38-40) and at Green Point where they were recovered 150 feet from the site seven feet below the Middle Woodland level in a level correlated with the "Early Woodland" level (Wright 1964:20) suggests that they could be easily missed in excavation and analysis. It is important to note that both of these items, pottery and squash, which are the two major traits of the "Early Woodland" are apparently seasonally specific and would not necessarily be expected on non-autumn sites.

While some of the variation between these assemblages can be explained by seasonal uses of particular artifact categories (i.e. pottery and cultigens), this does not account for all of the variation. We have noted that the Meadowood points from 20GR33 served a wide range of uses: projectiles, knives, and end scrapers. Similarly, the stemmed points from Schultz appear to have served a variety of uses. While Ozker did not suggest a use for the stemmed points at Schultz, she noted that they were often reworked into drills (Ozker 1982:105) and Fitting (1972:195-196) noted wear along the sides which might suggest use as knives. The wide range of variation in the reworking of these points indicates that they were used for a wide range of tasks. The reworking and use of Meadowood points at 20GR33 and stemmed points at Schultz as both projectiles and knives indicates that the variation between these point types is not "functional" but rather "stylistic".

While some of the variability projectile points take in these assemblages can be attributed to the particular use of the point (functional variation), we use "stylistic variability" here to denote the forms points take which can not be attributed to functional variation, despite the objections of Wobst (1977:317-318). In the assemblages being studied here style and use appear to vary independently of each other.

Wobst (1977) has noted that traditional archaeological practise has tended to equate stylistic form with social or cultural boundaries, though he connects style with processes of information exchange. As such the stylistic forms which artifacts take transmit simple messages of identification, etc. (*ibid.*: 323). He notes that these stylistic messages are more economical the greater the social distance (beyond relatives and close friends) and as societies increase in size and complexity.

> It is not surprising to find that certain aspects of band society material culture show so little evidence of "stylistic" elaboration. Either category 4 [socially distant] is completely lacking in the societies in question so that the functional matrix for stylistic behavior is only weakly developed, or few messages are sufficiently replicative to justify the energy and matter investment required by stylistic communication. As societies increase in size and complexity, more and more aspects of behavior become intertwined with personnel in category 4 [socially distant], and more and more of these behaviors become repetitious and anticipated. It is in the latter societies that stylistic behavior structures [are] important aspects of artifact form. (*ibid.*: 326)

This observation concerning "band societies" appears to be confirmed by the archaeological record from central Michigan in the first millennium B.C. Before the appearance of pottery, projectile points display the most variation among the various artifact types in use during the Archaic period. Examination of projectile point types from sites in the Saginaw Valley of Michigan dated to the middle of the first millennium B.C. indicates that several styles were in use in a limited geographic area over a fairly short period of time. Thus, 1) Meadowood points occur as the dominant point type at 20GR33 (summer) and the only point type at the Green Point site (fall), 2) Kramer stemmed points represent the dominant point type at the Schultz site (spring and fall), and 3) Dustin points occur as the dominant point type at 20GR176 (uncertain season).

It should be noted that while Kramer points and Dustin points dominate the Schultz and 20GR176 assemblages respectively, Meadowood points occur as a minor element in both assemblages. A variety of stemmed, corner-notched, and side-notched points also occur as minor elements in the 20GR33, Schultz, and 20GR176 assemblages.

The distribution of point styles at 20GR33 also indicates that the variation in point styles is not due to functional or social factors. Three areas (I-III) were defined above on the basis of cultural material and features. The C-14 dates indicate that all three areas are Terminal Archaic/Early Woodland and the floral remains from the features indicate mid-summer occupations (especially Areas I and II) with similar activities being performed in all areas. Differences in point styles were noted between these areas. Areas I and III were dominated by Meadowood points, while Area II contained *no* Meadowood points, three "expedient" points, one Dustin-like point, and one stemmed point. The unifacial blank (Meadowood primary preform) and lobate-stemmed point, both of Onondaga chert from Area II indicate that this distribution of Meadowood points is not the result of access to exotic cherts but rather the result of the stylistic preferences of the knappers in the various areas of the site.

With this intra-site/inter-cultural variation one would also expect to find mixing of the variables used to establish these point typologies. There are in fact several intermediate points which mix attributes and place the legitimacy of these typological classifications into question. These points combine variables of form and technology, raw materials, and use. The point types being discussed in this study (i.e. Meadowood, Kramer, Dustin, Turkey Tails) occur on many sites with hundreds and thousands of examples. The intermediate points occur in very small numbers, are often unique, and by combining distinctive attributes of two or more point types they fall between the boundaries. Because of the small sample sizes and their position between point types, they should not be given "type" names which would only obscure their relationships. Several examples from central Michigan are:

1) Double-notched Dustin point (Figure 59B). This point is in the collection of Don Simons and comes from a site in Saginaw County (20SA371) which has produced numerous Dustin points. Double-notching occurs fairly frequently on Meadowood points (see above page 26). This point combines the attributes of a Dustin Point (narrow side-notched/expanding stem, lamellar and contracting flake scars) with a Meadowood point attribute (double-notching) which is otherwise unknown on Dustin Points.

2) Narrow side-notched point of Onondaga chert (Figure 40A). This point is a reworked Meadowood tip found at 20GR33 (#139). It is narrow and has the unmodified base of Dustin points, though it lacks plano-triangular/convex or bi-triangular/convex transverse sections of Dustin points which is precluded by the thinness of the Meadowood point from which it is reworked.

3) Stemmed "Meadowood" point of Onondaga chert (Figure 59A). This point comes from site 20GR45 in Gratiot County, Michigan. This point combines attributes of a Meadowood point (thickness less than 7 mm, shallow ill-defined flake scars, and raw material - Onondaga chert) with an attribute of Kramer points (ground stem as opposed to Meadowood side-notching).

By combining variables of form, technology, and raw materials these points clearly cross the typological categories of Terminal Archaic/Early Woodland points.

In addition to this mixing of attributes between point types, there is also considerable variation within the Terminal Archaic/Early Woodland point types. Thus, the Meadowood points from 20GR33 range from examples with the small side-notches characteristic of New York examples (Figure 35A) to examples which are almost corner-notched (Figures 36B-D) to an example which has the appearance of a Jack's Reef Corner-notched point (Figure 35D). Dustin points when defined by lamellar flaking which forms a ridge on one face and a triangular transverse section are perhaps better considered as a variety of a larger narrow blade point type (cf. Lovis and Robertson 1989). Thus the 20GR176 points show a range of variability. These Dustin points differ from the 20GR33 Dustin-like points only in basal preparation and degree of curation.

This combination of attributes illustrated by the intermediate points and the variation within point types in individual assemblages indicates that these point types should be considered as rather gross categories with fuzzy boundaries.

The stylistic variability within and between Terminal Archaic/Early Woodland sites over a wide area indicates that these point styles do not mark social boundaries within and between band level societies. Rather, this stylistic variability should be viewed as a basic feature associated with band level Terminal Archaic/Early Woodland societies. We have noted that in the past the Archaic period has been described as having hunter-gatherer bands characterized by band exogamy, patrilocal postmarital residence, and band territoriality (cf. band society described by Service 1962) and a similar model of social organization has been suggested for "Early Woodland" Meadowood sites in New York (Granger 1978:267-297). While these models are adequate for viewing the ecology of hunter-gatherer bands within limited territories, they do not account for networks of contacts which go beyond local groups (cf. Lee 1976; Hill 1978).

Lee (1976) has argued that hunter-gatherer spatial and social boundaries are fluid and that this fluidity is a strategy for dealing with scarce resources, demographic stress, and resolution of conflict by fission. And in a study of hunter-gatherer language use, Hill (1978) has critiqued the "dialect tribe" model of language use which equates dialects with territorial groups. She argues that while the dialect tribe model accounts for "learned regional dialects," it does not account for various forms of multilingualism and fails "... to capture a major level of structural significance in the organization of human populations: areal units and network systems that go beyond the local group" (*ibid.*: 2-3). She concludes that the systems of multilingualism:

> ... facilitate the extensive networks of contacts which allow survival of human groups and ways

> of life even during periods of locally severe environmental stress, since they facilitate the movement of people as refugees and visitors into contact with groups in areas where the resource situation remains favorable, with an "edge" of improved access to the new language and a history of previous contact. (*ibid.*: 18-19)

Archaeologically, the regular use of exotic raw materials in Terminal Archaic/Early Woodland assemblages from sources up to 550-750 km away clearly indicates extensive trade networks. And the occurrence of various artifact styles over large areas (i.e. Meadowood points across New York, Ontario, and central Michigan; Dustin/Lamoka points in New York and Michigan; Kramer points throughout Michigan and Illinois together with other varieties of stemmed points; Turkey Tails from New York through Michigan, Ohio, Indiana, and Illinois; and thick interior-exterior cordmarked pottery throughout the northeastern United States) is a situation which should be expected in non-stratified societies with simple technologies that do not restrict access to raw materials and information on technology. This is in contrast to stratified societies where style can be used to indicate social group affiliation and status. The exchange networks represented in the Terminal Archaic/Early Woodland archaeological record by exotic raw materials and which results in variability in artifact styles would have provided an adaptive means for dealing with environmental and social stress similar to the systems discussed by Lee (1976) and Hill (1978).

This type of social system is also indicated by mortuary data from Meadowood sites in Ontario. Spence and Fox (1986) have shown considerable intra-population variability at the Bruce Boyd site indicating "a relatively open and flexible society."

Noting that the arguments made above are based on a limited number of sites (20GR33, 20GR176, Green Point, and Schultz), some observations on the structure of Terminal Archaic/Early Woodland societies may be offered. The Early Woodland is sometimes viewed as the beginning of the transition from hunter-gatherer bands of the Archaic period to more complex agricultural societies. While sites in other parts of the midwest may represent sedentary occupations at this time, based on presently available evidence all the sites from central Michigan were occupied on a seasonal basis and the artifact assemblages and faunal and floral remains indicate a hunting and gathering adaptation. Tropical cultigens (squash) appear on two of the sites (Green Point and Schultz) and while they do provide a seasonal source of food, they could also serve as containers (Ozker 1982). This together with the other major Early Woodland trait, ceramics, suggests that the Early Woodland can be viewed as a period of innovation in container technology in some archaeological assemblages in the Great Lakes. Present evidence indicates that it is not until the introduction of maize in the Late Woodland period that cultigens become an important subsistence element (Fitting 1975:144-145; cf. also Lynott *et al.* 1986). The rather large variability in artifact styles within and between site assemblages and the very fuzzy boundaries between "style zones" on regional levels, preclude the use of stylistic variation to define social groups during this period. This stylistic variation together with the non-status utilitarian use of exotic raw materials suggests egalitarian-band level societies integrated in wide ranging exchange networks.

TABLE 8

20GR33, AREA I, FEATURES

#	Depth	Dimensions	Color	F.C.R.	Flakes	C-14 Date	Comments
A	--	ca. 53-61 cm	Black?	4.5+ kg	?	---	
B	--	ca. 46 cm	Black?	few	?	---	
C	--	ca. 53-61 cm	Black?	8.6+ kg	?	---	Biface Fragment (20-GR-33-5).
D	--	76 X 84 cm	7.5YR2/0	7.6 kg	23	---	
E	23 cm	61 X 61 cm	7.5YR2/0 10YR7/2	27.0 kg	25	---	First noted at base of plow zone.
F	11 cm	67 X 52 cm	10YR3/1	4.1 kg	7	2515 +- 145 b.p.	First noted 9 cm below plow zone.
G	32 cm	1.06 X 1.16 m	7.5YR2/0 10YR5/1	8.4 kg	20	2570 +- 65 b.p.	Figure 13. First noted 9 cm below plow zone.
H	52 cm	49 X 64 cm	10YR2/1	2 frags	7	---	First noted 9 cm below plow zone.
O	15 cm	76 (NS) X 84 (EW) cm	10YR5/3	3 frags	1	---	First noted at bottom of plow zone.

TABLE 8 (CONTINUED)

#	Depth	Dimensions	Color	F.C.R.	Flakes	C-14 Date	Comments
P	35 cm	49 (NS) X 46 (EW) cm	10YR3/1 10YR5/3	10.0 kg	--	2445 +- 95 b.p.	First noted 6 cm below plow zone.
Q	30 cm	99 cm (NS) X 1.03 m (EW)	10YR4/1 10YR5/3	22.9 kg	1	---	First noted 3-6 cm below plow zone.
R	12 cm	---	---	4.6 kg	--	---	Concenrtation of F.C.R. 6-18 cm below plow zone. No soil stain.
NN	91 cm	82+ X 46+ cm	10YR6/4 10YR7/2	--	622	---	Probably large pit. Only corner excavated.

TABLE 9

20GR33, AREA II, FEATURES

#	Depth	Dimensions	Color	F.C.R.	Flakes	C-14 Date	Comments
I	58 cm	79+ X 97+ cm	10YR2/1	few	14	2690 +- 150 b.p.	First noted at bottom of plow zone. Contained 1 sherdlet (intrusive). 1/4 excavated.
L	20 cm	40 X 24 cm	7.5YR2/0	none	1	---	First noted at bottom of plow zone.
M	15 cm	37 X 43+ cm	7.5YR2/0 10YR4/3	none	1	---	First noted 15 cm below plow zone. Possibly a rodent burrow.
N	9 cm	49 X 52 cm	7.5YR2/0	none	1	---	First noted at bottom of plow zone.

TABLE 10

20GR33, AREA III, FEATURES

#	Depth	Dimensions	Color	F.C.R.	Flakes	C-14 Date	Comments
J	52 cm	76 cm X 1.04 m	7.5YR2/0 7.5YR3/2	14.5 kg	18	2560 +- 65 b.p.	First noted at bottom of plow zone.
K	30 cm	46 cm X 1.04 m	7.5YR2/0 10YR4/2	0.5 kg	12	---	First noted at bottom of plow zone. Contained tip of Meadowood point (20GR33-225).
S	21 cm	84 X 97 cm	7.5YR2/0	8.1 kg	4	2450 +- 100 b.p.	First noted at bottom of plow zone.
T	24 cm	94 cm X 1.07+ m	7.5YR2/0 10YR3/2 10YR4/4	1.8 kg	2	2820 +- 65 b.p.	Figure 14. First noted at bottom of plow zone.
U	27 cm	40 X 46 cm	7.5YR2/0	none	none	---	First noted 15 cm below plow zone.
V	37 cm	49 cm X 1.07 m	7.5YR2/0 10YR5/3	few	14	---	First noted at bottom of plow zone.
W	27 cm	76 X 97 cm	7.5YR2/0 10YR4/6	1.8 kg	1	---	First noted at bottom of plow zone.
X	29 cm	78 cm X 1.16 m	7.5YR2/0 7.5YR5/4	1.4 kg	1	---	First noted at bottom of plow zone.

TABLE 10 (CONTINUED)

#	Depth	Dimensions	Color	F.C.R.	Flakes	C-14 Date	Comments
Y	15 cm	44 X 46 cm	7.5YR4/2	none	none	---	First noted 8 cm below bottom of plow zone.
Z	30 cm	1.07 X 1.13 m	7.5YR2/0 10YR3/2 10YR3/3 10YR5/3	few	8	---	Figure 15. First noted at bottom of plow zone.
AA	12 cm	47 X 49 cm	10YR2/1 10YR3/4	7.7 kg	none	---	First noted at bottom of plow zone.
BB	6 cm	43+ X 49+ cm	10YR3/4	1 frag.	none	---	First noted at bottom of plow zone.
CC	37 cm	1.07 X 1.22 m	7.5YR3/4 10YR2/1	1.8 kg	1	---	First noted 6 cm below plow zone. Contained 2 pieces of green slate.
DD	15 cm	37 X 47 cm	7.5YR2/0 10YR3/3 10YR4/4	none	none	---	First noted 3-6 cm below plow zone.
EE	--	61+ X 84 cm	7.5YR2/0 10YR3/4	--	--	---	Not excavated.
FF	29 cm	85 cm X 1.02 m	7.5YR2/0 10YR3/2	4.4 kg	3	---	First noted at bottom of plow zone.

TABLE 10 (CONTINUED).

#	Depth	Dimensions	Color	F.C.R.	Flakes	C-14 Date	Comments
GG	--	53 X 69 cm	7.5YR2/0 10YR2/1	--	--	---	Not excavated.
HH	55 cm	33 X 40 cm	10YR5/3 10YR5/6 10YR7/4	1 frag.	none	---	First noted at bottom of plow zone. 1 utilized flake in fill. Half of feature excavated.
II	--	91 cm X 1.07+ m	7.5YR2/0 10YR4/3	--	--	---	Not excavated.
JJ	--	61 X 67 cm	7.5YR2/0	--	--	---	Not excavated.
KK	--	61 X 30+ cm	7.5YR2/0	--	--	---	Not excavated.
LL	--	46+ X 76+ cm	--	--	--	---	Not excavated. Historic feature. First noted in plow zone just below sod.

TABLE 11

20GR33, WASTE FLAKES - CHERT TYPE PERCENTAGES

Chert Type	1/4" Screen	1/8" Screen
Bayport	74.5%	78.0%
Pebble	24.8%	17.3%
Charity Island / Norwood	0.1%	0.3%
Onondaga	0.3%	4.0%
Flint Ridge	0.1%	0.1%
Pipe Creek	--*	0.1%
Indiana Hornstone	--*	--
Unidentified Exotic	0.1%	0.1%
Total	99.9%	99.9%

*Less than 0.1%.

TABLE 12

20GR33, AREA I, WASTE FLAKES - 1/4" SCREEN (189.7 m^2)

Chert Type	Cortex #	Cortex Wt.	Flat #	Flat Wt.	Ridged #	Ridged Wt.	Battered #	Battered Wt.	Fragment #	Fragment Wt.	Shatter #	Shatter Wt.	Total #	Total Wt.
Bayport	--	--	439	225.5g	535 (unground) 155 (ground)	138.2g 129.2g	201	72.9g	2011	575.5g	49	48.7g	3390	1190.0g
w/ outer cortex	46	93.6g	103	231.1g	3 (unground)	2.7g	7	10.6g	48	52.2g	8	18.8g	215	409.0g
w/ cortex	--	--	275	195.1g	127 (unground) 77 (ground)	24.3g 87.6g	64	37.8g	494	191.2g	33	42.7g	1070	578.7g
cortex	--	--	262	199.8g	65 (unground) 38 (ground)	27.3g 20.0g	48	25.2g	428	138.3g	18	23.7g	859	434.3g
HM (pink)	--	--	15	13.2g	23 (unground) 9 (ground)	9.3g 7.9g	4	0.9g	66	30.9g	--	--	117	62.2g
w/ outer cortex	--	--	3	4.5g	--	--	--	--	3	6.6g	--	--	6	11.1g
w/ cortex	--	--	7	7.1g	--	--	2	0.3g	13	8.3g	1	8.8g	23	24.5g

TABLE 12 (CONTINUED).

Chert Type	Cortex #	Cortex Wt.	Flat #	Flat Wt.	Ridged #	Ridged Wt.	Battered #	Battered Wt.	Fragment #	Fragment Wt.	Shatter #	Shatter Wt.	Total #	Total Wt.
cortex	--	--	2	0.7g	1	0.3g (ground)	2	0.5g	7	9.0g	--	--	12	10.5g
HM (potlid)	--	--	8	2.5g	6	1.8g (ground)	--	--	72	35.2g	1	1.2g	87	40.7g
w/ outer cortex	1	0.8g	--	--	--	--	--	--	1	2.1g	--	--	2	2.9g
w/ cortex	--	--	--	--	--	--	--	--	3	2.9g	--	--	3	2.9g
Dark (HM)	--	--	48	15.9g	70	16.6g (unground)	24	7.4g	368	107.4g	4	4.6g	515	152.1g
					1	0.2g (ground)								
w/ outer cortex	6	4.9g	3	6.3g	--	--	--	--	3	2.8g	--	--	12	14.0g
w/ cortex	--	--	24	14.0g	12	5.1g (unground)	5	4.2g	44	21.6g	--	--	85	44.9g
cortex	--	--	2	3.4g	1	0.1g	--	--	11	7.4g	--	--	14	10.9g
Total	53	99.3g	1191	919.1g	1123	470.6g	357	159.8g	3572	1191.4g	114	148.5g	6410	2988.7g
Charity Island	--	--	2	0.2g	1	0.2g	1	0.3g	--	--	--	--	4	0.7g
Pebble	9	10.4g	191	99.2g	89	31.0g	39	16.1g	351	80.5g	186	296.2g	865	533.4g
HM (pink)	--	--	4	4.6g	1	0.4g	1	0.1g	7	3.2g	3	7.3g	16	15.6g
HM (potlid)	--	--	1	0.2g	--	--	--	--	1	0.1g	--	--	2	0.3g

TABLE 12 (CONTINUED).

Chert Type	Cortex #	Cortex Wt.	Flat #	Flat Wt.	Ridged #	Ridged Wt.	Battered #	Battered Wt.	Fragment #	Fragment Wt.	Shatter #	Shatter Wt.	Total #	Total Wt.
Pebble (cont.)														
Total	9	10.4g	196	104.0g	90	31.4g	40	16.2g	359	83.8g	189	303.5g	883	549.3g
Onondaga	--	--	4	0.9g	9	0.9g	5	0.8g	6	0.8g	--	--	24	3.4g
HM (potlid)	--	--	--	--	--	--	--	--	1	0.3g	--	--	1	0.3g
Total			4	0.9g	9	0.9g	5	0.8g	7	1.1g			25	3.7g
Flint Ridge	--	--	1	0.5g	1 (unground) 2 (ground)	0.1g 0.8g	1	0.5g	6	1.9g	1	0.5g	12	4.3g
Indiana Hornstone	--	--	--	--	--	--	1	0.6g	--	--	--	--	1	0.6g
TOTAL	62	109.7g	1394	1024.7g	1226	504.0g	405	178.2g	3944	1278.2g	304	452.5g	7335	3547.3g

TABLE 13

20GR33, AREA I, WASTE FLAKES - 1/8" SCREEN (69.0 m^2)

Chert Type	Cortex #	Cortex Wt.	Flat #	Flat Wt.	Ridged #	Ridged Wt.	Battered #	Battered Wt.	Fragment #	Fragment Wt.	Shatter #	Shatter Wt.	Total #	Total Wt.
Bayport	--	--	275	18.1g	556	25.1g	102	10.1g	1911	65.6g	19	3.2g	2869	122.1g
w/ outer cortex	--	--	--	--	--	--	--	--	1	0.5g	--	--	1	0.5g
w/ cortex	--	--	87	7.7g	111	6.0g	35	1.9g	305	15.7g	--	--	538	31.3g
cortex	--	--	66	3.7g	74	3.7g	20	1.1g	278	11.8g	2	0.2g	440	20.5g
HM (pink)	--	--	5	0.4g	6	0.4g	1	0.1g	20	1.4g	--	--	32	2.3g
w/ cortex	--	--	1	0.1g	1	0.1g	1	0.1g	6	0.7g	--	--	9	1.0g
cortex	--	--	--	--	--	--	--	--	1	0.1g	--	--	1	0.1g
HM (potlid)	--	--	--	--	--	--	1	0.1g	7	0.8g	--	--	8	0.9g
Dark (HM)	--	--	15	1.2g	18	1.1g	3	0.3g	79	4.7g	1	0.2g	116	7.5g
w/ outer cortex	--	--	--	--	--	--	--	--	1	0.3g	--	--	1	0.3g
w/ cortex	--	--	3	0.2g	1	0.2g	--	--	8	0.5g	--	--	12	0.9g
cortex	--	--	--	--	--	--	--	--	1	0.1g	--	--	1	0.1g
Total			452	31.4g	767	36.6g	163	13.7g	2624	102.2g	22	3.6g	4028	187.5g
Charity Island	--	--	2	0.1g	10	0.7g	--	--	1	0.1g	--	--	13	0.9g
Pebble	--	--	126	8.4g	45	2.7g	17	1.5g	334	16.8g	34	4.1g	565	33.5g
HM (pink)	--	--	--	--	--	--	--	--	1	0.1g	2	0.2g	3	0.3g
HM (potlid)	--	--	--	--	--	--	--	--	1	0.1g	--	--	1	0.1g

TABLE 13 (CONTINUED)

Chert Type	Cortex #	Cortex Wt.	Flat #	Flat Wt.	Ridged #	Ridged Wt.	Battered #	Battered Wt.	Fragment #	Fragment Wt.	Shatter #	Shatter Wt.	Total #	Total Wt.
Pebble (cont.) Total			126	8.4g	45	2.7g	17	1.5g	336	17.0g	36	4.3g	568	33.9g
Onondaga	--	--	32	1.8g	106	4.4g	11	0.6g	40	2.2g	--	--	189	9.0g
Flint Ridge	--	--	--	--	--	--	1	0.1g	2	0.2g	--	--	3	0.3g
Exotic	--	--	--	--	--	--	--	--	3	0.2g	--	--	3	0.2g
TOTAL			612	41.7g	928	44.4g	192	15.9g	3015	121.9g	58	7.9g	4805	231.8g

TABLE 14

20GR33, AREA II, WASTE FLAKES - 1/4" SCREEN (33.1 m^2)

Chert Type	Cortex #	Cortex Wt.	Flat #	Flat Wt.	Ridged #	Ridged Wt.	Battered #	Battered Wt.	Fragment #	Fragment Wt.	Shatter #	Shatter Wt.	Total #	Total Wt.
Bayport	--	--	47	13.8g	13	4.7g	17	6.5g	58	11.6g	9	6.4g	144	43.0g
w/ outer cortex	2	3.0g	3	6.6g	--	--	--	--	2	2.5g	--	--	9	12.1g
w/ cortex	--	--	19	12.7g	4	0.7g	1	0.2g	29	12.2g	1	0.5g	54	26.3g
cortex	--	--	7	2.1g	1	0.5g	--	--	16	6.9g	--	--	24	9.5g
HM (pink)	--	--	1	0.1g	5	1.9g	--	--	5	3.2g	--	--	11	5.2g
Dark (HM)	--	--	1	0.2g	1	0.3g	1	0.2g	4	0.8g	1	0.2g	8	1.7g
w/ cortex	--	--	1	0.3g	--	--	--	--	--	--	--	--	1	0.3g
Total	2	3.0g	79	35.8g	24	8.1g	19	6.9g	99	37.2g	11	7.1g	249	98.1g
Charity Island	--	--	2	0.4g	1	0.1g	1	0.9g	--	--	--	--	4	1.4g
Pebble	--	--	196	98.8g	14	3.1g	42	14.8g	136	40.2g	171	231.7g	562	388.6g
HM (pink)	--	--	2	0.5g	1	0.2g	--	--	1	0.1g	--	--	4	0.8g
Total			198	99.3g	15	3.3g	42	14.8g	137	40.3g	171	231.7g	566	389.4g
TOTAL	2	3.0g	279	135 5g	40	11.5g	62	22.6g	236	77.5g	182	238.8g	819	488.9g

TABLE 15

20GR33, AREA III, WASTE FLAKES - 1/4" SCREEN (190.3 m^2)

Chert Type	Cortex #	Cortex Wt.	Flat #	Flat Wt.	Ridged #	Ridged Wt.	Battered #	Battered Wt.	Fragment #	Fragment Wt.	Shatter #	Shatter Wt.	Total #	Total Wt.
Bayport	--	--	91	47.2g	85	21.5g	17	3.5g	163	57.5g	21	25.7g	378	155.4g
w/ outer cortex	1	2.0g	7	9.4g	--	--	--	--	4	2.5g	1	1.0g	13	14.9g
w/ cortex	--	--	26	17.9g	15	7.9g	4	1.2g	17	10.4g	6	5.6g	68	43.0g
cortex	--	--	9	7.2g	6	1.5g	1	0.3g	9	3.3g	--	--	25	12.3g
HM (pink)	--	--	1	1.7g	5	7.1g	--	--	3	0.5g	--	--	9	9.3g
HM (potlid)	--	--	--	--	--	--	--	--	6	1.4g	1	0.8g	7	2.2g
Dark (HM)	--	--	7	2.1g	3	0.5g	2	0.4g	12	6.6g	--	--	24	9.6g
w/ cortex	--	--	--	--	--	--	--	--	1	2.3g	--	--	1	2.3g
Total	1	2.0g	141	85.5g	115	38.5g	24	5.4g	215	84.5g	29	33.1g	525	249.0g
Charity Island	--	--	--	--	--	--	1	4.2g	--	--	--	--	1	4.2g
Pebble	2	3.5g	268	118.9g	102	21.7g	34	14.9g	255	72.9g	174	76.9g	835	308.8g
HM (pink)	--	--	1	0.7g	--	--	1	0.4g	--	--	--	--	2	1.1g
HM (potlid)	--	--	--	--	--	--	1	0.3g	1	0.1g	1	0.9g	3	1.3g
Total	2	3.5g	269	119.6g	102	21.7g	36	15.6g	256	73.0g	175	77.8g	840	311.2g
Onondaga	--	--	2	1.7g	1	0.2g	--	--	2	0.8g	--	--	5	2.7g
Pipe Creek	--	--	1	0.6g	1	0.3g	--	--	1	0.2g	--	--	3	1.1g

TABLE 15 (CONTINUED)

Chert Type	Cortex #	Cortex Wt.	Flat #	Flat Wt.	Ridged #	Ridged Wt.	Battered #	Battered Wt.	Fragment #	Fragment Wt.	Shatter #	Shatter Wt.	Total #	Total Wt.
Exotic	--	--	1	0.2g	2	0.3g	2	0.5g	1	0.2g	2	0.7g	8	1.9g
TOTAL	3	5.5g	414	207.6g	221	61.0g	66	25.7g	475	158.7g	206	111.6g	1382	570.1g

TABLE 16

20GR33, AREA III, WASTE FLAKES - 1/8" SCREEN (65 m^2)

Chert Type	Cortex		Flat		Ridged		Battered		Fragment		Shatter		Total	
	#	Wt.	#	Wt.	#	Wt.	#	Wt.	#	Wt.	#	Wt.	#	Wt.
Bayport	--	--	24	1.0g	40	1.6g	4	0.2g	107	5.1g	--	--	175	7.9g
w/ cortex	--	--	1	0.2g	2	0.1g	--	--	3	0.2g	--	--	6	0.5g
cortex	--	--	2	0.1g	--	--	--	--	1	0.1g	--	--	3	0.2g
HM (potlid)	--	--	--	--	--	--	1	0.1g	--	--	--	--	1	0.1g
Dark (HM)	--	--	--	--	--	--	--	--	1	0.1g	--	--	1	0.1g
Total			27	1.3g	42	1.7g	5	0.3g	112	5.5g			186	8.8g
Charity Island	--	--	2	0.1g	1	0.1g	--	--	--	--	--	--	3	0.2g
Pebble	--	--	47	2.7g	12	0.7g	12	0.8g	222	11.0g	13	1.4g	306	16.6g
Onondaga	--	--	4	0.2g	12	0.6g	--	--	2	0.3g	--	--	18	1.1g
Flint Ridge	--	--	--	--	1	0.1g	2	0.1g	--	--	--	--	3	0.2g
Pipe Creek	--	--	3	0.2g	1	0.1g	2	0.2g	1	0.1g	--	--	7	0.6g
TOTAL			83	4.5g	69	3.3g	21	1.4g	337	16.9g	13	1.4g	523	27.5g

TABLE 17

20GR33, EXPLORATORY UNITS, WASTE FLAKES - 1/4" SCREEN

Chert Type	Cortex #	Cortex Wt.	Flat #	Flat Wt.	Ridged #	Ridged Wt.	Battered #	Battered Wt.	Fragment #	Fragment Wt.	Shatter #	Shatter Wt.	Total #	Total Wt.
Bayport	--	--	3	3.0g	1	0.3g (ground)	--	--	4	2.8g	1	0.2g	9	6.3g
w/ cortex	--	--	--	--	1	0.1g (ground)	1	0.1g	1	0.1g	--	--	3	0.3g
HM (potlid)	--	--	--	--	--	--	--	--	1	0.1g	--	--	1	0.1g
Total			3	3.0g	2	0.4g (ground)	1	0.1g	6	3.0g	1	0.2g	13	6.7g
Pebble	--	--	14	8.0g	--	--	4	1.1g	11	3.8g	14	12.1g	43	25.0g
Onondaga	--	--	--	--	--	--	--	--	1	0.1g	--	--	1	0.1g
Exotic			--	--	1	0.5g	--	--	--	--	--	--	1	0.5g
TOTAL			17	11.0g	3	0.9g	5	1.2g	18	6.9g	15	12.3g	58	32.2g

TABLE 18

20GR33, EXPLORATORY UNITS, WASTE FLAKES - 1/8" SCREEN

Chert Type	Cortex #	Cortex Wt.	Flat #	Flat Wt.	Ridged #	Ridged Wt.	Battered #	Battered Wt.	Fragment #	Fragment Wt.	Shatter #	Shatter Wt.	Total #	Total Wt.
Bayport	--	--	2	0.2g	8	0.7g	2	0.2g	18	0.6g	--	--	30	1.7g
w/ cortex	--	--	--	--	--	--	--	--	1	0.1g	--	--	1	0.1g
Charity Island	--	--	--	--	1	0.1g	--	--	--	--	--	--	1	0.1g
Pebble	--	--	6	0.2g	2	0.1g	6	0.3g	48	2.5g	2	0.3g	64	3.4g
Onondaga	--	--	3	0.1g	5	0.3g	2	0.1g	2	0.1g	--	--	12	0.6g
Pipe Creek	--	--	--	--	1	0.1g	--	--	--	--	--	--	1	0.1g
Flint Ridge	--	--	--	--	--	--	--	--	1	0.1g	--	--	1	0.1g
Exotic	--	--	3	0.1g	--	--	--	--	--	--	--	--	3	0.1g
TOTAL			14	0.6g	17	1.3g	10	0.6g	66	3.4g	2	0.3g	113	6.2g

TABLE 19

20GR33, TRAIL ALONG RIVER, WASTE FLAKES - 1/4" SCREEN

Chert Type	Cortex #	Cortex Wt.	Flat #	Flat Wt.	Ridged #	Ridged Wt.	Battered #	Battered Wt.	Fragment #	Fragment Wt.	Shatter #	Shatter Wt.	Total #	Total Wt.
Bayport	--	--	27	33.1g	13	6.1g	3	0.4g	56	17.1g	5	4.2g	106	63.0g
					(unground) 2	2.1g								
w/ outer cortex	--	--	4	12.4g	--	--	--	--	--	--	--	--	4	12.4g
w/ cortex	--	--	19	15.2g	6	2.9g	1	0.2g	10	5.0g	2	2.8g	38	26.1g
cortex	--	--	2	1.0g	1	0.1g	1	0.5g	4	2.8g	3	9.7g	11	14.1g
HM (pink)	--	--	1	0.1g	--	--	--	--	--	--	--	--	1	0.1g
w/ cortex	--	--	2	3.7g	--	--	--	--	1	1.9g	--	--	3	5.6g
HM (potlid)	--	--	--	--	--	--	1	0.1g	2	0.5g	--	--	3	0.6g
w/ cortex	--	--	--	--	--	--	--	--	1	0.9g	--	--	1	0.9g
Dark (HM)	--	--	1	2.2g	--	--	1	0.2g	12	2.9g	--	--	14	5.3g
w/ cortex	--	--	1	0.7g	--	--	--	--	1	0.7g	--	--	2	1.4g
Total			57	68.4g	22	11.2g	7	1.4g	80	31.8g	10	16.7g	183	129.5g
Pebble	--	--	37	32.2g	14	4.5	7	2.8g	37	18.7g	27	80.2g	122	138.4g
HM (potlid)	--	--	1	0.3g	--	--	--	--	--	--	--	--	1	0.3g
TOTAL			95	100.9g	36	15.7g	14	4.2g	117	50.5g	37	96.9g	306	268.2g

TABLE 20

20GR33 MEADOWOOD POINT METRICS

(In Centimeters)

#	Width			Length			Thickness	Chert Type
	Base	Tang	Shoulder	Axis	Tang	Notch		
7	(1.61)	--	--	(1.00)	--	--	0.53	Onondaga
11	(1.41)	--	--	(0.78)	--	--	(0.40)	Onondaga
12/24	2.50	1.80 bottom -- top	--	(2.97)	1.82	0.69 bottom 0.77 top	0.59	Onondaga
87	--	--	(2.25)	(3.68)	--	--	0.67	Onondaga
138	2.35	1.83	2.62	(3.10)	0.76	0.50/ 0.43	0.51	Onondaga
140	2.51	1.70	--	(0.81)	--	--	(0.43)	Onondaga
141	2.29	1.82	--	(0.95)	(0.79)	(0.45)	(0.34)	Onondaga
144	(1.65)	--	--	(2.43)	--	--	0.54	Onondaga
147	(2.00)	--	--	(3.37)	--	--	(0.46)	Exotic
155	(1.25)	--	--	(0.96)	--	--	(0.30)	Onondaga
156	(1.40)	--	--	(1.43)	--	--	(0.32)	Bayport
161	1.71	1.61	2.29	4.03	0.83	0.50	0.56	Pipe Creek
165	(1.73)	--	--	(1.05)	--	--	(0.46)	Bayport
169	(1.97)	1.44	--	(0.93)	--	--	0.48	Onondaga (?)
170	1.64	1.08	1.51	3.19	1.00	0.80/ 0.68	0.55	Exotic

TABLE 20 (CONTINUED)

#	Width			Length			Thickness	Chert Type
	Base	Tang	Shoulder	Axis	Tang	Notch		
189	2.23	1.68 bottom	(2.57) bottom	(3.68)	1.85	0.69 bottom	0.63	Onondaga
		2.00 top	2.73 top			0.65 top		
194	1.98	1.56	1.69	3.39	0.93	0.51	0.58	Onondaga
199	(1.43)	--	--	(0.82)	--	--	(0.43)	Onondaga
220	--	--	2.02	(3.60)	--	--	0.60	Exotic
225	(1.60)	--	--	(3.08)	--	--	0.54	Onondaga
226	(1.74)	1.23	--	(0.97)	--	--	(0.37)	Onondaga
230	(1.76)	--	--	(1.84)	--	--	0.50	Exotic
240	1.70	1.30	(2.18)	3.32	0.80	0.73	0.51	Onondaga (?)
242	(1.21)	(1.53)	--	(1.70)	--	--	0.54	Exotic
255	(1.74)	--	--	(0.70)	--	--	(0.39)	Onondaga
257	(2.07)	1.45	--	(0.89)	--	--	(0.44)	Bayport
259	--	1.68	--	(3.23)	--	--	0.60	Onondaga (?)
263	--	1.43	2.57	(0.93)	--	--	0.49	Bayport
264	2.59	2.12 bottom	2.82 bottom	(3.01)	1.96	0.87 bottom	0.76	Bayport
		1.89 top	2.67 top			0.78 top		
269	(0.98)	--	--	(2.02)	--	--	(0.48)	Onondaga
270	(1.18)	1.12	1.89	(2.48)	0.89	0.73	0.54	Pipe Creek
283	(2.14)	--	--	(2.44)	--	--	0.53	Exotic
294	1.61	1.50	2.18	(2.81)	0.72	0.53	(0.54)	Bayport
296	(2.20)	--	--	(1.25)	--	--	(0.30)	Onondaga

TABLE 21

20GR33 PROJECTILE POINT METRICS

(in Centimeters)

#	Width			Length			Thickness	Chert Type
	Base	Tang	Shoulder	Axis	Tang	Notch		
Miscellaneous Narrow Notched Points								
A)139	1.34	0.86	1.10	4.37	0.92	0.57/ 0.45	0.51	Onondaga
B) 1	(0.99)	0.94	1.53	(2.82)	0.92	0.73	0.75	Pebble
174	1.58	1.11	1.35	2.75	1.00	0.70/ 0.77	0.70	Pebble
295	1.52	1.18	1.81	(3.86)	1.46	1.13/ 0.99	0.97	Ten Mile Creek
C)235	(1.16)	1.11	1.93	(2.75)	1.00	0.75	0.61	Bayport
236	(1.61)	1.23	(1.78)	(1.34)	0.86	--	(0.46)	Bayport
D) 97	1.42	1.11	1.50	3.42	0.86	0.46/ 0.64	0.51	Bayport
E)173	1.24	1.14	1.41	2.69	0.97	0.61	0.57	Bayport
175	1.33	1.25	1.68	2.81	1.18	0.77	0.60	Pebble (?)
209	1.54	1.31	1.74	3.95	1.14	0.59/ 0.79	0.75	Onondaga
241	1.34	1.16	1.71	4.43	1.01	0.50	0.70	Onondaga
Stemmed Point								
168	1.44	1.55	2.20	4.75	1.60	1.16	1.04	Onondaga

TABLE 21 (CONTINUED)

#	Width			Length			Thickness	Chert Type
	Base	Tang	Shoulder	Axis	Tang	Notch		
Corner-Notched Points								
62	1.46	1.24	2.15	(2.20)	0.81	0.58	0.67	Bayport
99	--	1.28	2.39	(2.61)	--	--	0.75	Charity Island
284	--	1.35	2.22	(5.62)	--	--	0.77	Bayport
Late Woodland Triangular Points								
216	1.73			3.00			0.48	Charity Island (?)
217	1.92			3.40			0.41	Exotic
Miscellaneous Point Blades and Tips								
17	(1.58)			(1.61)			(0.48)	Bayport
27	(1.90)			(2.40)			0.84	Bayport
38	(0.98)			(1.74)			(0.70)	Bayport
143	(1.92)			(3.57)			(0.43)	Bayport
254	(1.79)			(2.38)			(0.58)	Bayport
285	(1.57)			(2.13)			0.55	Bayport (?)

() Broken attribute

TABLE 22

20GR33 HAFTED SCRAPER AND KNIFE METRICS

(in Centimeters)

#	Width			Length			Thickness	Chert Type
	Base	Tang	Shoulder	Axis	Tang	Notch		
Hafted Scrapers								
219	(1.32)	1.28 bottom 1.49 top	2.00	3.64	1.70	(0.43) bottom 0.56/ 0.44 top	0.64	Bayport
265	--	1.10	1.99	(3.38)	--	--	0.69	Bayport
Hafted Knife								
286	(2.14)	2.00	3.32	(3.49)	1.42	0.88	1.20	Charity Island or Norwood

() Broken Attribute

TABLE 23

20GR33 BIFACE METRICS

(in Centimeters)

#	Width	Maximum Width	Length	Thickness	Chert
Trianuglar Bifaces					
146	1.50		1.69	0.34	Bayport
160	1.43		1.39	0.28	Bayport
171	2.39		3.44	0.52	Bayport
224	1.43		2.41	0.49	Bayport
238	(1.50)		2.18	0.32	Bayport
Large Bifacial Preforms					
5/16	5.24		(9.37)	0.98	Bayport
148/150	(3.69)		7.33	0.62	Bayport
151/152	(2.84)		(7.20)	0.60	Bayport
192/193	(4.81)		(7.87)	0.85	Bayport
202	3.18		(2.90)	0.73	Bayport
Medium/Small Bifacial Preforms					
135		3.59	6.64	1.71	Bayport
6	2.85		(3.01)	0.82	Bayport
276	2.72		4.45	0.85	Bayport
232	2.08	2.37	4.16	0.64	Charity Island
67	2.48	2.74	(3.37)	0.52	Bayport
Bifacial Scrapers					
200	1.29		(1.60)	0.32	Bayport
117	2.45		3.67	1.12	Bayport
221	2.38		2.30	0.48	Bayport
287	1.89		2.42	0.42	Bayport
159	4.39		2.71		Bayport
229	2.99		2.67	0.91	Pebble
Miscellaneous Bifaces					
19	2.21	2.30	2.53	1.22	Pebble
20	(2.18)		(2.51)	1.11	Pebble

() Broken Attribute

TABLE 24

20GR33 BIFACE FRAGMENTS

	Tips	Mid-Sections	Bases
Area I			
Bayport	3	7	4
Charity Island	1	--	--
Pebble	--	4	2
Area II			
Pebble	--	1	--
Area III			
Bayport	1	21	3
Onondaga	--	1	--
Exotic	1	--	--
Pebble	--	1	--
Exploratory			
Bayport	--	1	--
Flint Ridge ?	--	--	--
Exotic	--	1	--

TABLE 25

20GR33 BIPOLAR CORE METRICS

(in Centimeters)

Area	Width	Length	Thickness	Chert Type
Surface				
1	1.81	1.62	1.12	Bayport
2	1.00	2.70	0.78	Bayport (?)
3	1.67	1.69	0.77	Pebble
4	0.89	1.68	0.37	Pebble
Area I				
5	1.81	4.87	1.54	Pebble
6	1.56	1.60	0.60	Pebble
7	1.84	2.36	1.29	Pebble
8	1.45	1.55	0.40	Bayport
9	2.78	4.52	1.99	Pebble
10	1.24	1.88	1.11	Pebble
11	1.88	3.05	0.85	Bayport w/ cortex
12	2.19	2.36	0.87	Bayport w/ cortex
13	2.14	3.24	0.79	Bayport cortex HM (pink)
14	1.30	2.17	0.92	Pebble
15	1.80	2.52	0.78	Pebble
16	1.44	1.81	0.58	Bayport
17	2.00	2.06	0.64	Bayport w/ outer cortex
18	1.12	2.48	0.72	Bayport
19	0.82	3.19	0.55	Pebble
20	0.90	2.25	0.55	Bayport
21	1.16	1.57	0.52	Bayport HM (dark)
22	2.08	2.14	0.57	Bayport
23	0.99	2.70	0.62	Pebble
24	0.99	1.46	0.49	Pebble
25	1.70	3.00	0.70	Pebble
26	0.75	2.59	0.50	Pebble
27	2.25	2.12	0.46	Pebble
28	1.84	1.48	0.59	Pebble
29	1.75	2.20	0.56	Bayport
30	1.44	2.14	0.78	Pebble
Area II				
31	3.14	4.10	1.91	Pebble

TABLE 25 (CONTINUED)

Area	Width	Length	Thickness	Chert Type
Area II	1.62	2.86	0.54	Pebble
32				
33	1.75	3.78	1.14	Pebble
34	1.00	2.79	0.67	Bayport
35	2.36	5.14	1.89	Pebble
Area III				
36	3.31	3.38	1.19	Pebble
37	1.00	1.62	0.31	Pebble
38	0.63	1.42	0.38	Pebble
39	1.75	2.38	0.49	Bayport
40	1.10	1.49	0.37	Pebble
41	1.51	1.93	0.39	Bayport (?) also used as utilized flake.
42	0.95	3.39	0.76	Pebble
43	1.04	2.12	0.64	Pebble
44	0.98	1.94	0.73	Pebble
45	1.43	2.05	0.68	Pebble
46	1.69	1.87	0.29	Pebble
Exploratory				
47	1.52	3.50	0.58	Pebble

TABLE 26

20GR33 UNIFACE METRICS

(in Centimeters)

#	Width	Length	Thickness	Chert Type
Unifacial Blank				
167	3.17	5.78	0.97	Onondaga
Hafted End Scraper				
198	1.71	1.95	0.92	Pebble
End Scrapers				
3	3.40	(2.60)	1.26	Bayport
164	2.04	(1.93)	0.76	Bayport
213	1.61	2.32	0.88	Pebble
Side Scrapers				
4	(2.00)	(1.68)	0.60	Pebble
107	1.62	2.53	0.66	Bayport w/ outer cortex
113	2.91	4.15	1.78	Bayport w/ outer cortex
End/Side Scrapers				
292	2.05	2.30	0.67	Bayport
Scraper Fragments				
108	2.93	(1.09)	0.52	Bayport
172	2.88	(3.87)	0.78	Bayport
246	0.74	(1.41)	0.39	Pebble
Unifacial Blades				
75	1.96	5.14	0.53	Bayport w/ outer cortex
86	2.13	5.42	0.92	Bayport w/ outer cortex
126	2.13	5.11	0.79	Bayport
176	2.34	4.36	0.52	Bayport w/ outer cortex

() Broken Attribute

TABLE 27

20GR33 UTILIZED FLAKES

Position of Retouch	Area I #	Area I %	Area II #	Area II %	Area III #	Area III %	Surface #	Surface %	Total #	Total %
1 lateral edge	18	36.0%	--	--	5	41.7%	--	--	23	35.4%
2 lateral edges	1	2.0	--	--	--	--	--	--	1	1.5
1 lateral edge - inner face	2	4.0	--	--	--	--	--	--	2	3.1
1 lateral edge & distal end	1	2.0	1	50.0%	1	8.3	--	--	3	4.6
2 lateral edges & distal end	--	--	--	--	2	16.7	--	--	2	3.1
distal end	26	52.0	1	50.0	4	33.3	--	--	31	47.7
1 lateral edge & proximal end	--	--	--	--	--	--	1	100.0%	1	1.5
uncertain	2	4.0	--	--	--	--	--	--	2	3.1
TOTAL	50	100.0%	2	100.0%	12	100.0%	1	100.0%	65	100.0%

TABLE 28

20GR33 POTTERY

Area	Grams	% Grams	Grams/m^2	#Vessels	Vessels/m^2
Area I	69.0	6.0	0.4	1	0.005
Area II	956.1	83.0	8.9	3	0.09
Area III	68.8	6.0	0.4	2	0.01
90N90E	22.2	1.9	--	1	0.005
190S145E	8.3	0.7	--	--	--
190S180E	3.1	0.3	--	--	--
340S340E	24.5	2.1	--	--	--
TOTAL	1152.0g	100.0	2.6	8	0.02

TABLE 29

20GR33 FIRE CRACKED ROCK

Area	Kilograms	Kilograms/m^2
Area I	343.8	1.8
Area II	40.7	1.4
Area III	215.3	1.1
Exploratory	19.7	0.5
TOTAL	619.5kg	1.4

TABLE 30

20GR33 RADIOCARBON DATES

Feature	Lab Number	C-14 Age (b.p.)	C13/C12	C-13 Corrected Age (b.p.)	Calibrated Age*	Calibrated Age - 1 sigma	Calibrated Age - 2 sigma
F	GX-5746	2515 +- 145	---	---	766, 676, 622 B.C.	830-410 B.C.	973-233 B.C.
G	Beta-9644	2560 +- 60	-25.38	2570 +- 65	792 B.C.	805-598 B.C.	889-434 B.C.
I	Beta-10508	2750 +- 150	-28.87	2690 +- 150	831 B.C.	1010-664 B.C.	1290-410 B.C.
J	Beta-9646	2530 +- 60	-23.08	2560 +- 65	790 B.C.	803-594 B.C.	830-492 B.C.
P	Beta-9645	2400 +- 90	-22.01	2445 +- 95	750, 724, 536, 535, 519, 464, 446 B.C.	787-402 B.C.	810-365 B.C.
S	Beta-10509	2490 +- 100	-27.45	2450 +- 100	752, 720, 708, 695, 586, 585, 538, 533, 521, 463, 447 B.C.	790-400 B.C.	820-264 B.C.
T	Beta-9648	2760 +- 90	-21.26	2820 +- 95	1002, 989, 975, 947 B.C.	1208-836 B.C.	1309-800 B.C.
Average	---	---	---	---	792 B.C.	799-664 B.C.	811-595 B.C.

*Stuiver and Becker 1986.

TABLE 31

20GR33 ARTIFACTS

	Area I #	Area I %	Area II #	Area II %	Area III #	Area III %	Exploratory #	Exploratory %	Total #	Total %
Projectile Points										
Meadowood Points	16	10.8%	--	--	17	19.3%	--	--	33	12.3%
Side-Notched Points	2	1.4	4	21.0%	4	4.5	1	7.7%	11	4.1
Stemmed Points	--	--	1	5.3	--	--	--	--	1	0.4
Corner-Notched Points	2	1.4	--	--	--	--	1	7.7	3	1.1
Late Woodland Triangular	--	--	1	5.3	1	1.1	--	--	2	0.7
Blades and Tips	4	2.7	--	--	2	2.3	1	7.7	7	2.6
Total - Projectile Points	24	16.2%	6	31.6%	24	27.3%	3	23.1%	57	21.6%
Bifaces										
Turkey Tails	1	0.7%	--	--	--	--	--	--	1	0.4%
Hafted End Scrapers	--	--	--	--	2	2.3	--	--	2	0.7
Trianguloid Bifacial End Scrapers	--	--	--	--	1	1.1	--	--	1	0.4
Bifacial Scrapers	3	2.0	--	--	2	2.3	--	--	5	1.9
Drill Blanks	1	0.7	--	--	--	--	--	--	1	0.4
Blanks/Preforms	3	2.0	--	--	1	1.1	--	--	4	1.5
Hafted Knife	--	--	--	--	--	--	1	7.7	1	0.4
Bifacial Blades	4	2.7	--	--	--	--	--	--	4	1.5
Triangular Bifaces	2	1.4	--	--	3	3.4	--	--	5	1.9
Miscellaneous Bifaces	1	0.7	1	5.3	--	--	--	--	2	0.7
Biface Fragments	19	12.8	3	15.8	28	31.8	4	30.8	54	20.1
Total - Bifaces	34	23.0%	4	21.0%	37	42.0%	5	38.5%	80	29.9%

TABLE 31 (CONTINUED)

	Area I		Area II		Area III		Exploratory		Total	
	#	%	#	%	#	%	#	%	#	%
Bipolar Cores	26	17.6%	5	26.3%	10	11.4%	5	38.5%	46	17.2%
Unifaces										
End Scrapers	3	2.0%	1	5.3%	--	--	--	--	4	1.5%
Side Scrapers	4	2.7	1	5.3	--	--	--	--	5	1.9
End/Side Scrapers	1	0.7	--	--	1	1.1%	--	--	2	0.7
Scraper Fragments	1	0.7	--	--	2	2.3	--	--	3	1.1
Unifacial Blades	4	2.7	--	--	--	--	--	--	4	2.7
Utilized Flakes										
Side Retouch	21	14.2	--	--	5	5.7	--	--	26	9.7
End Retouch	26	17.6	1	5.3	4	4.5	--	--	31	11.6
End/Side Retouch	1	0.7	1	5.3	3	3.4	--	--	5	1.9
Uncertain	2	1.4	--	--	--	--	--	--	2	1.4
Total - Unifaces	63	42.6%	4	21.0%	15	17.0%	--	--	82	30.6%
Adze	1	2.7%	--	--	--	--	--	--	1	2.7%
Sandstone Artifact	--	--	--	--	1	1.1%	--	--	1	0.4%
Gorgets	--	--	--	--	1	1.1%	--	--	1	0.4%
TOTAL - ALL ARTIFACTS	148	100.1%	19	99.9%	88	99.9%	13	100.1%	268	100.2%

TABLE 32

20GR33 OCCUPATIONAL INTENSITY INDICES

Index	Area I	Area II	Area III	Total
Artifacts/m^2	0.6	0.6	0.5	0.6
Projectile Points/m^2	0.1	0.2	0.1	0.1
kg F.C.R./m^2	1.8	1.2	1.1	1.5
Flakes/m^2	38.7	24.5	7.2	23.0
Features/m^2	0.1	0.1	0.1	0.1

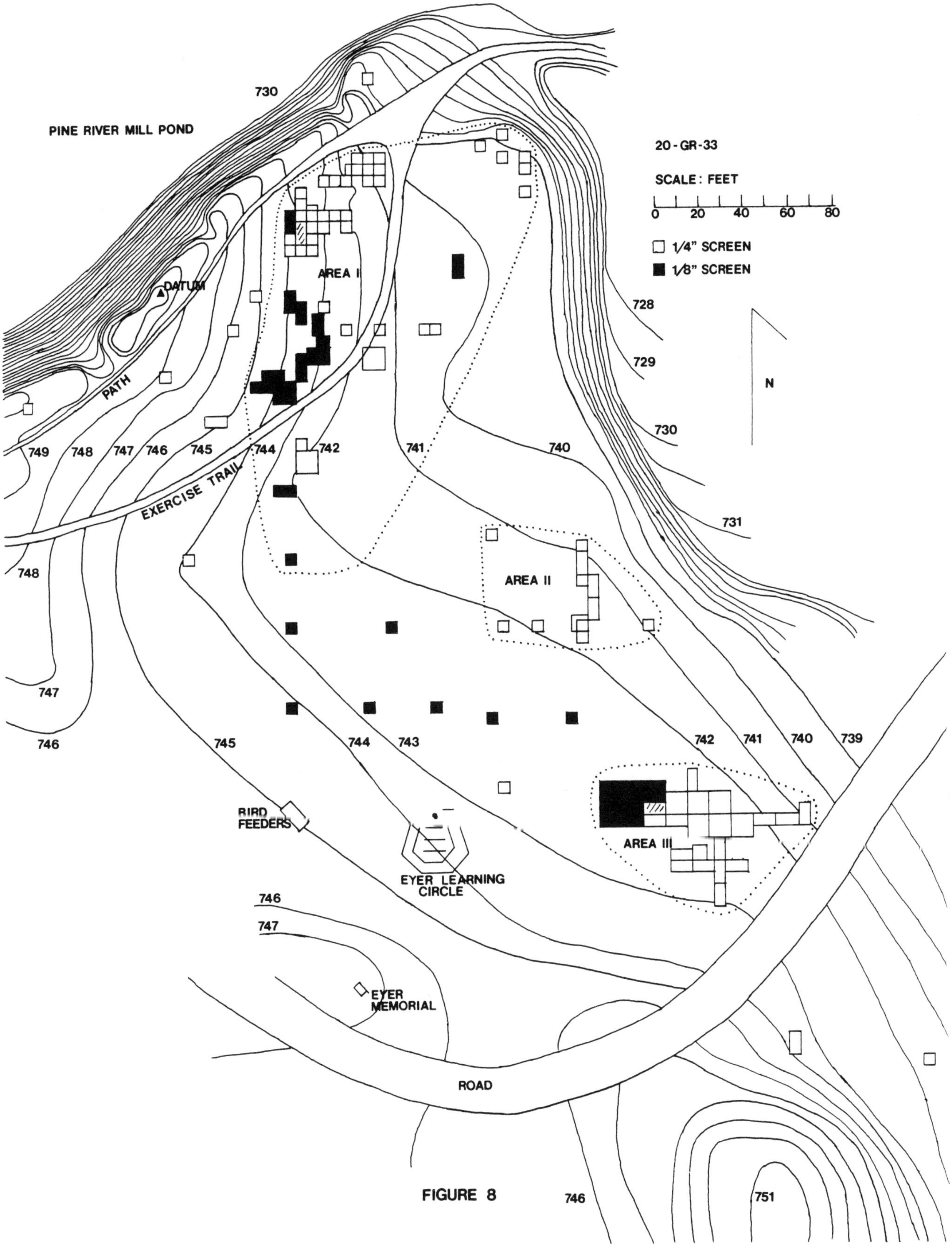
730
PINE RIVER MILL POND
20-GR-33
SCALE: FEET
0 20 40 60 80
1/4" SCREEN
1/8" SCREEN
AREA I
DATUM
PATH
728
729
N
730
749 748 747 746 745 744 742
741
740
EXERCISE TRAIL
731
748
AREA II
747
746
745
744 743
742 741 740 739
BIRD FEEDERS
AREA III
EYER LEARNING CIRCLE
746
747
EYER MEMORIAL
ROAD
746
751

FIGURE 8

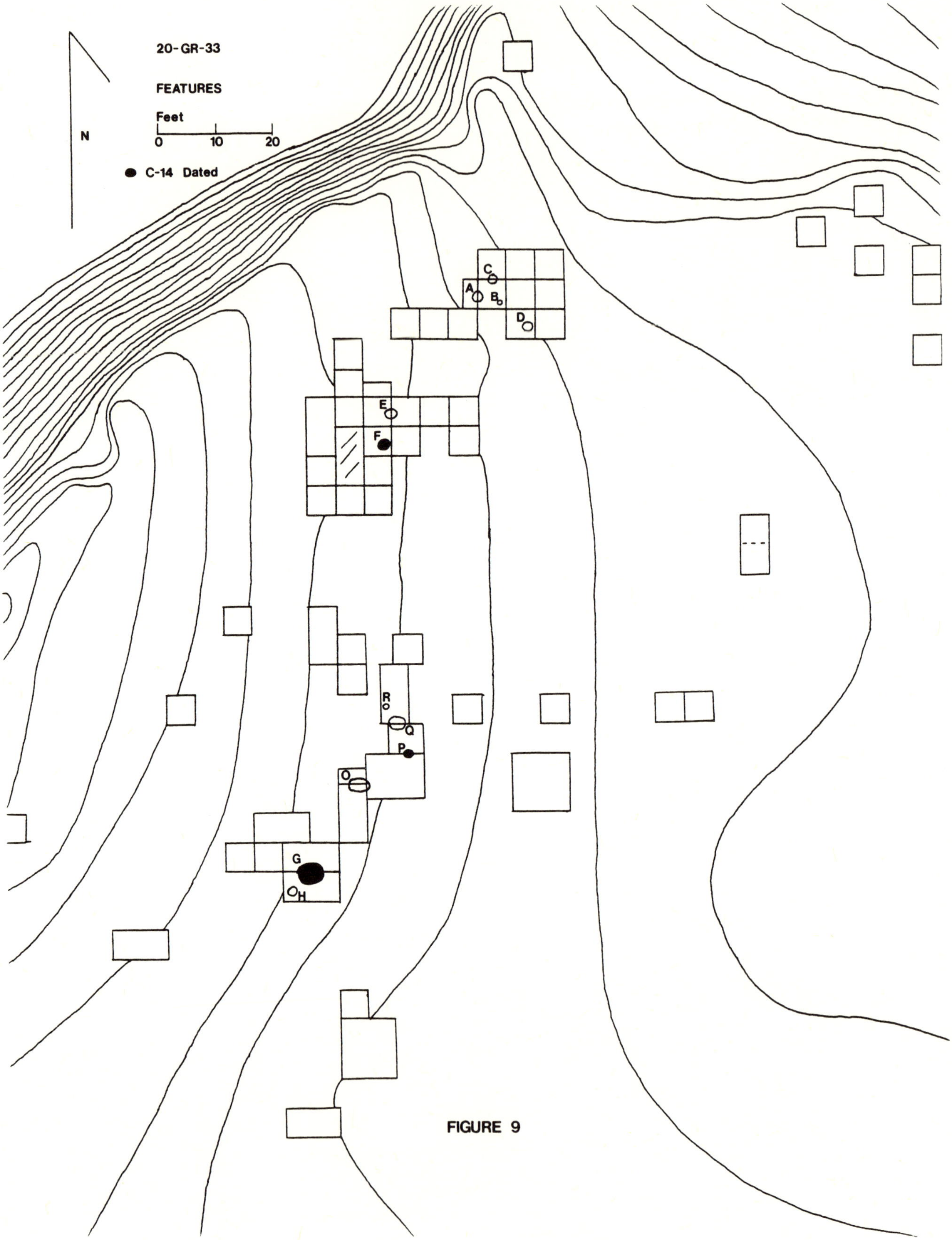

FIGURE 9

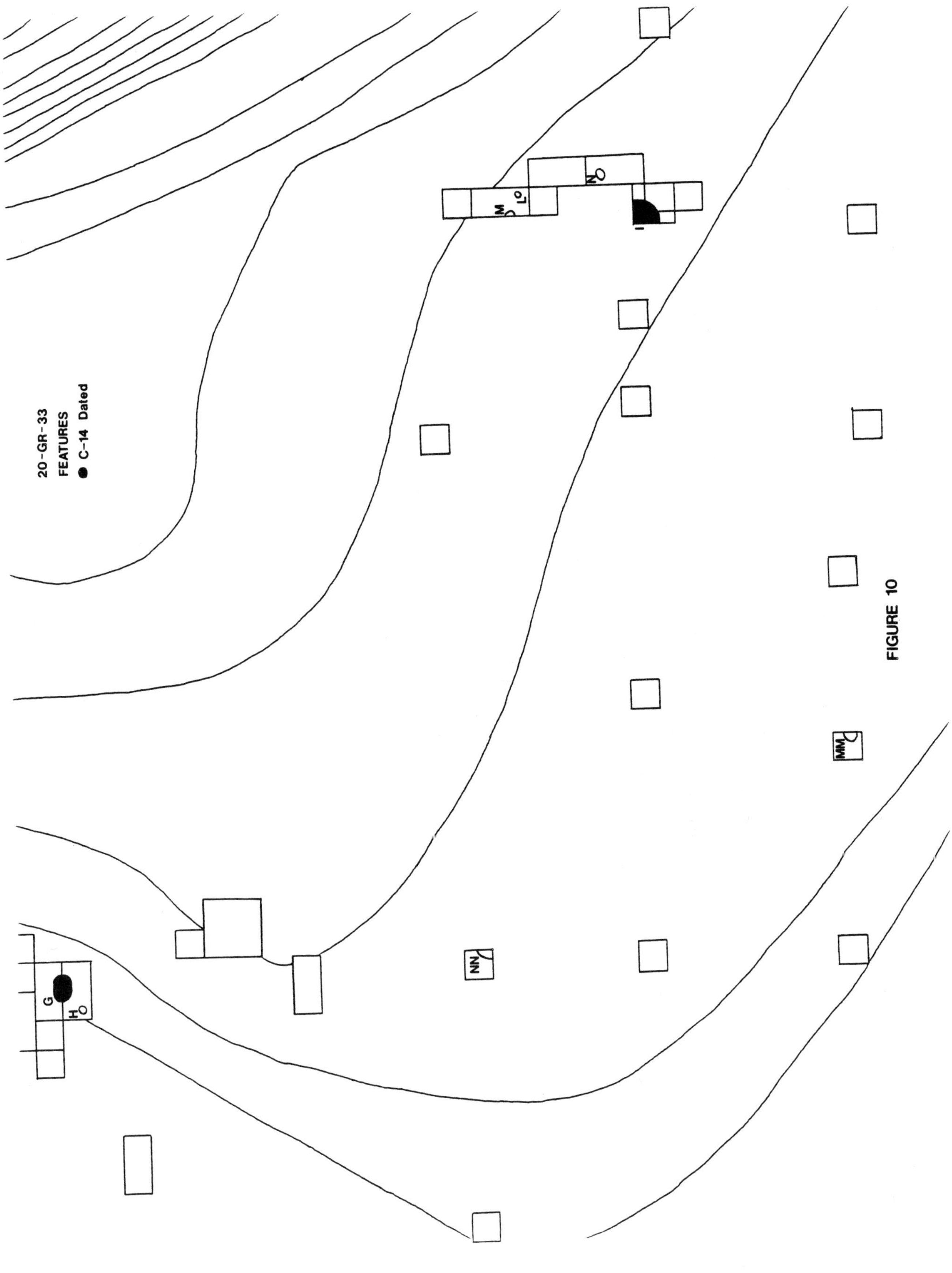

FIGURE 10

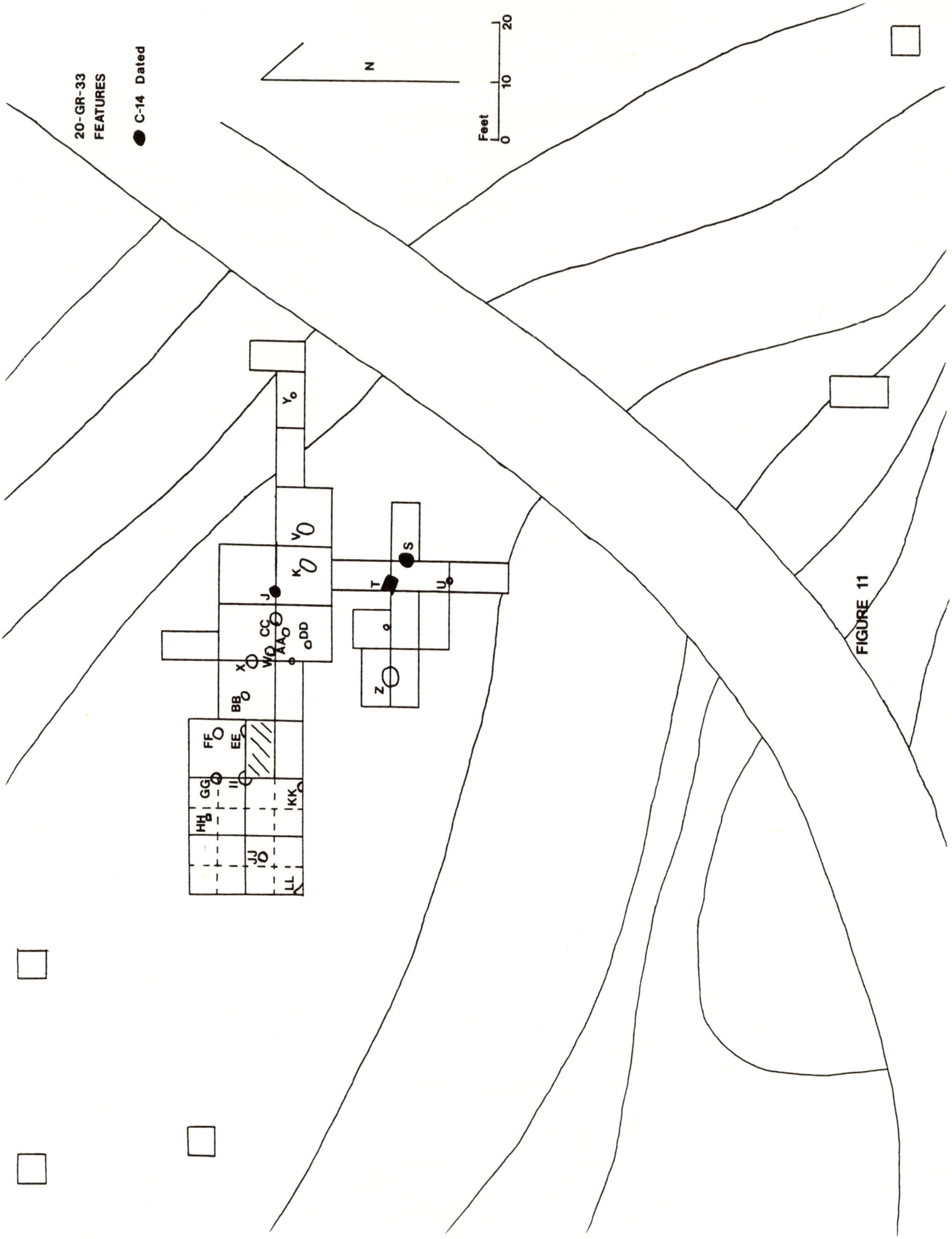
20-GR-33
FEATURES
C-14 Dated
N
Feet
0
10
20
Y
V
K
J
CC
DD
AA
W
X
BB
FF
EE
GG
II
HH
KK
JJ
LL
S
T
U
Z

FIGURE 11

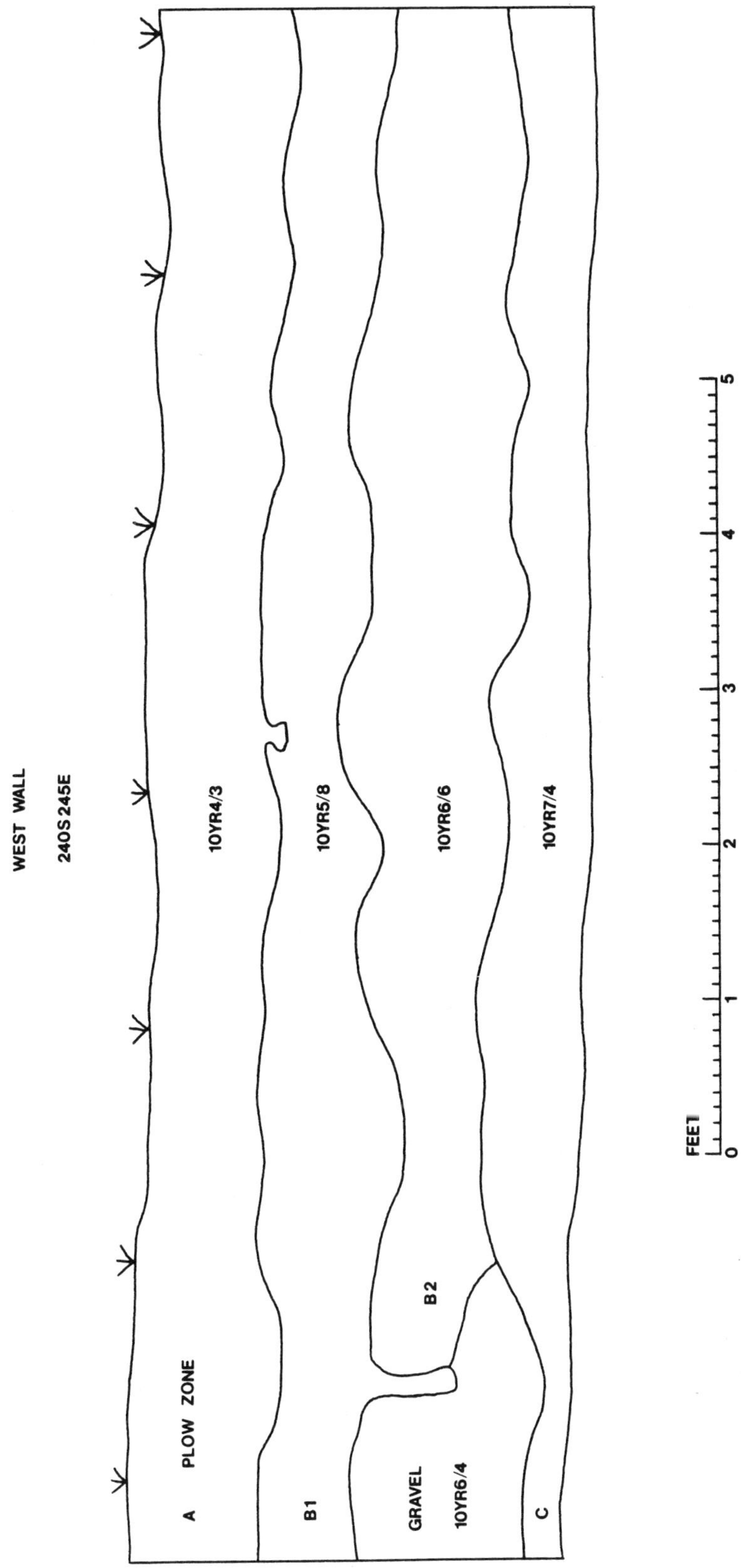
WEST WALL
240S 245E
A
PLOW ZONE
10YR4/3
B1
10YR5/8
B2
GRAVEL
10YR6/4
10YR6/6
C
10YR7/4
FEET
0
1
2
3
4
5

FIGURE 12

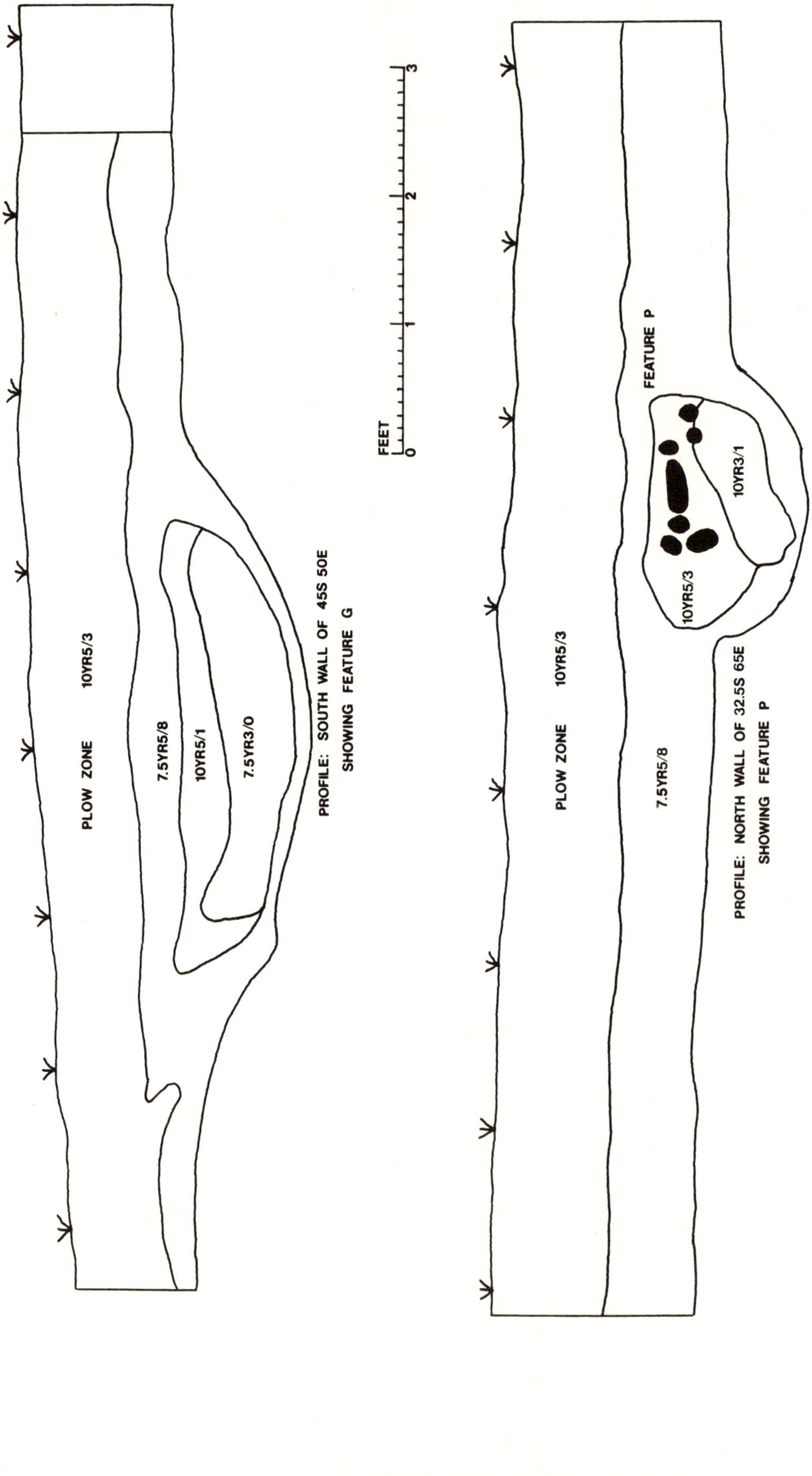
PLOW ZONE 10YR5/3
7.5YR5/8
10YR5/1
7.5YR3/0
PROFILE: SOUTH WALL OF 45S 50E
SHOWING FEATURE G
FEET
0
1
2
3
FEATURE P
10YR3/1
10YR5/3
PLOW ZONE 10YR5/3
7.5YR5/8
PROFILE: NORTH WALL OF 32.5S 65E
SHOWING FEATURE P

FIGURE 13

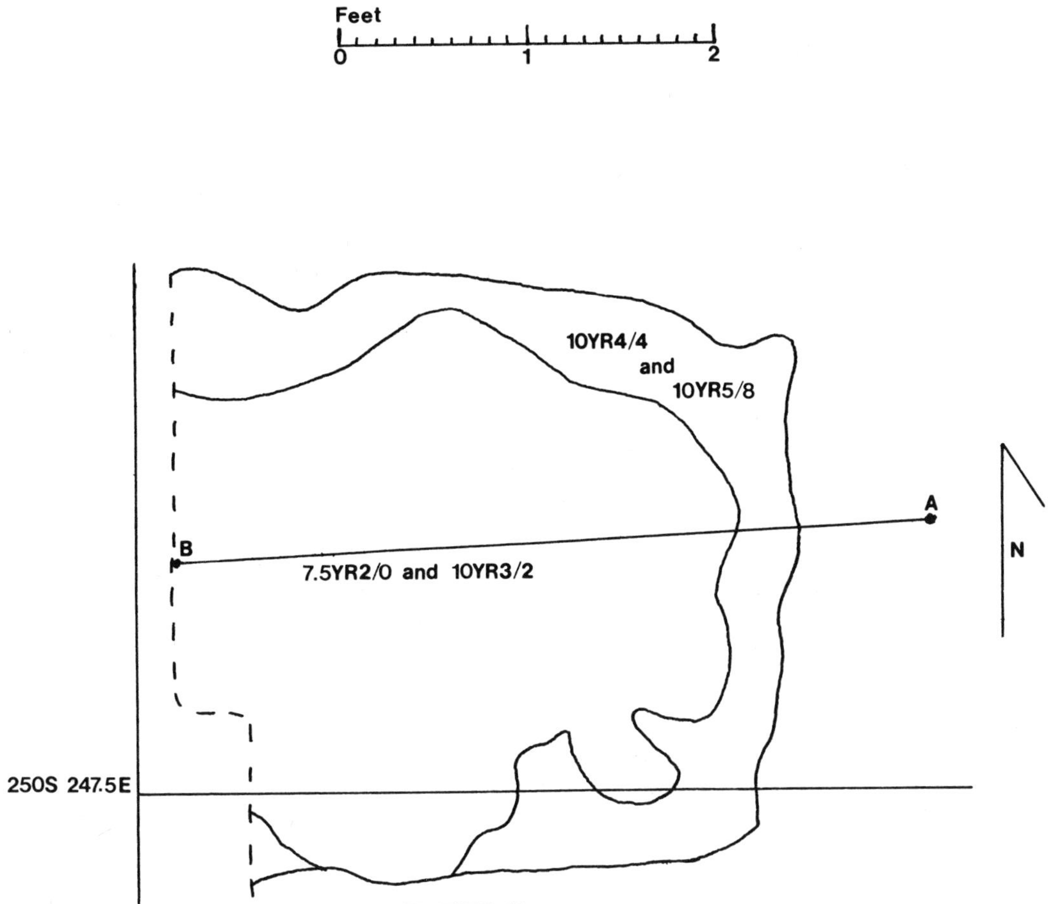

FEATURE T

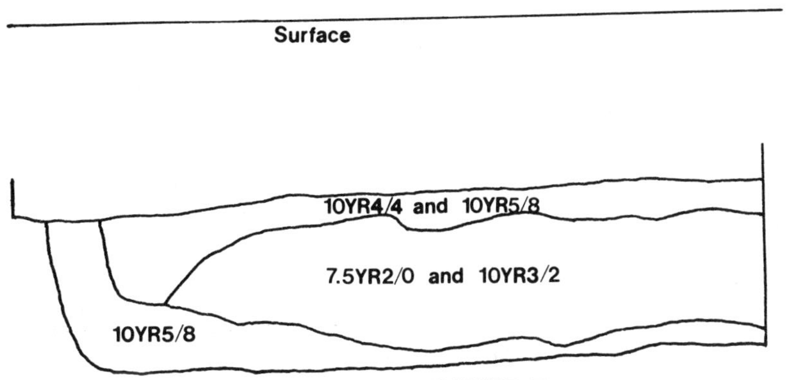

PROFILE FEATURE T

FIGURE 14

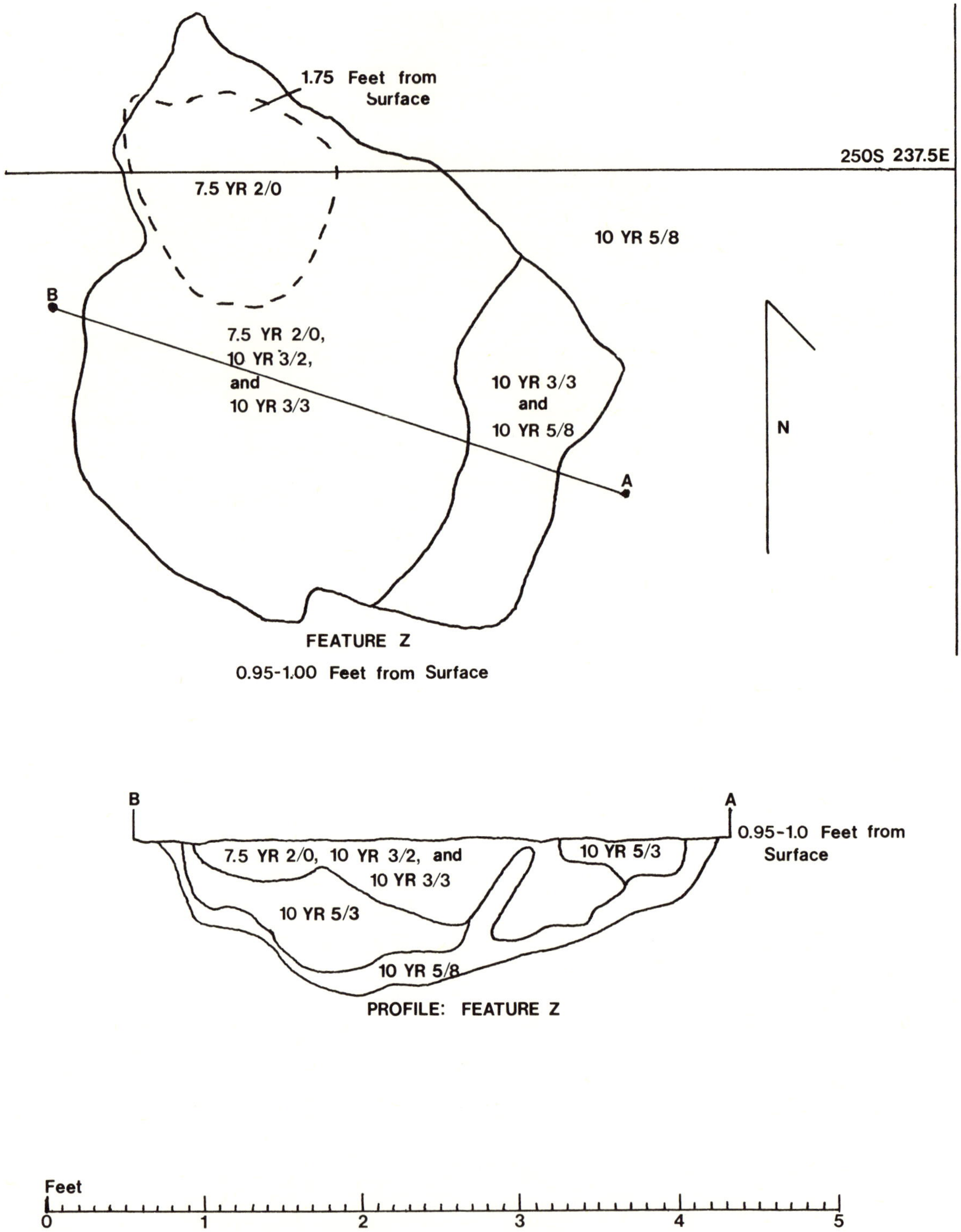
1.75 Feet from Surface
250S 237.5E
7.5 YR 2/0
10 YR 5/8
B
7.5 YR 2/0, 10 YR 3/2, and 10 YR 3/3
10 YR 3/3 and 10 YR 5/8
N
A
FEATURE Z
0.95-1.00 Feet from Surface
B
A
0.95-1.0 Feet from Surface
7.5 YR 2/0, 10 YR 3/2, and 10 YR 3/3
10 YR 5/3
10 YR 5/3
10 YR 5/8
PROFILE: FEATURE Z
Feet
0
1
2
3
4
5

FIGURE 15

20 GR 33
Flakes per Unit
1/4" Screen
Feet
0 10 20
N
41
6
26
19
52
16
10
251 118 118
223 235 243 224
92 278 271 219 148
166
231 109
293 232 379 138 202 142
466 293 76
78 90
42 40 106
17
11
5
71 85
21
293
61
3
6
3
4 6
29
29 107
9
6
148
65
14 24 97
126
5
8
35
45

FIGURE 16

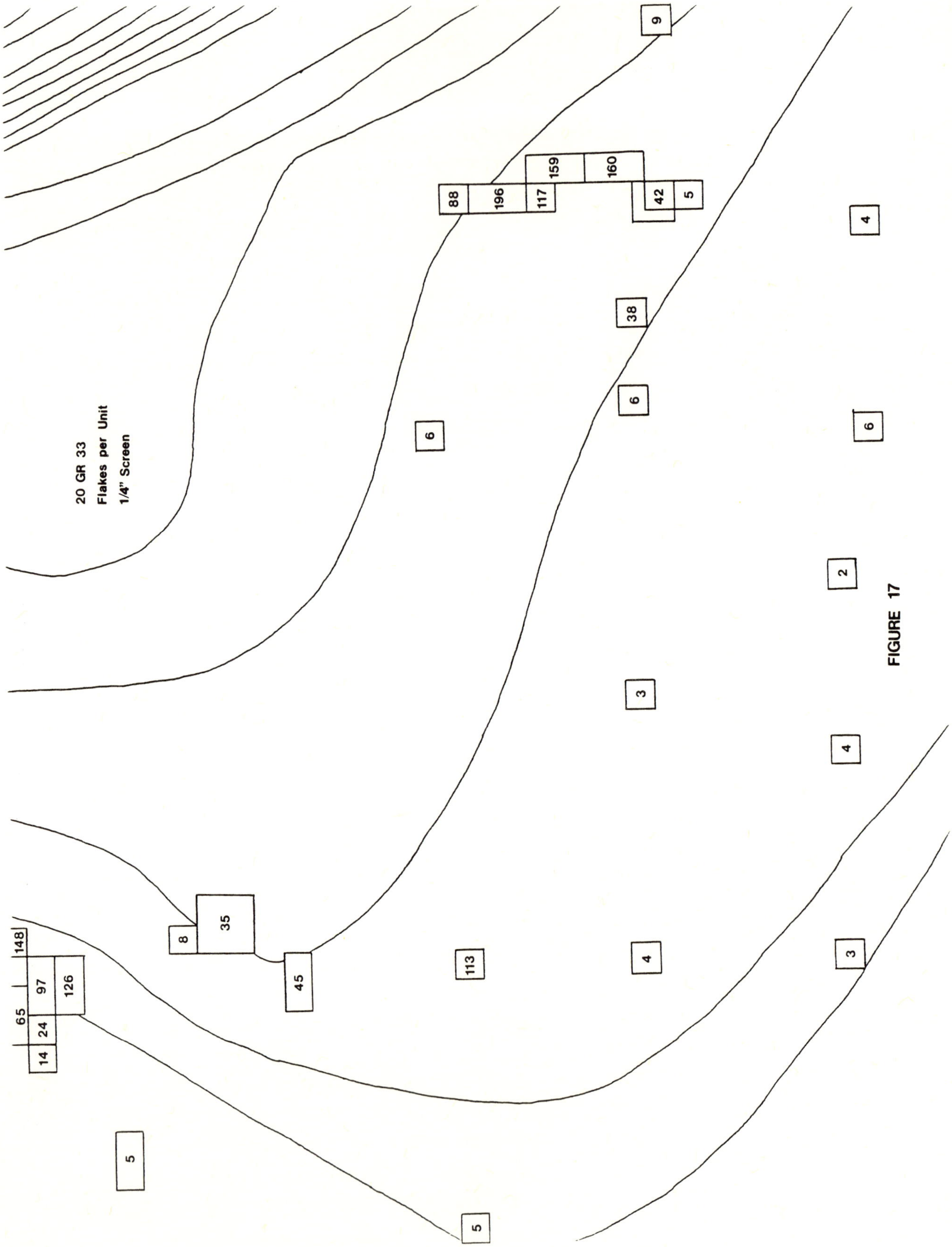

FIGURE 17

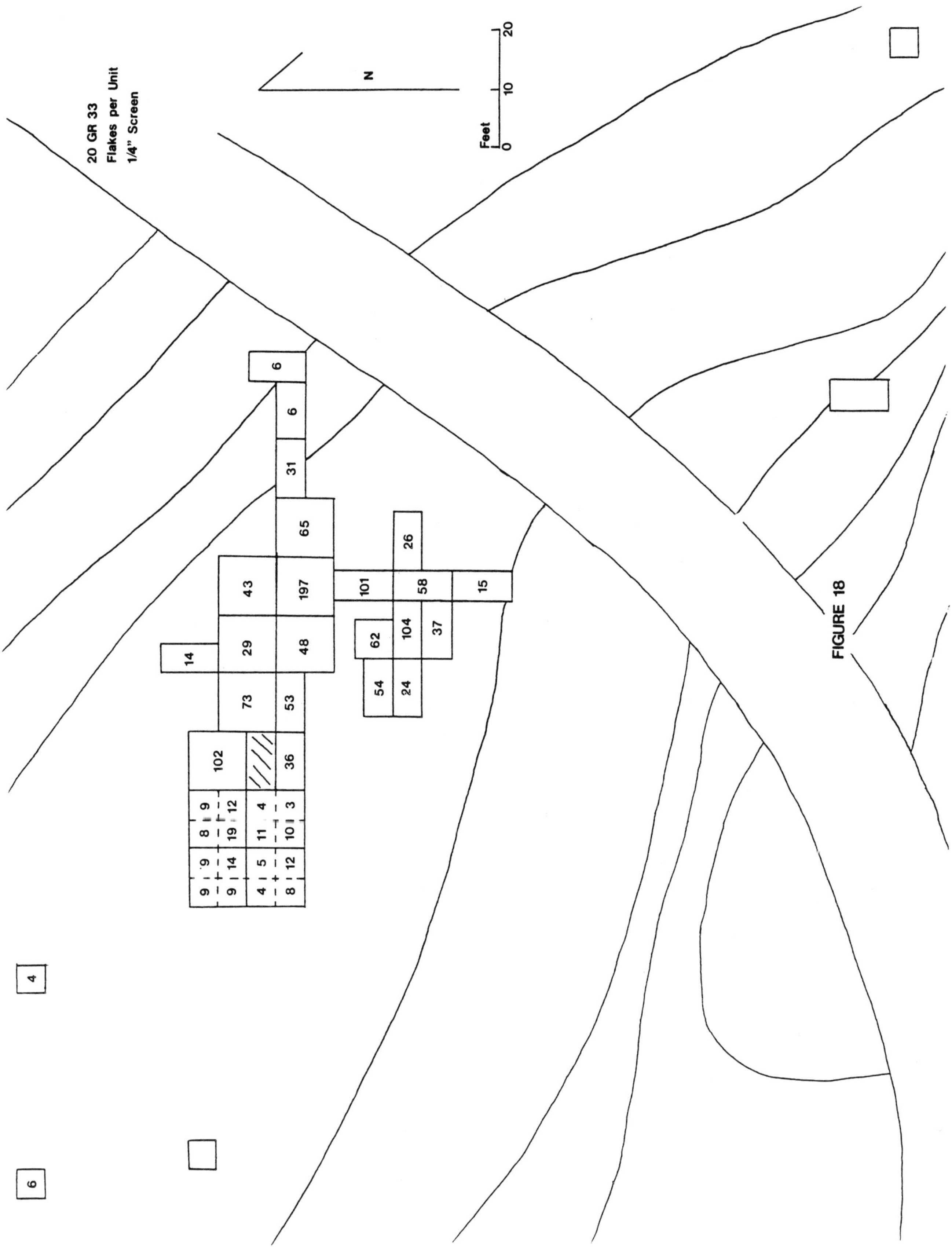

FIGURE 18

20 GR 33
Flakes per Unit
1/8" Screen
Feet
0 10 20
N
408
110
80
18
198
62
77
400
466
252
18
35
204
292
135

FIGURE 19

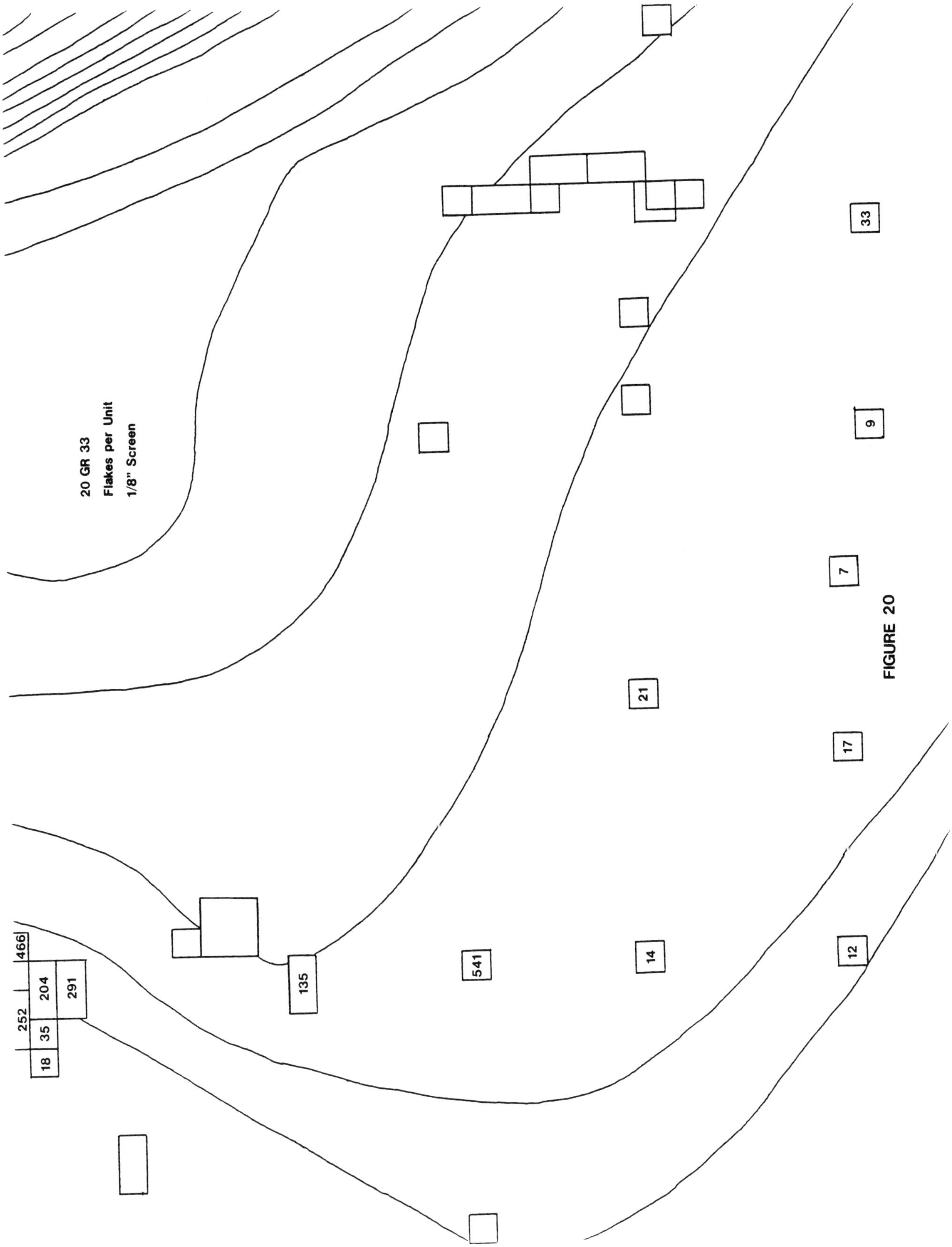
20 GR 33
Flakes per Unit
1/8" Screen
33
9
7
21
17
466
252
204
291
35
18
135
541
14
12

FIGURE 20

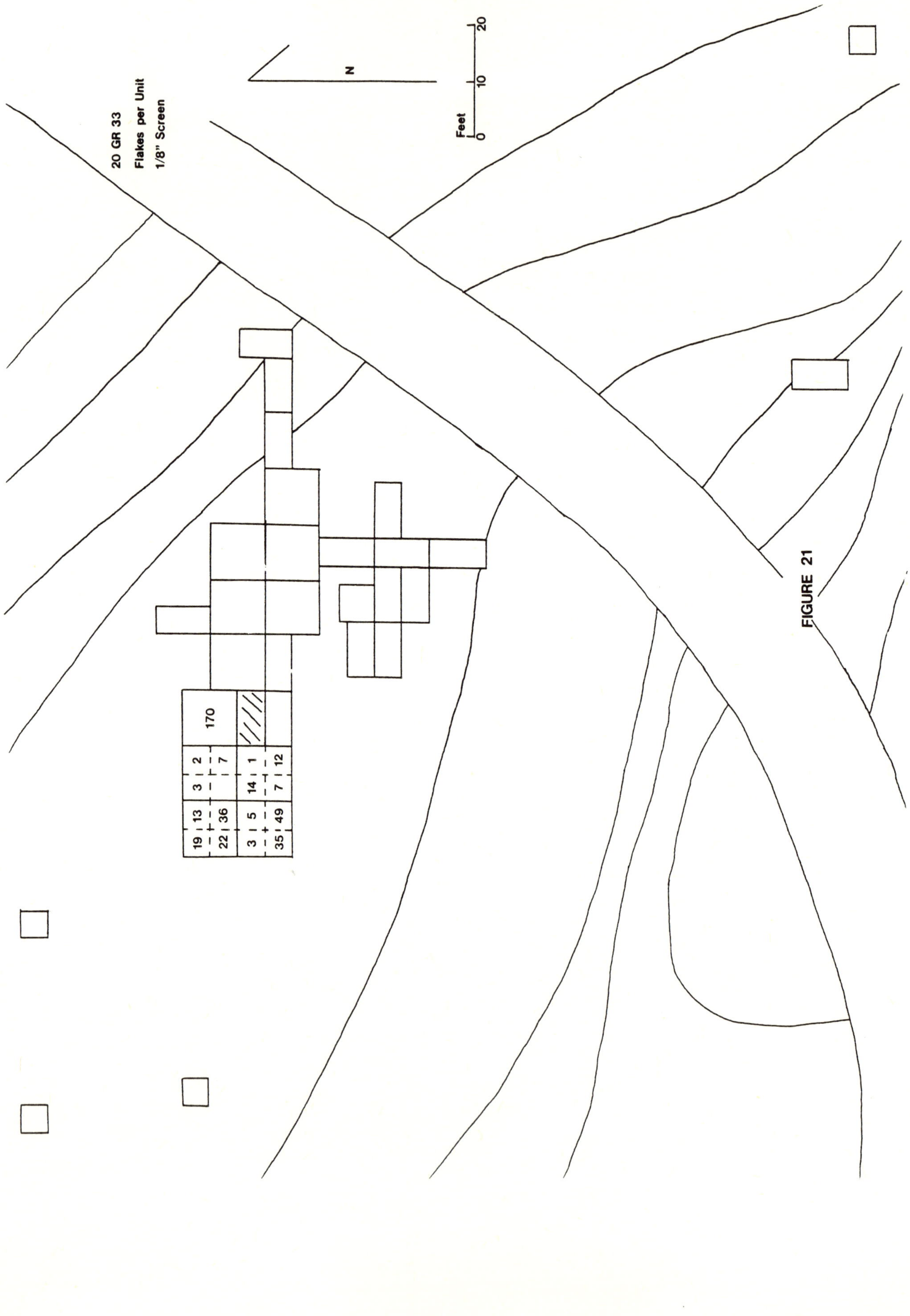
20 GR 33
Flakes per Unit
1/8" Screen
N
Feet
0
10
20
170
19
13
22
36
3
2
7
3
5
35
49
14
1
7
12

FIGURE 21

20 GR 33
Bayport Flakes with Outer
Cortex per Unit
Feet
0 10 20
N
4 2 1
10 3 10 7
4 8 6 7 3
3
11 1
11 23 9 14 7
16 16 18 3
3 2
3 8
1
3
1
1
1
2 2
2
1
1 1
2

FIGURE 22

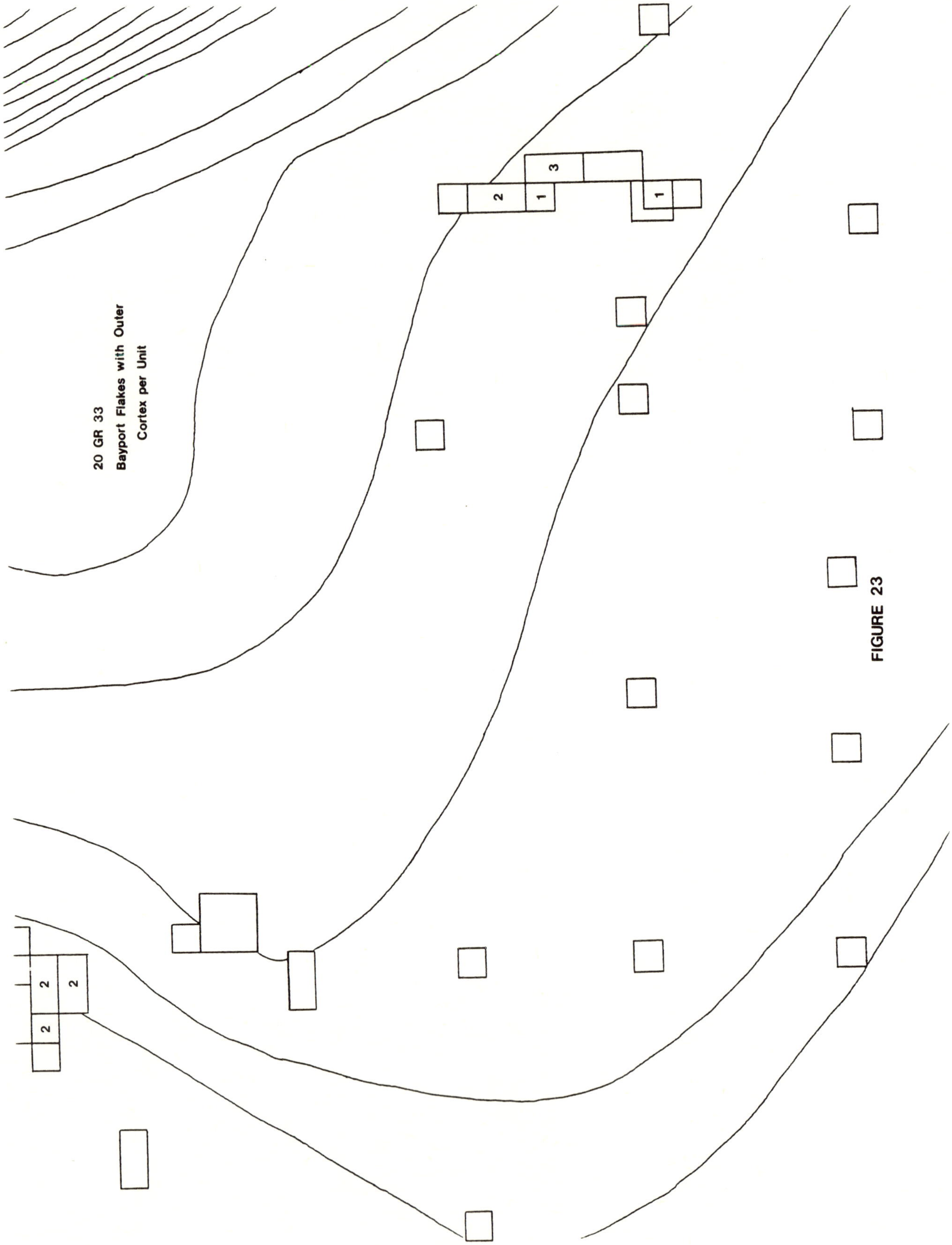

FIGURE 23

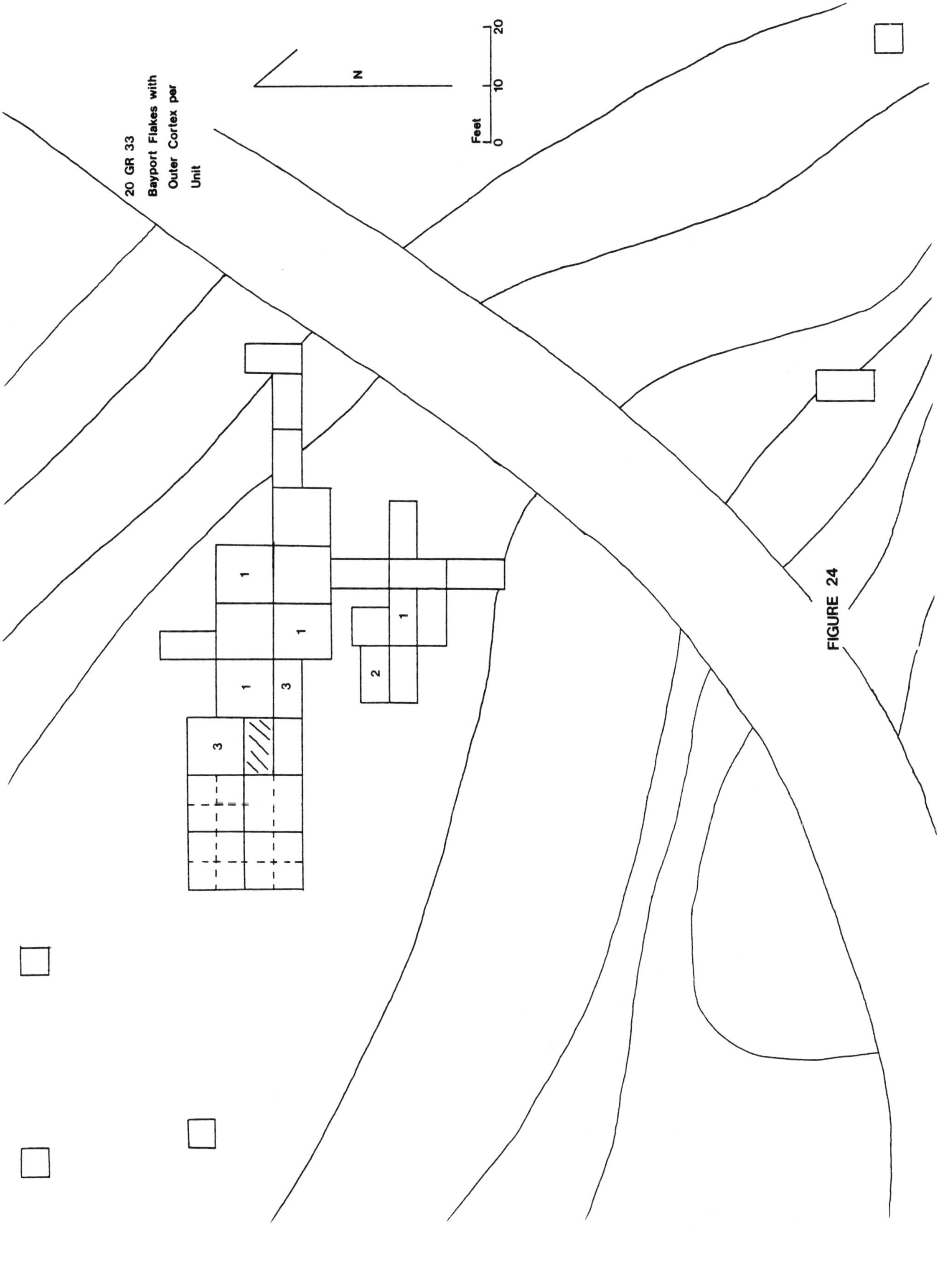
20 GR 33
Bayport Flakes with
Outer Cortex per
Unit
N
Feet
0
10
20
1
1
1
3
3
1
2

FIGURE 24

20 GR 33
Flakes with Ground Striking
Platforms per Unit
Feet
0 10 20
N
2
2
2
2
1
2
6 2 4
2 3 9 7 8
6
1
4 7 1 4 2
4
4 4
3 2
1
4 16
1
40
9
1
6 18
20
4
9
3
2

FIGURE 25

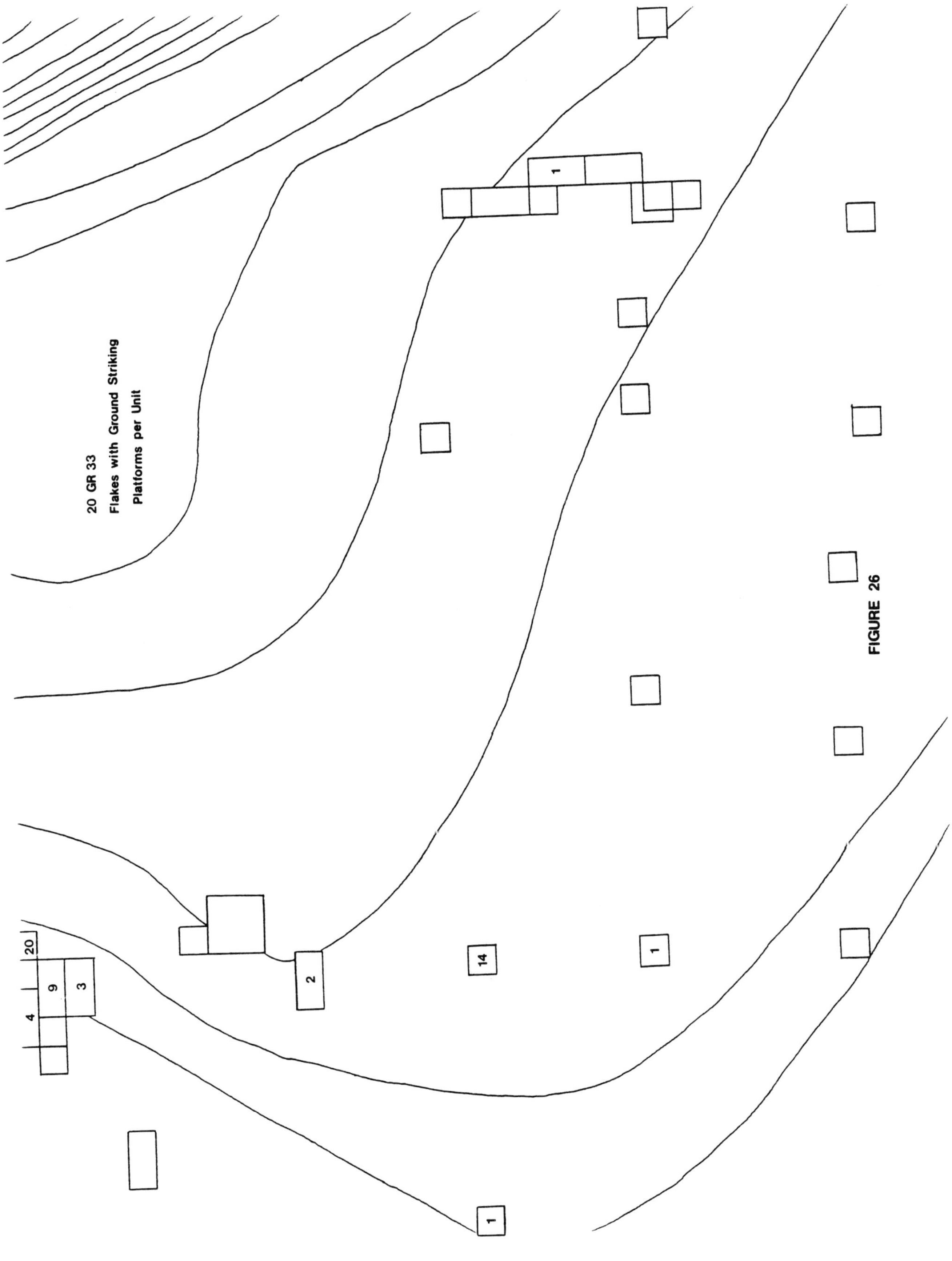
20 GR 33
Flakes with Ground Striking
Platforms per Unit
1
2
14
1
20
9
3
4
1

FIGURE 26

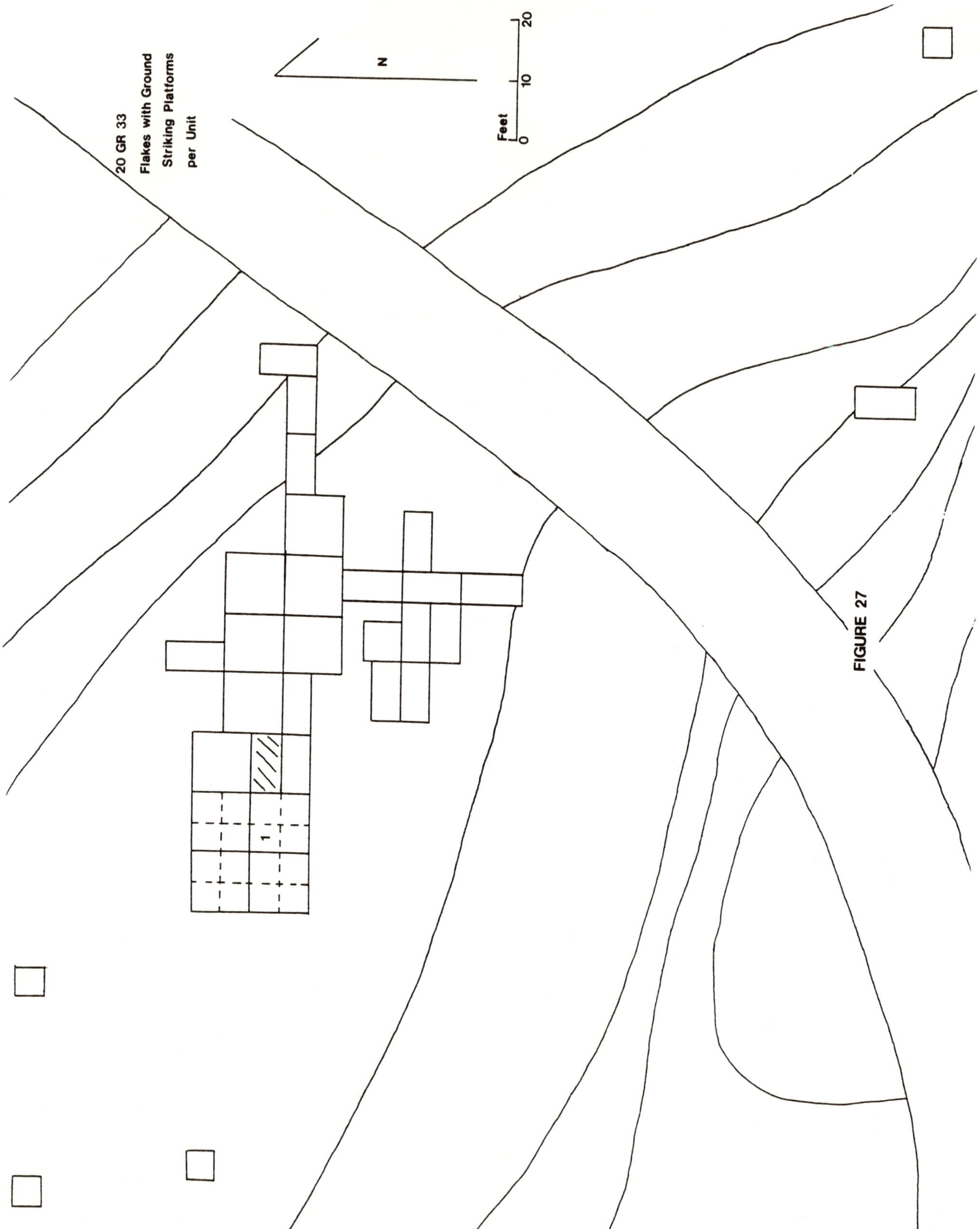
20 GR 33
Flakes with Ground
Striking Platforms
per Unit
N
Feet
0
10
20
1

FIGURE 27

20 GR 33
Grams of Pottery per Unit
Feet
0 10 20
N
22
3
12
16
1
0.4
3
3
0.5
5
2
3
1
6
1
10

FIGURE 28

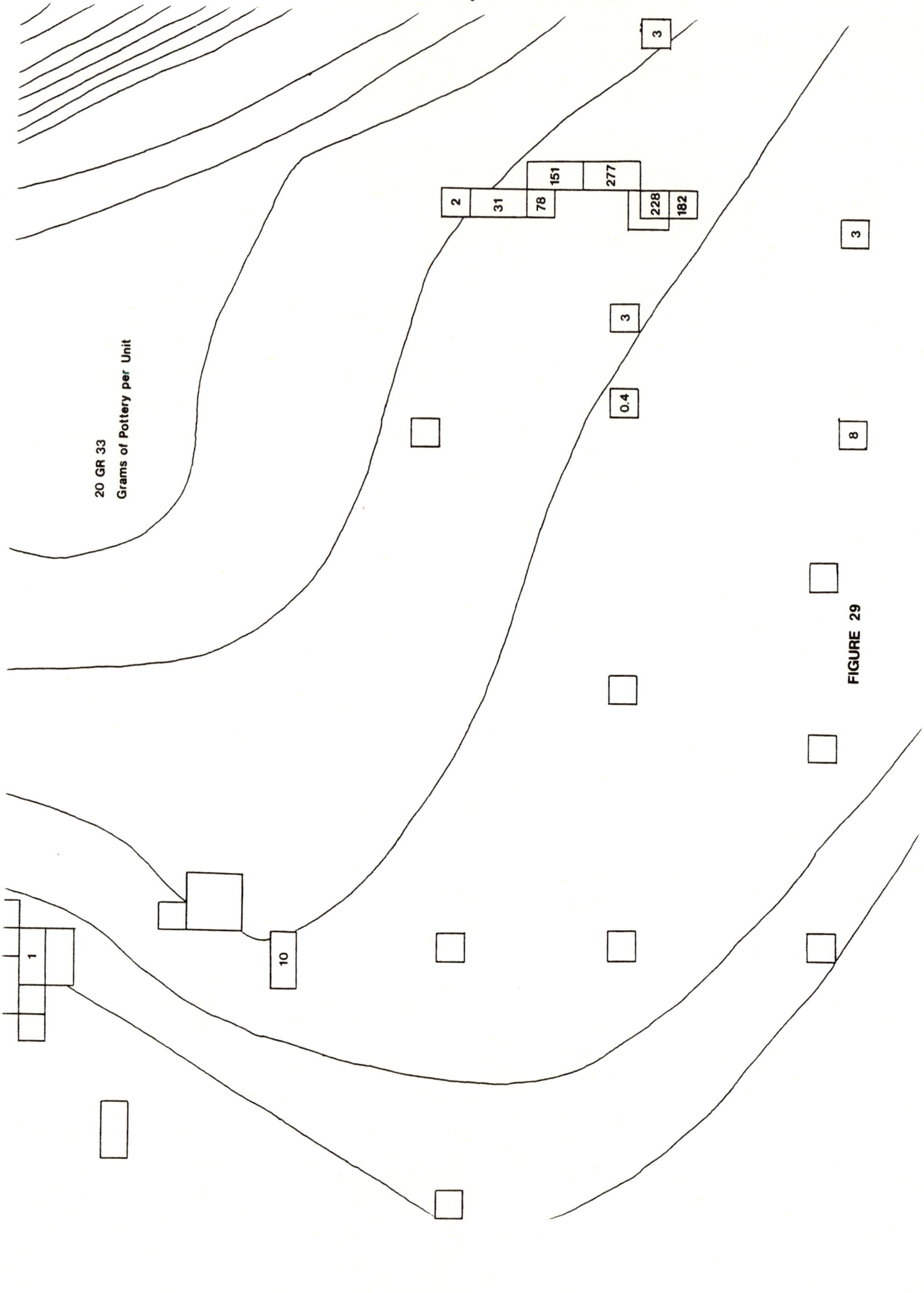
20 GR 33
Grams of Pottery per Unit
3
151
277
2
31
78
228
182
3
3
0.4
8
10
1

FIGURE 29

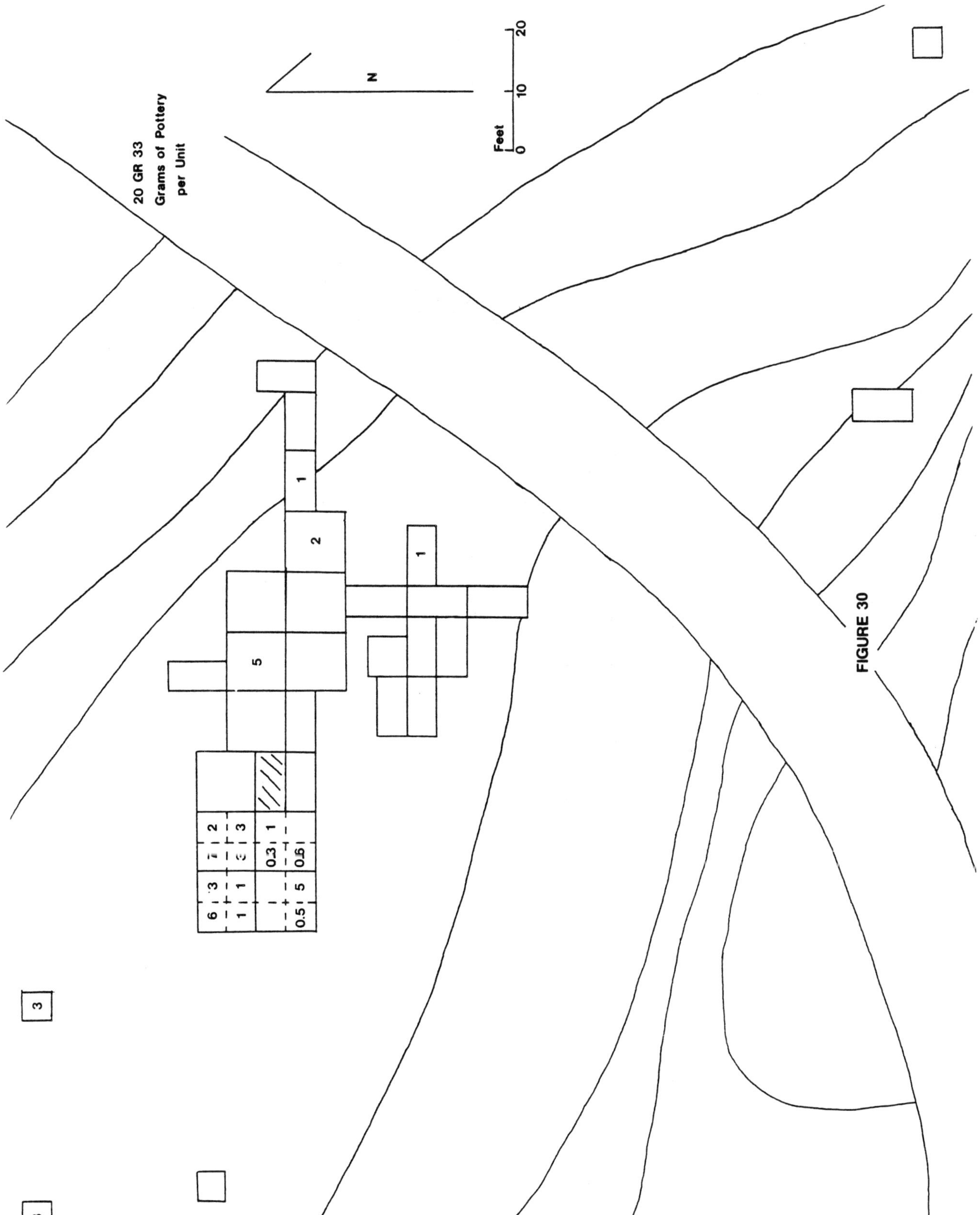

FIGURE 30

FIGURE 31

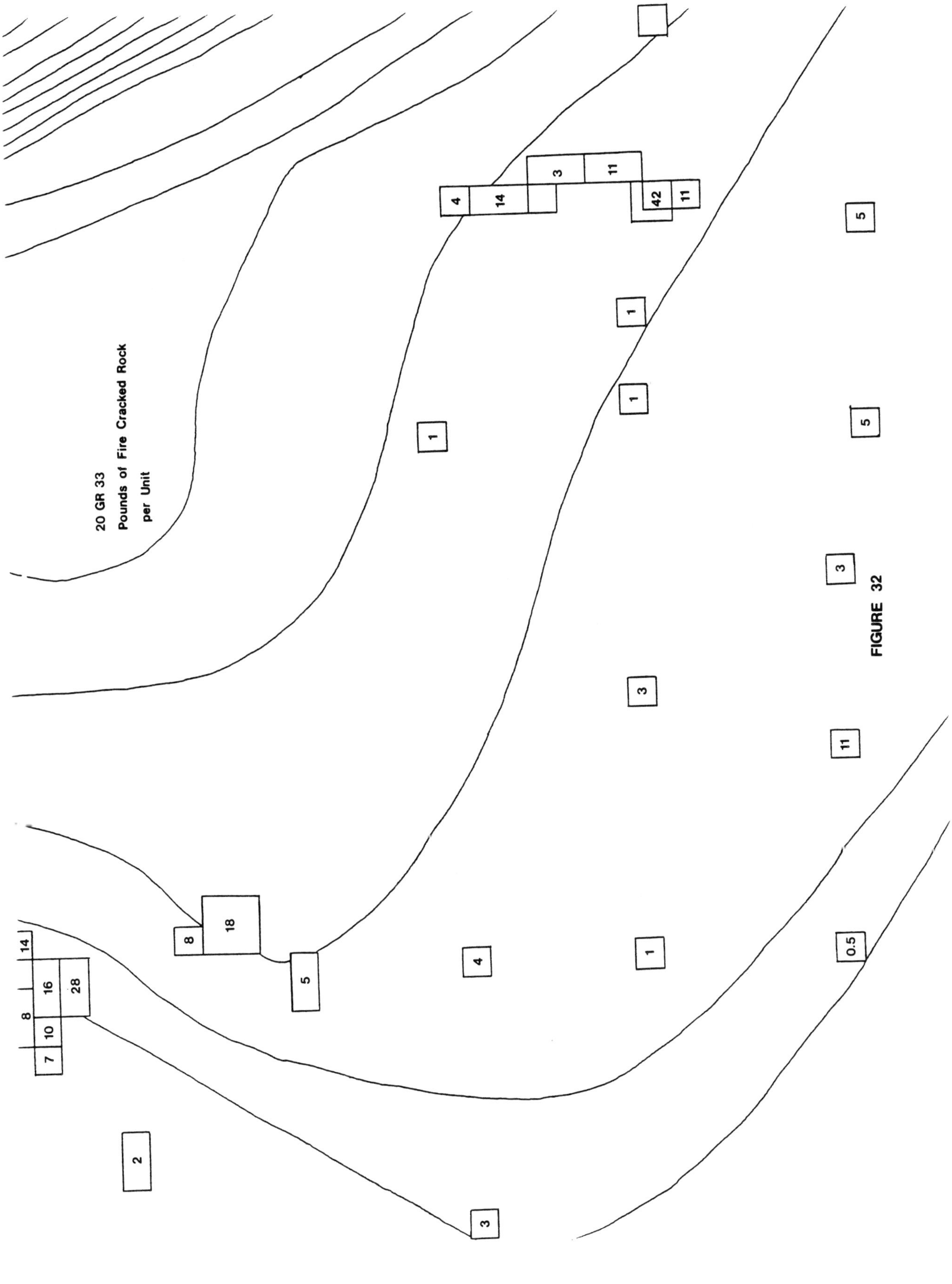

FIGURE 32

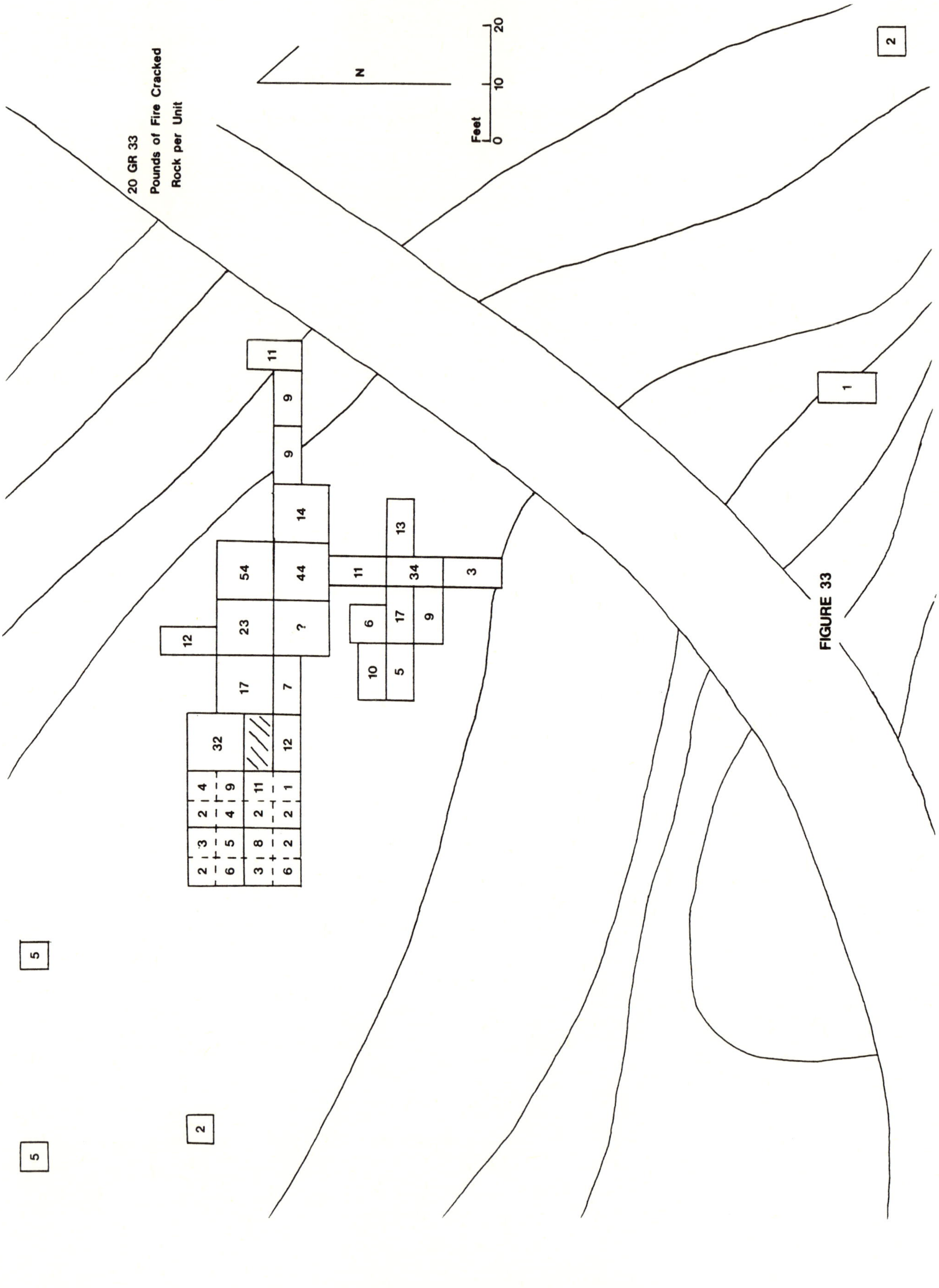

FIGURE 33

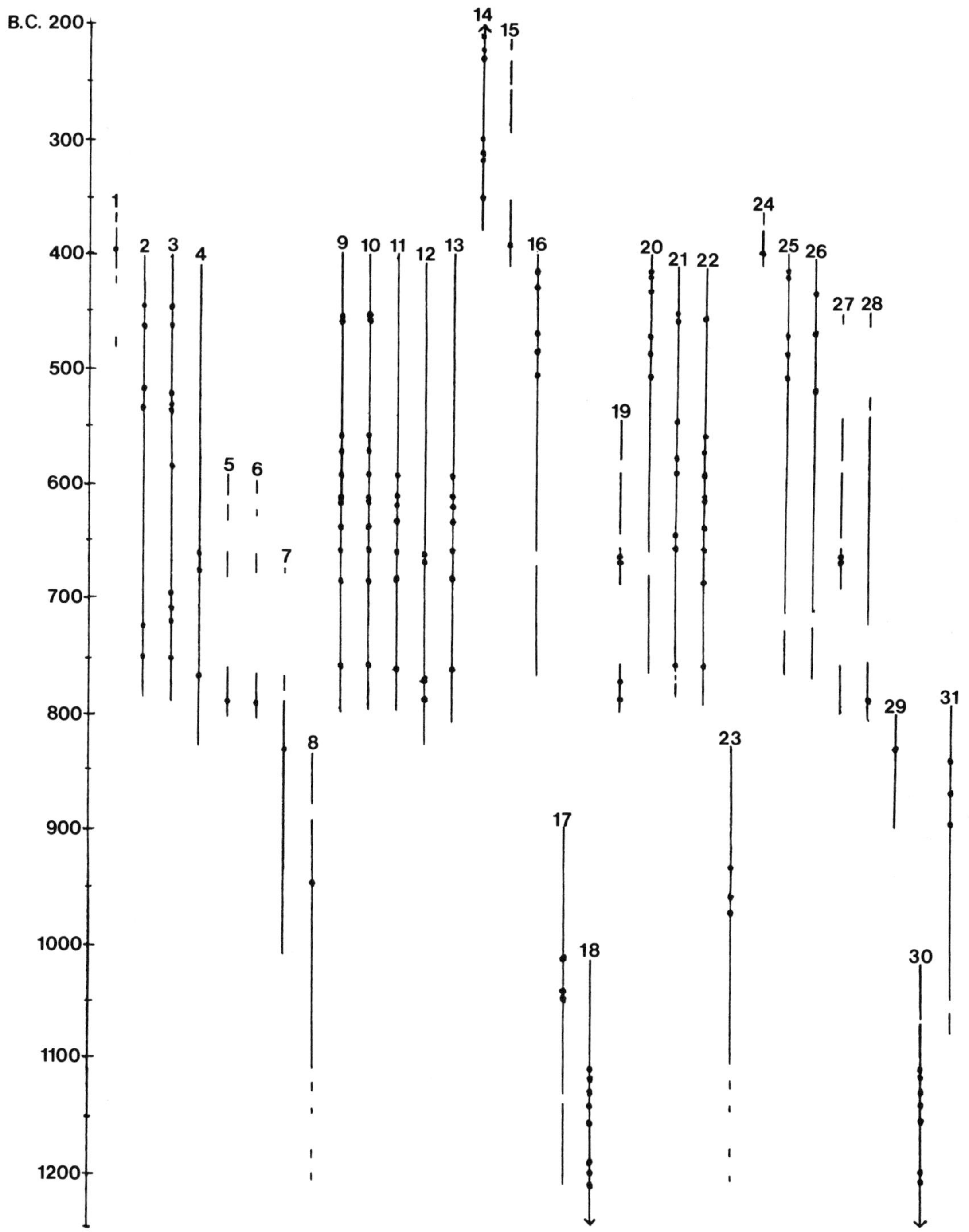

CALIBRATED EARLY WOODLAND
C-14 DATES

FIGURE 34

Figure 34

Calibrated Early Woodland C-14 Dates - Key

Michigan

1	20-GR-176 (this volume).
2-8	Conservation Park (this volume).
9	Green Point (Wright 1964:20).
10-11	Schultz (Speth 1972:61).
12-13	Croton Dam Mounds (Fitting 1975:95).
14-18	Eidson (Garland 1986:52).
19	Elam (Garland 1986:52).

Ontario

20	Ferris (Spence and Fox 1986:15).
21	Bruce Boyd (Jackson 1980:28; Spence and Fox 1986:15).
22	Wyoming Rapids (Spence and Fox 1986:15).
23	Boyd Lakefront (Spence and Fox 1986:15).
24-30	Dawson Creek (Jackson 1980:16; Spence and Fox 1986:15).

Ohio

31	Asmus No. 3 (Stothers 1975:5).

Dates calibrated according to Stuiver and Becker (1986).

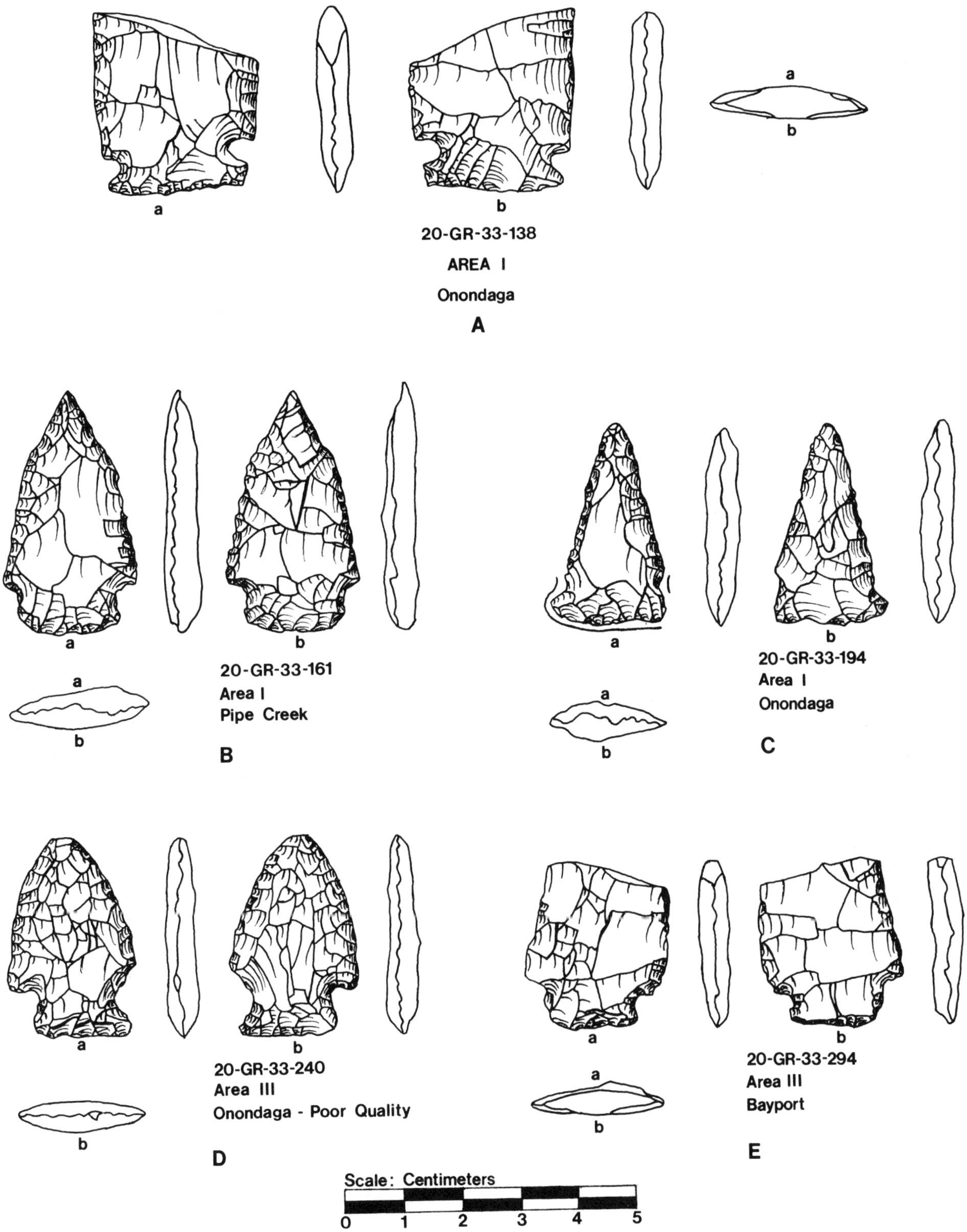

MEADOWOOD POINTS

FIGURE 35

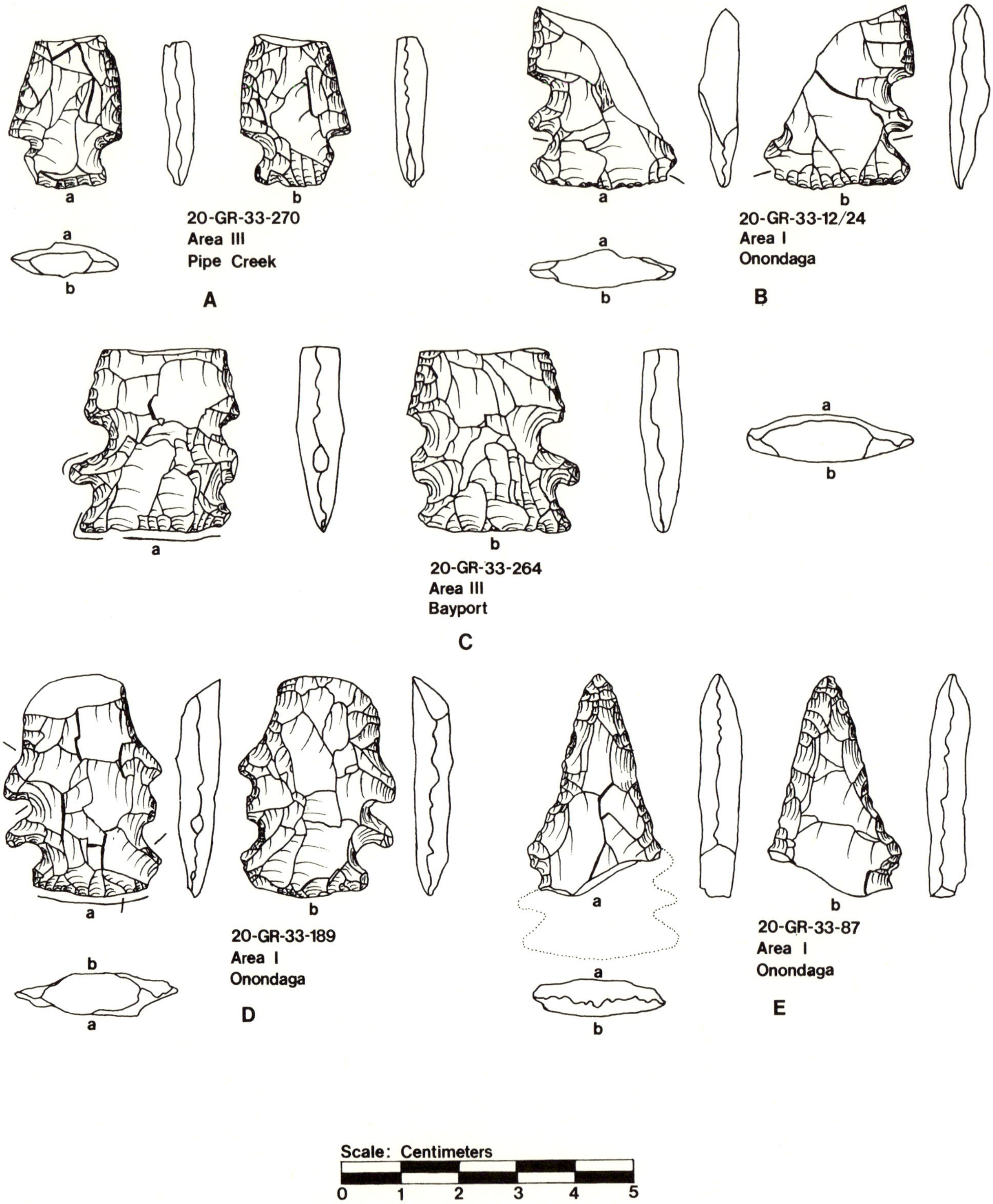

MEADOWOOD POINTS

FIGURE 36

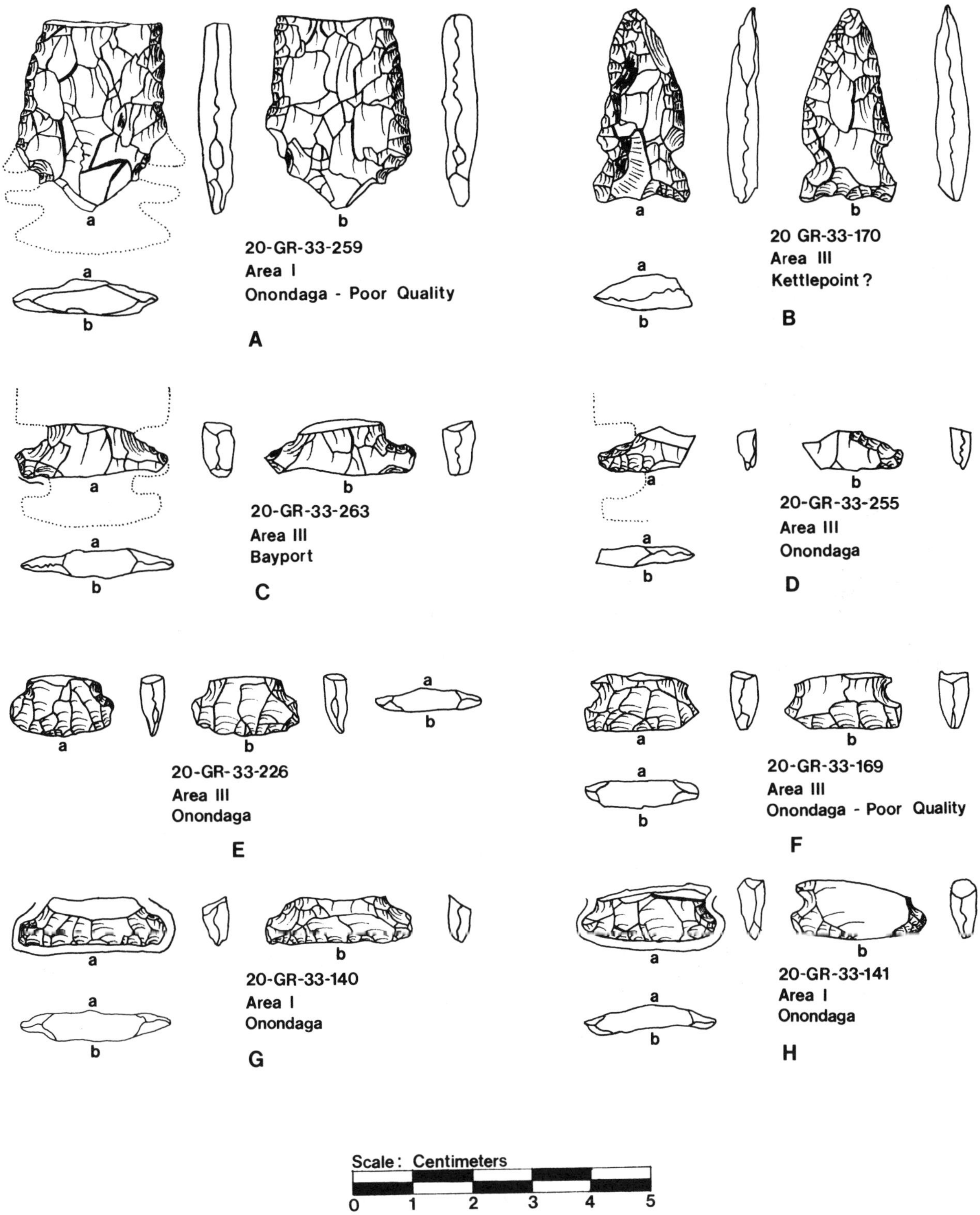

MEADOWOOD POINTS

FIGURE 37

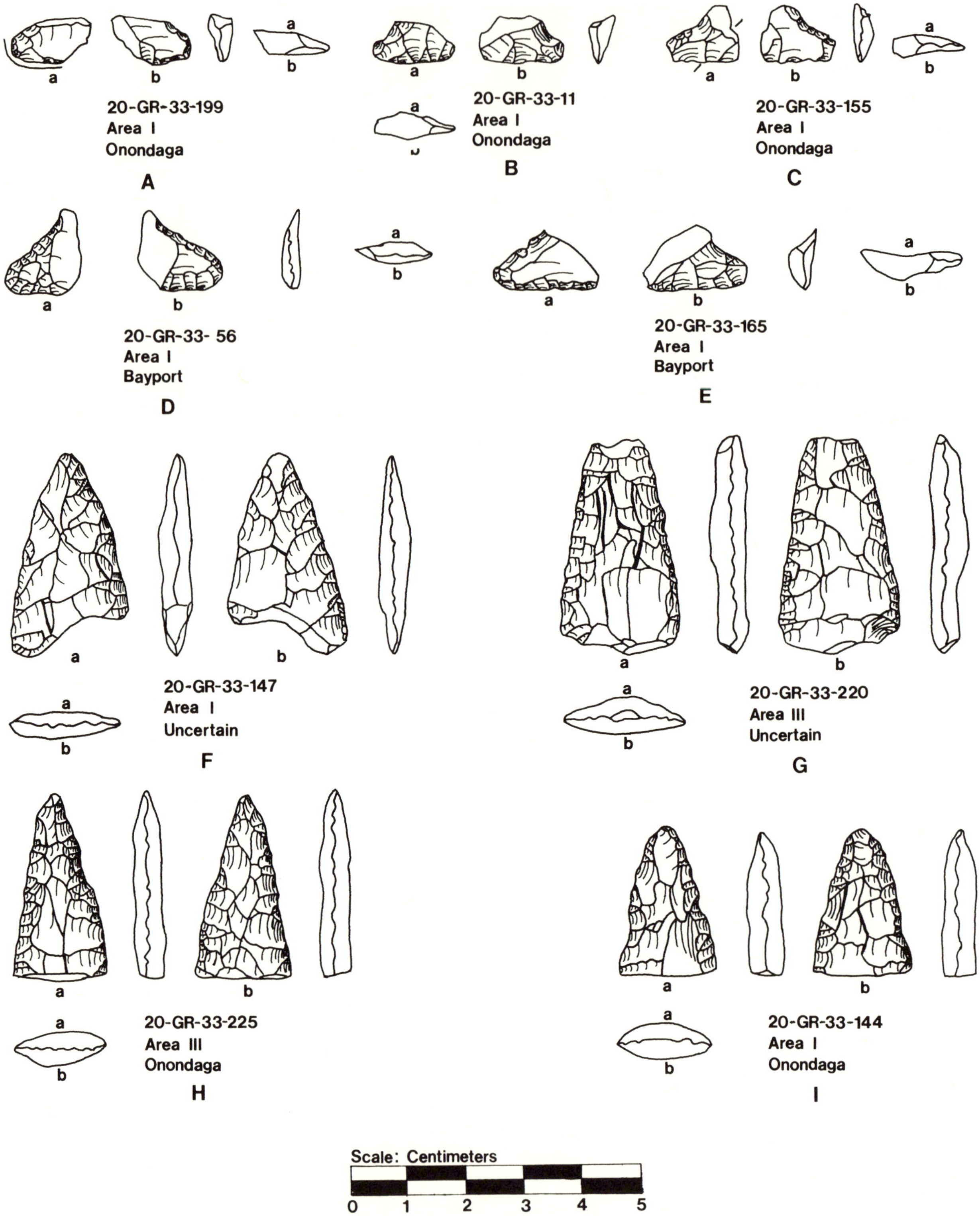

MEADOWOOD POINTS

FIGURE 38

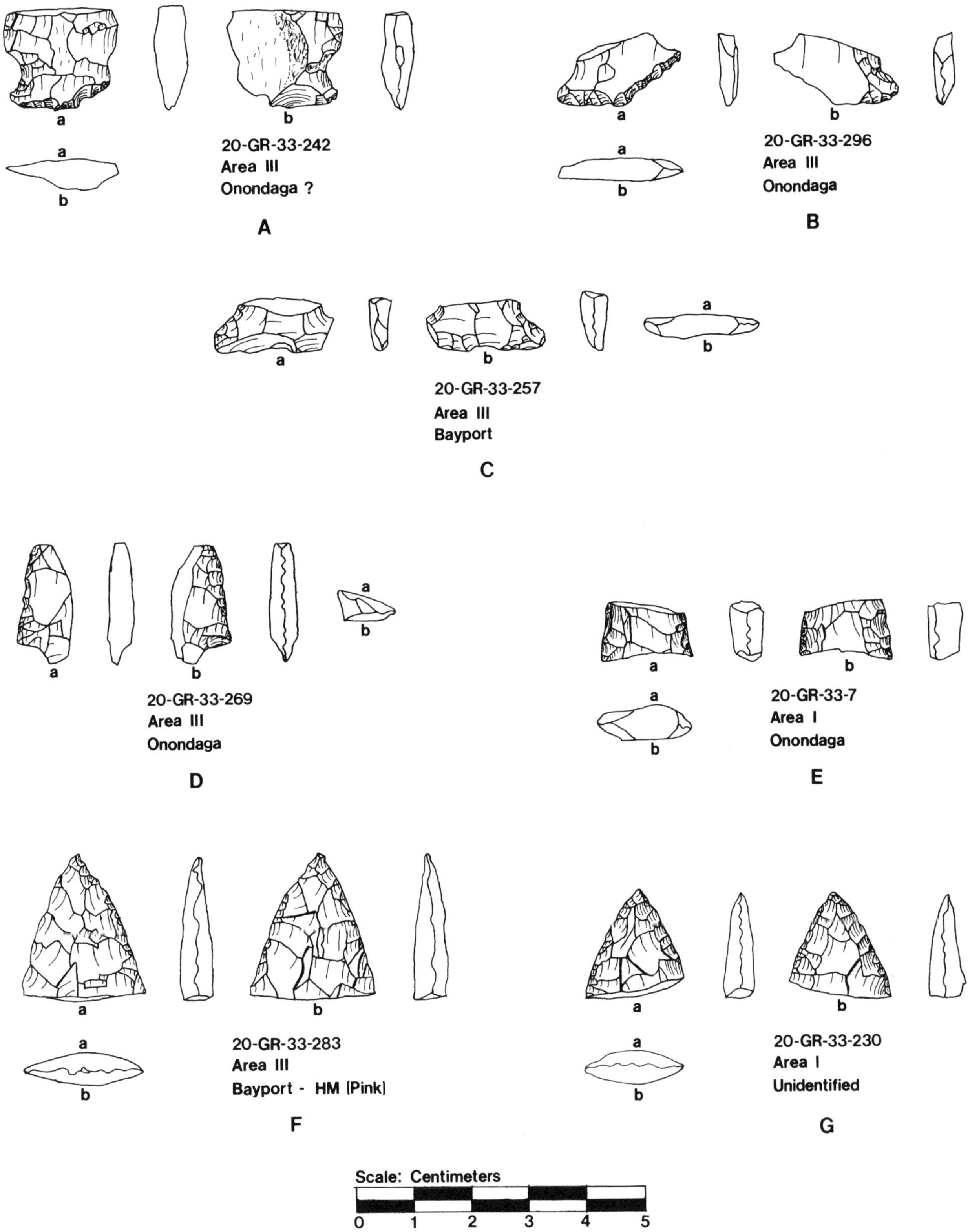

MEADOWOOD POINTS

FIGURE 39

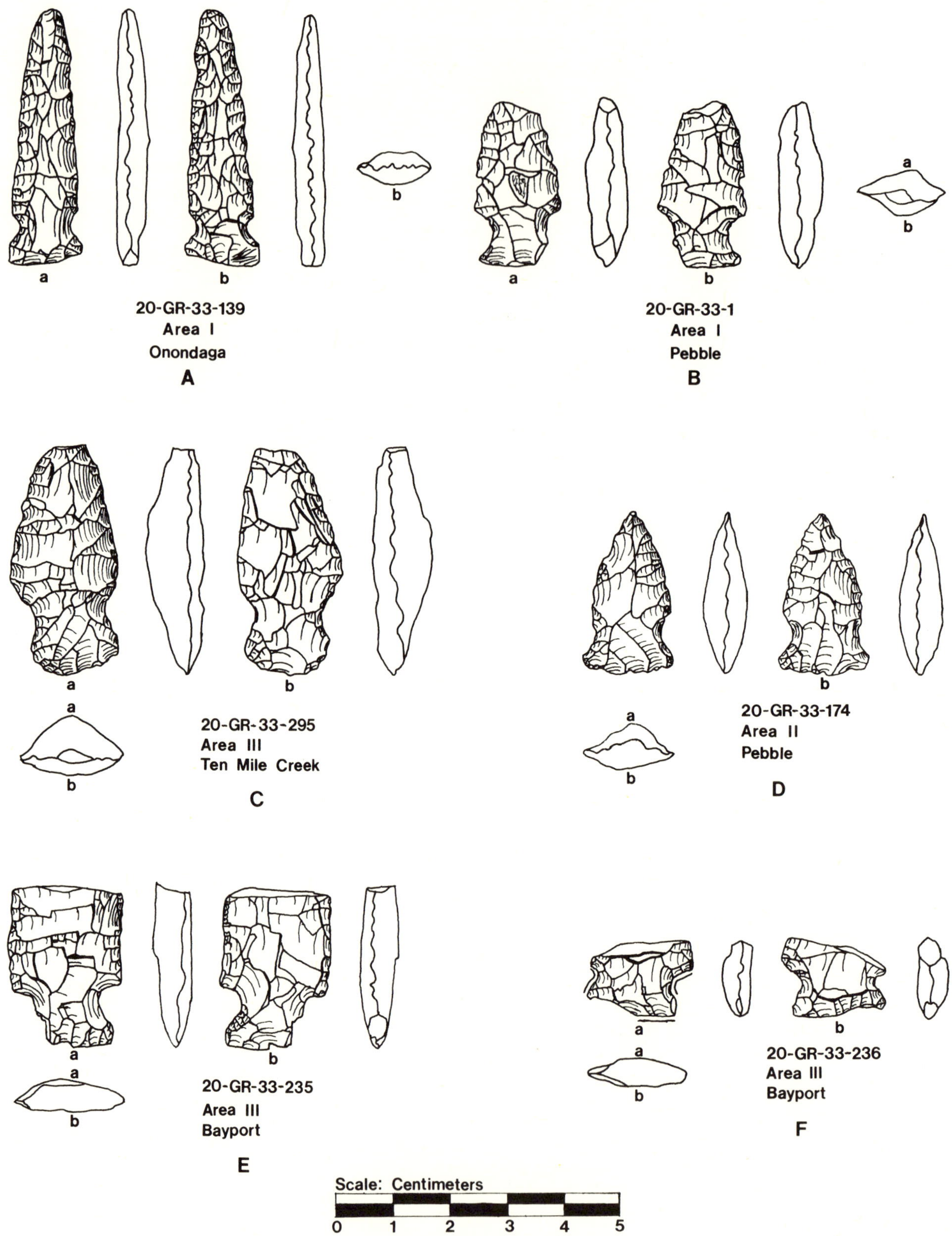

SIDE-NOTCHED POINTS

FIGURE 40

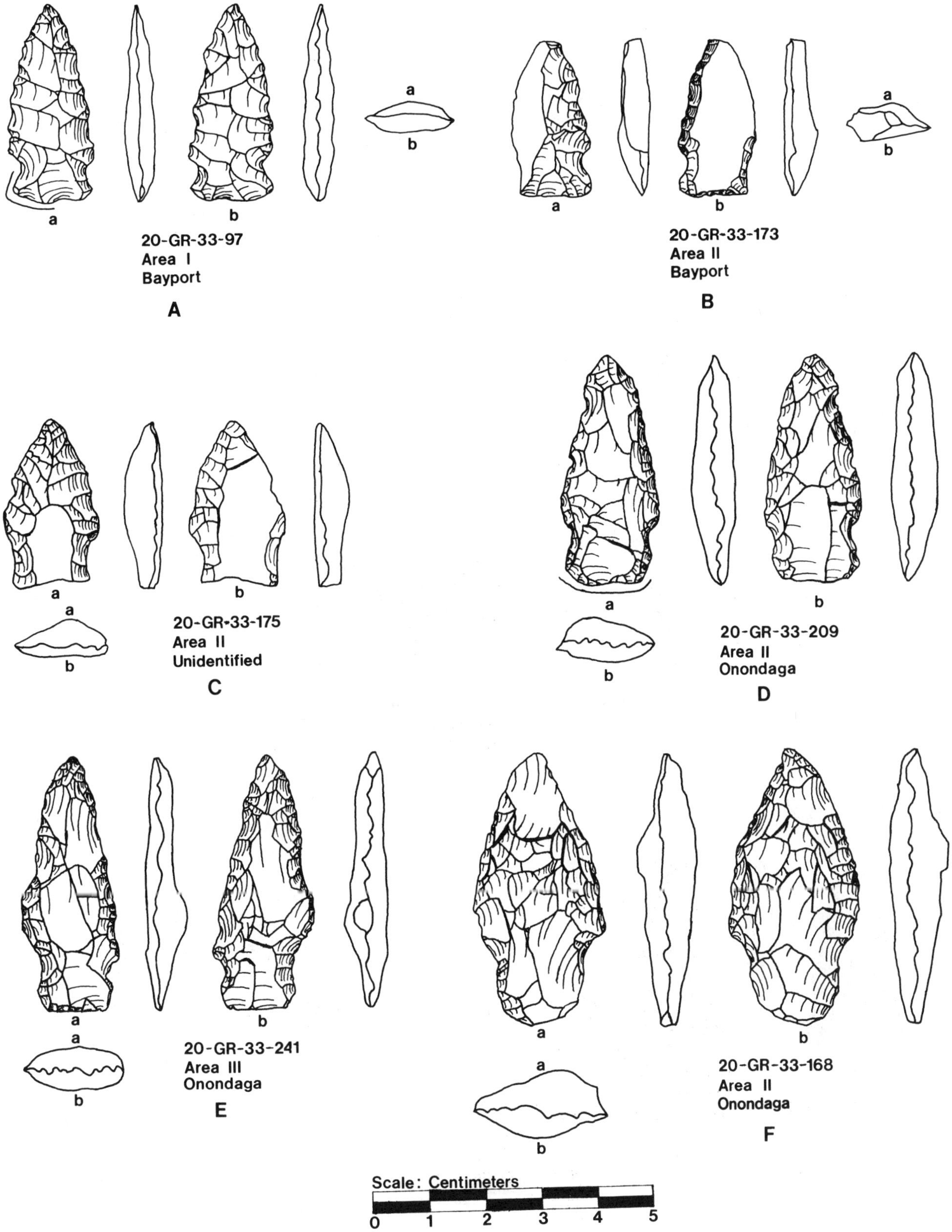

SIDE-NOTCHED and STEMMED POINTS

FIGURE 41

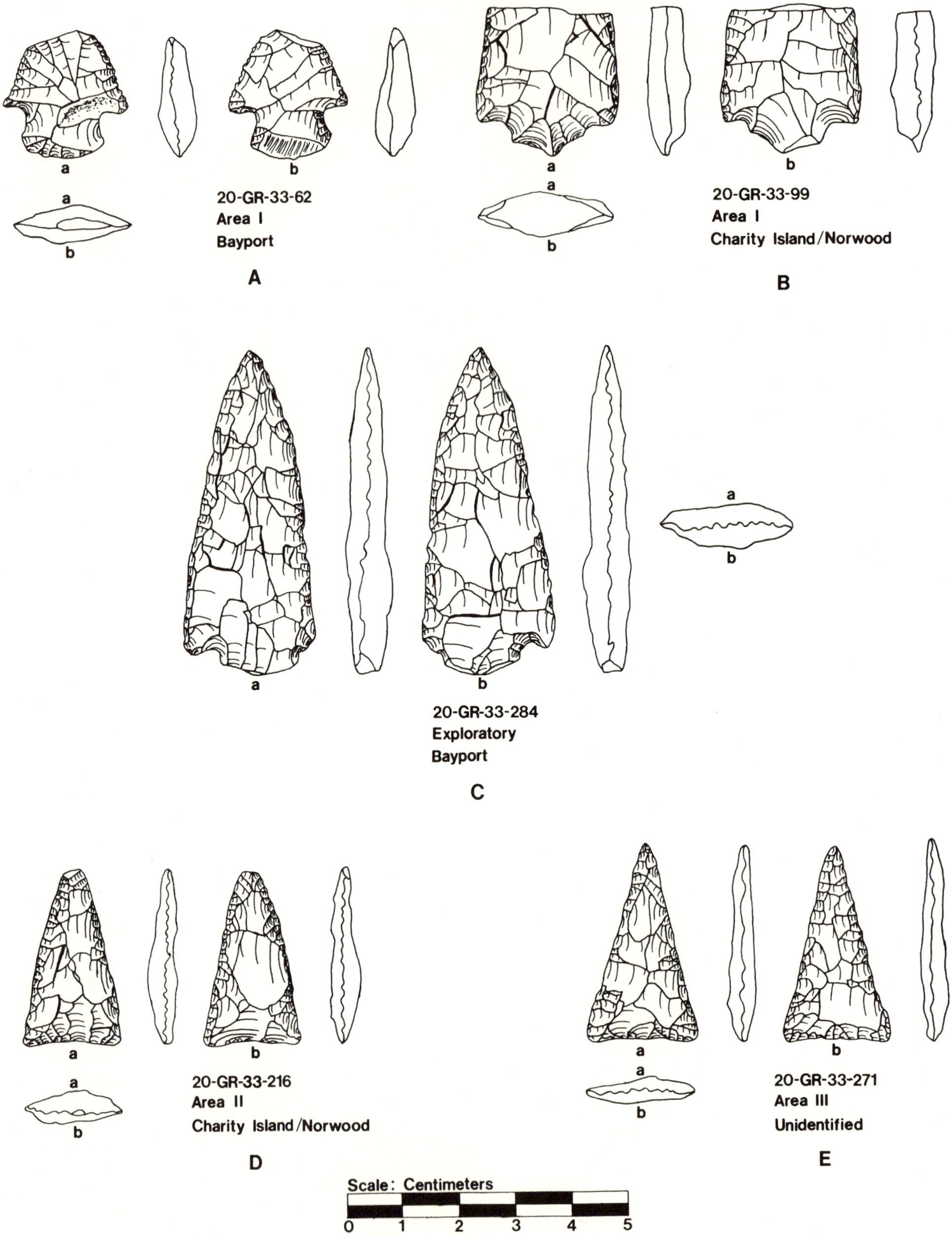

CORNER-NOTCHED and TRIANGULAR POINTS

FIGURE 42

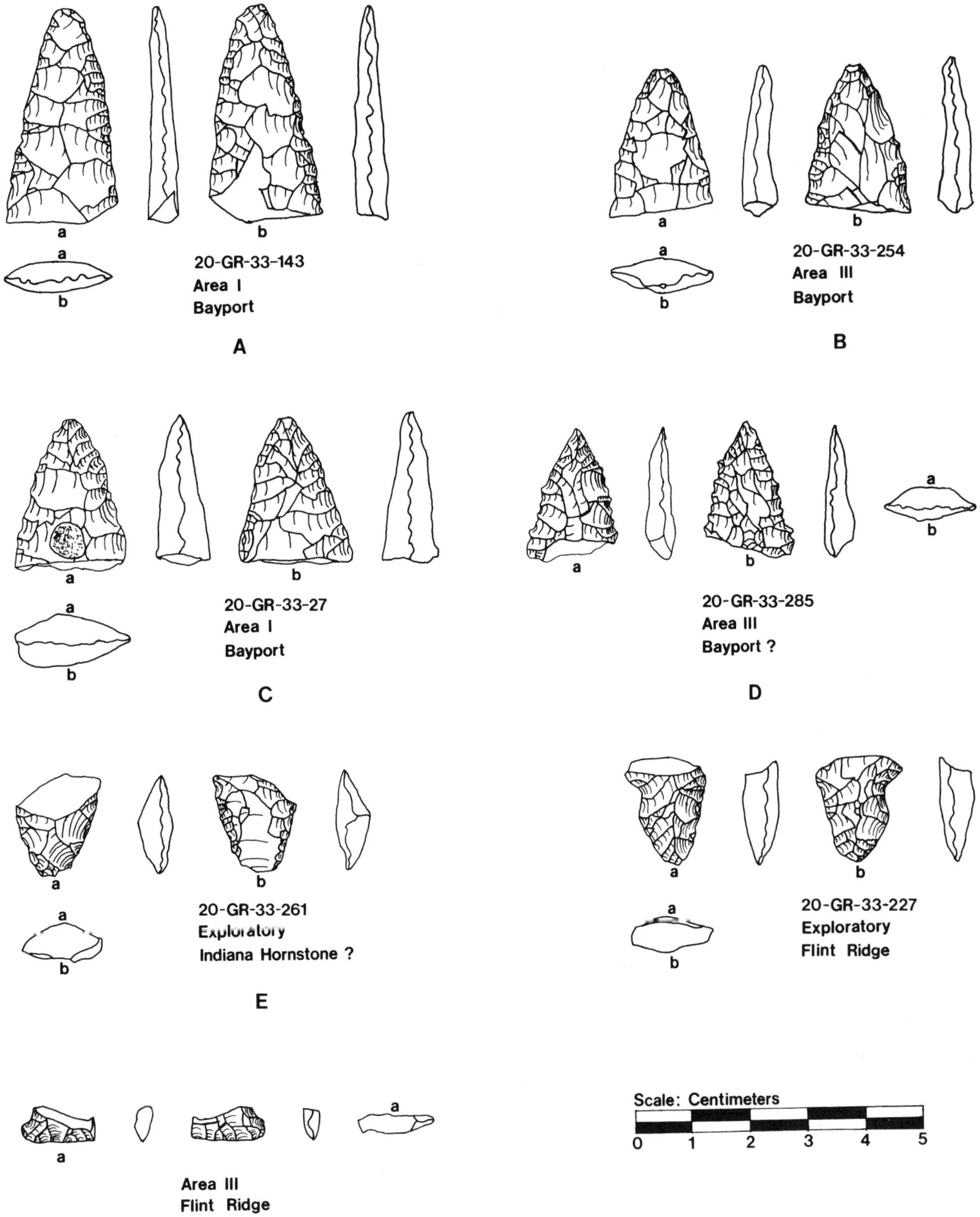

POINT TIPS and BASES

FIGURE 43

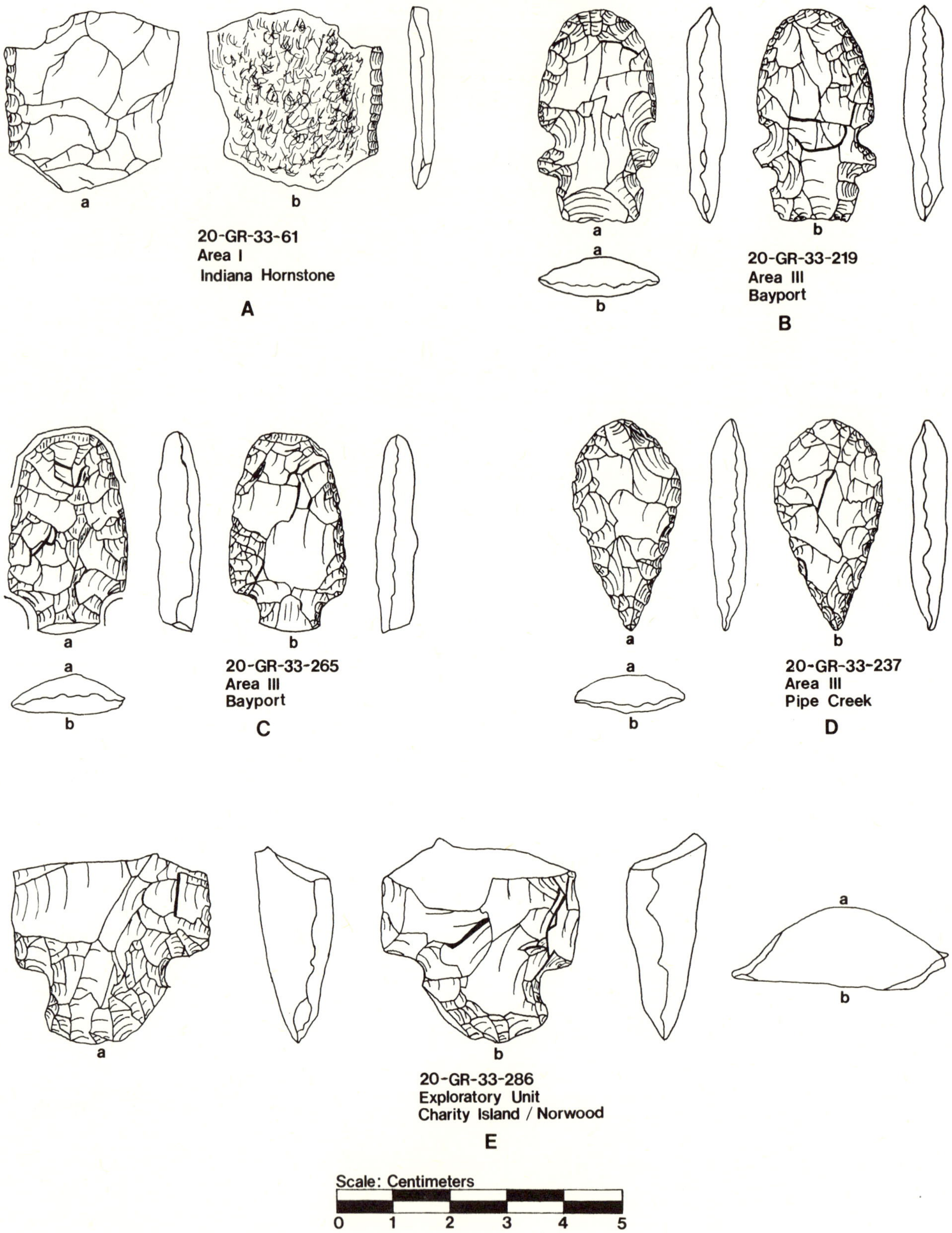

TURKEY TAIL FRAGMENT, HAFTED SCRAPERS and KNIFE

FIGURE 44

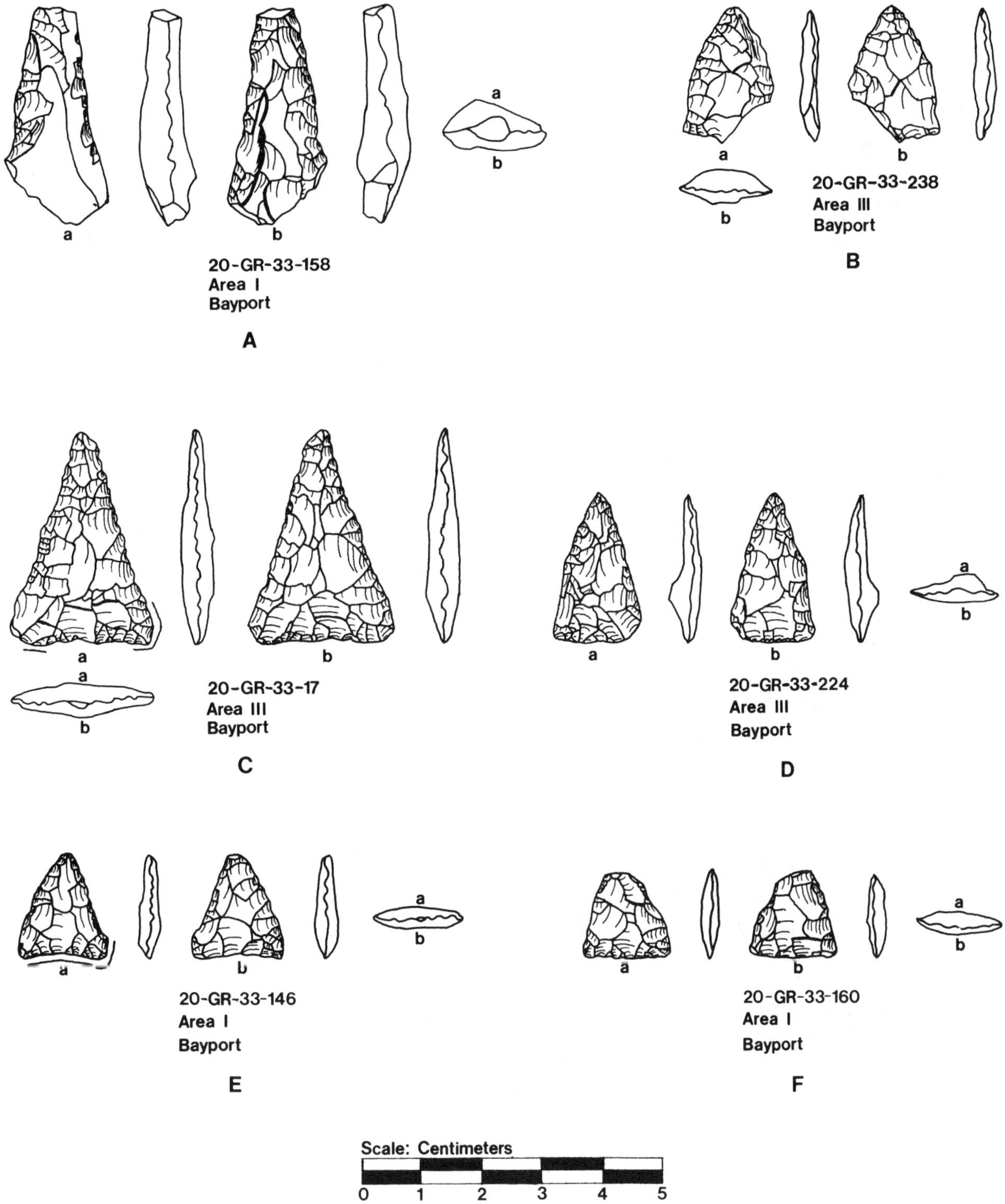

DRILL BLANK and TRIANGULAR BIFACES

FIGURE 45

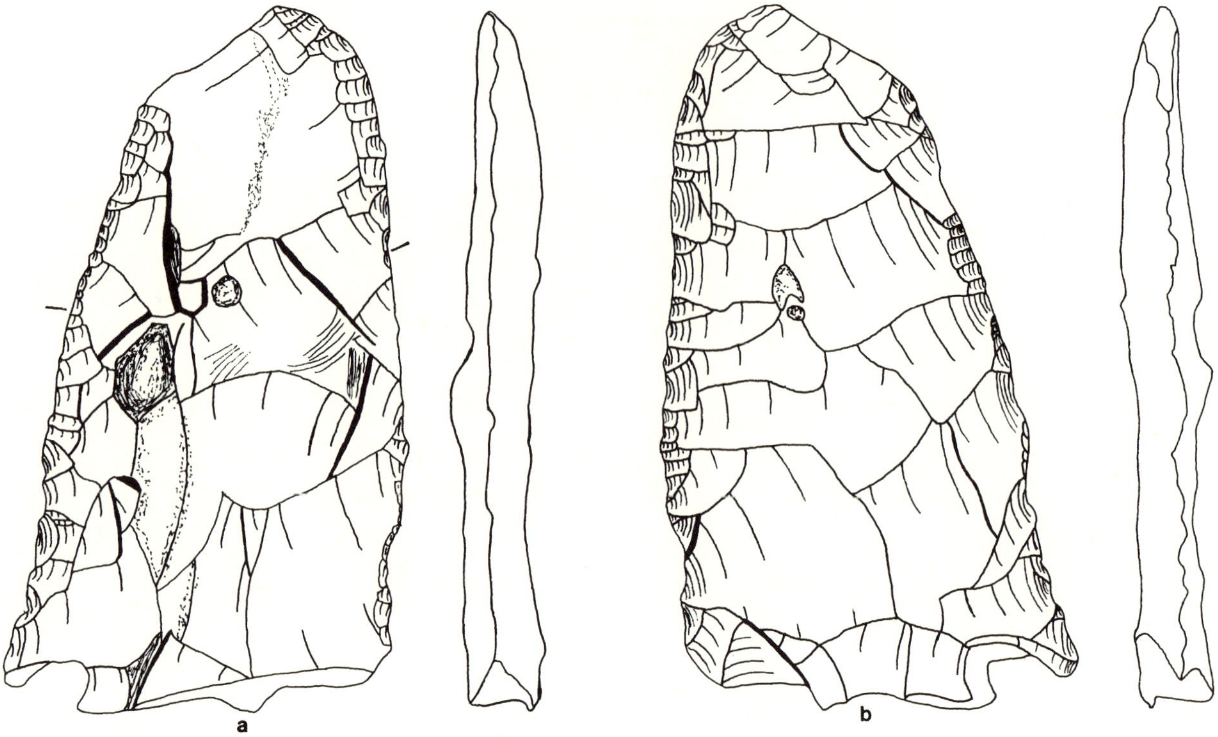

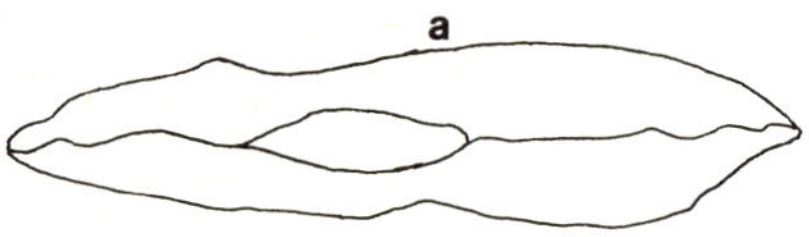

20-GR-33-5/16
Area I
Bayport

A

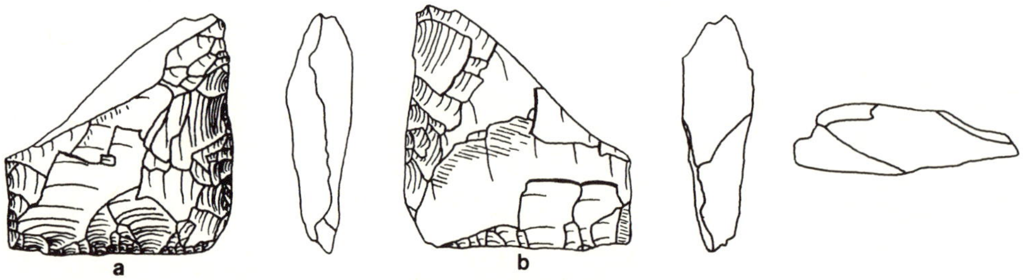

20-GR-33-6
Area I
Bayport

B

BIFACES

FIGURE 46

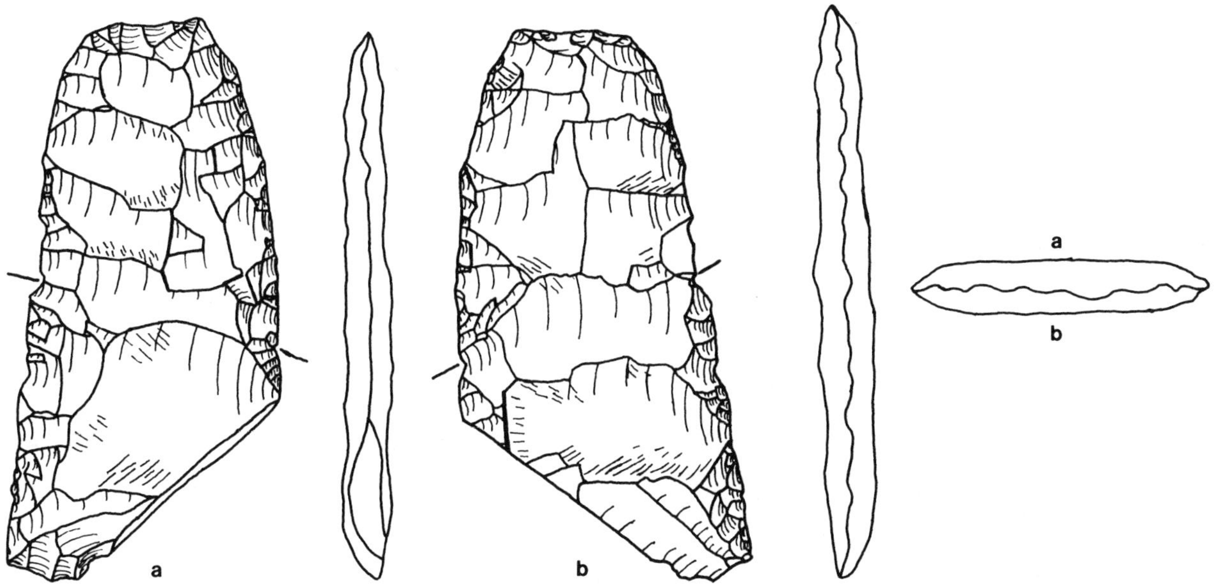

20-GR-33-148/150
Area I
Bayport

A

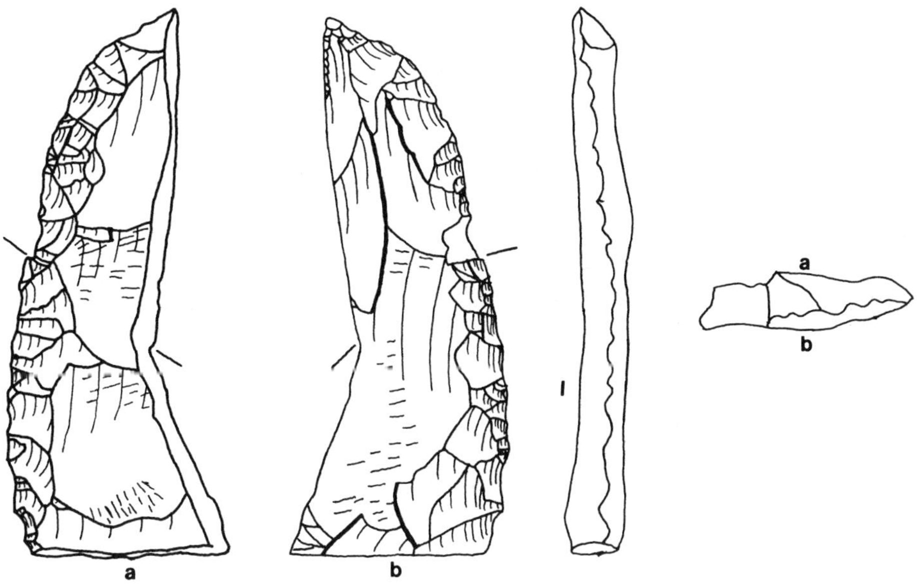

20-GR-33-151/152
Area I
Bayport

B

BIFACES
FIGURE 47

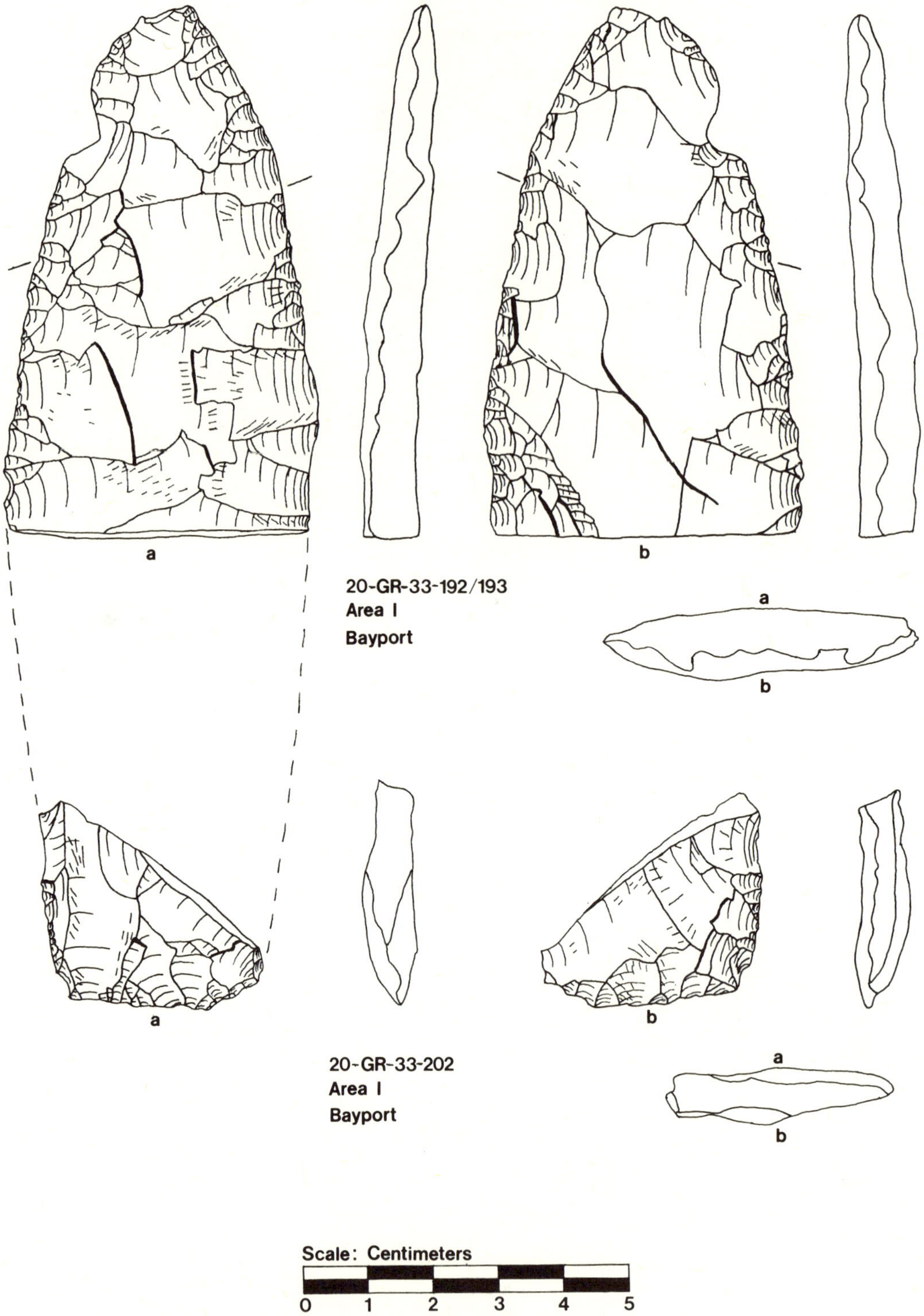

BIFACE

FIGURE 48

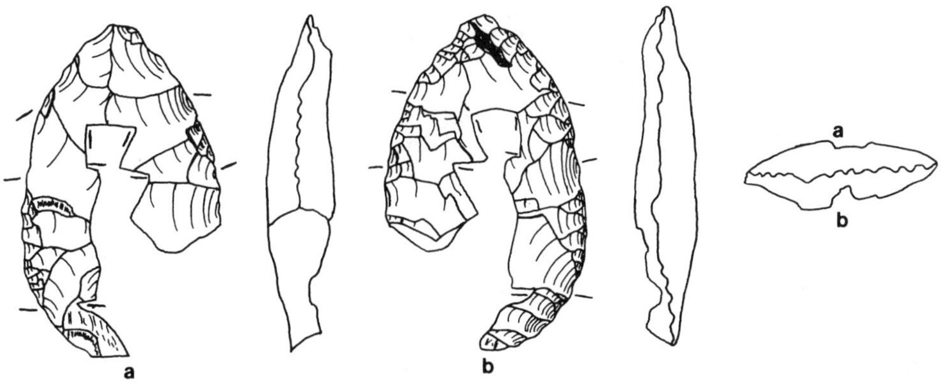

20-GR-33-276
Area III
Bayport

A

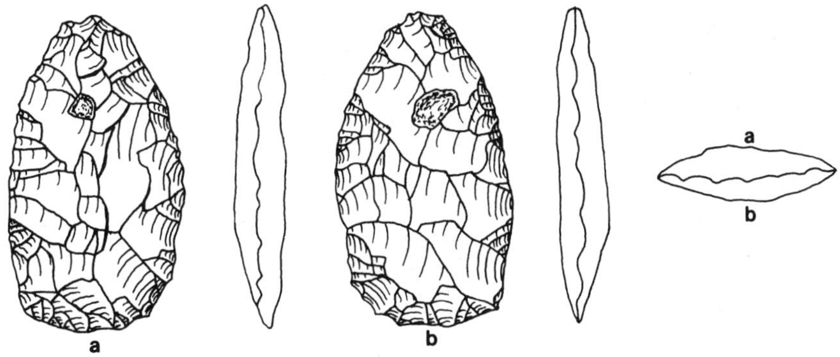

20-GR-33-232
Area I
Charity Island / Norwood

B

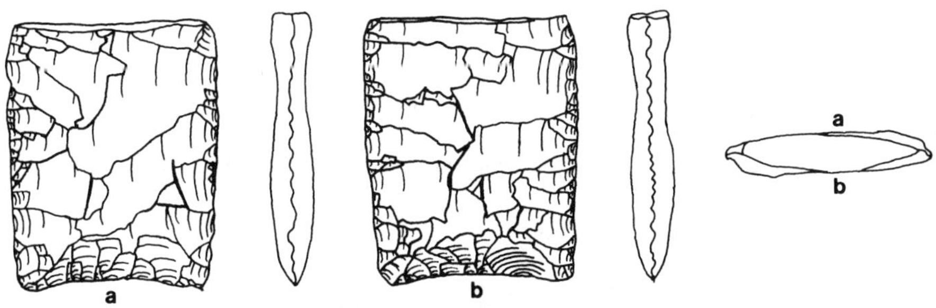

20-GR-33-67
Area I
Bayport

C

BIFACES
FIGURE 49

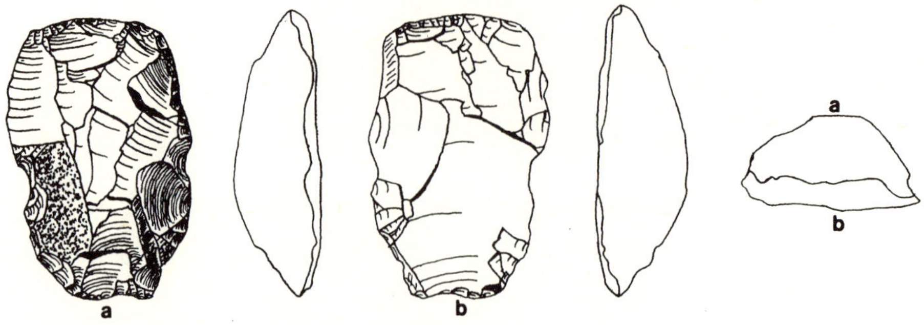

20-33-GR-117
Area I
Bayport

A

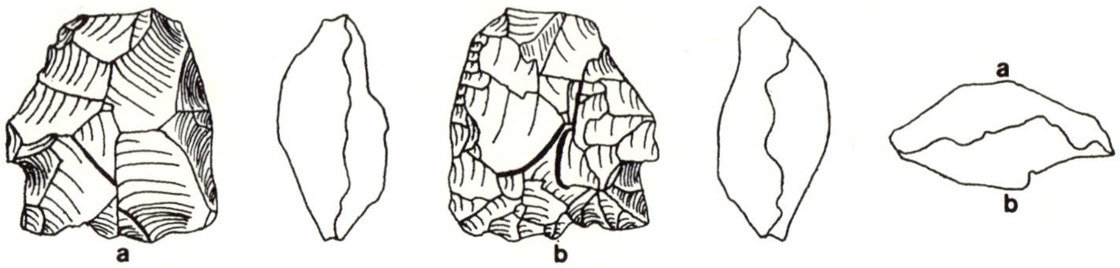

20-33-GR-19
Area I
Pebble

B

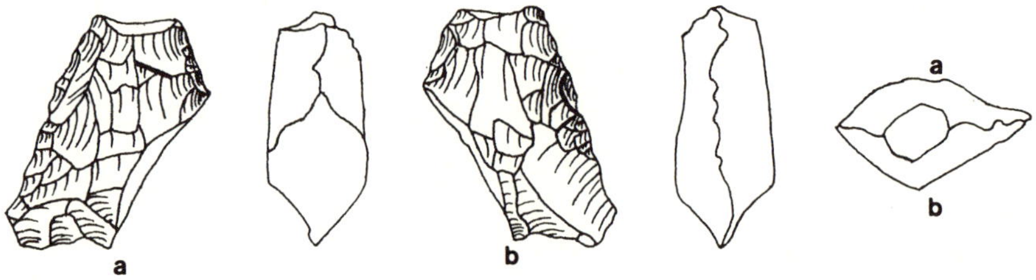

20-33-GR-166
Area II
Pebble

C

BIFACES

FIGURE 50

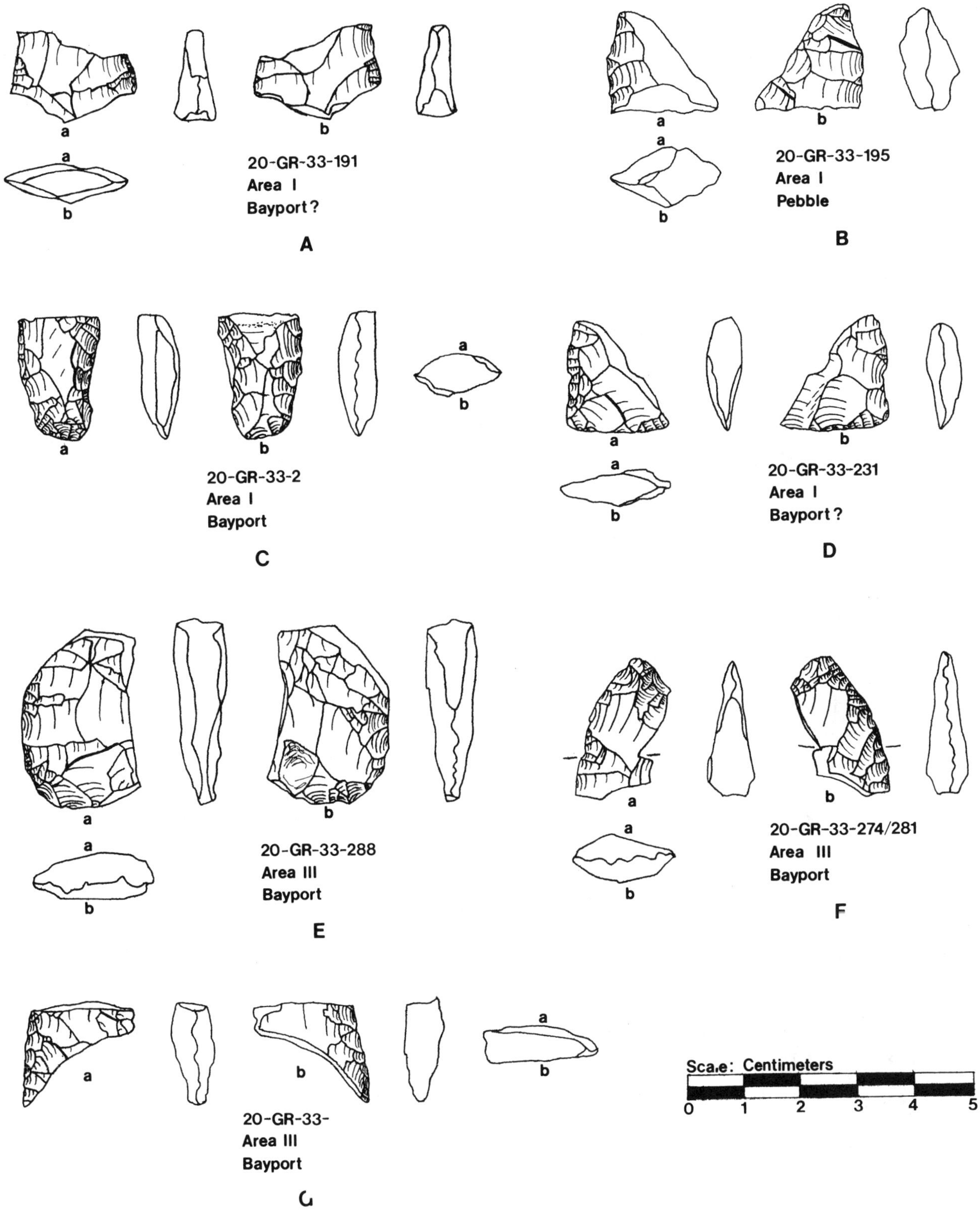

BIFACE FRAGMENTS

FIGURE 51

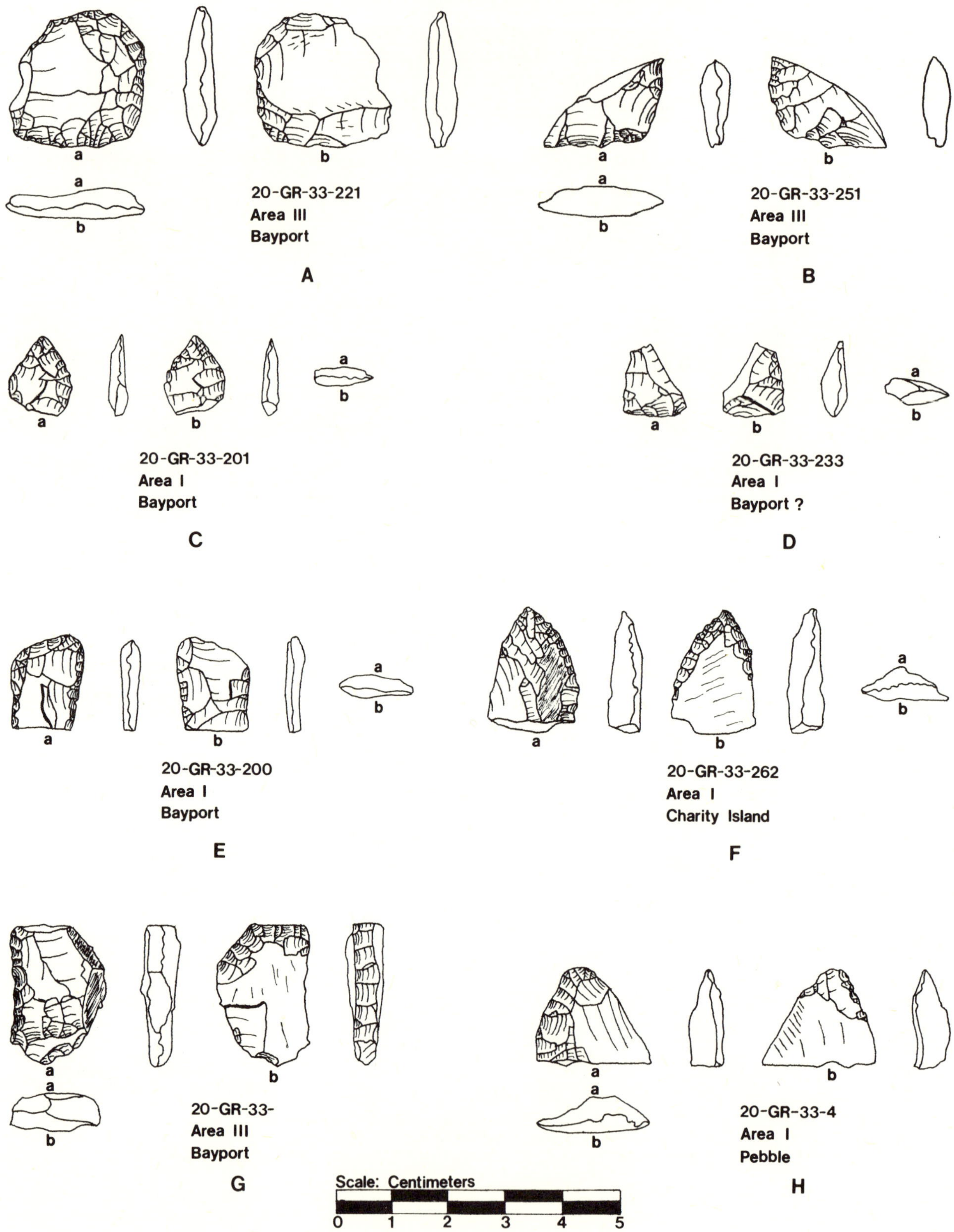

BIFACE FRAGMENTS

FIGURE 52

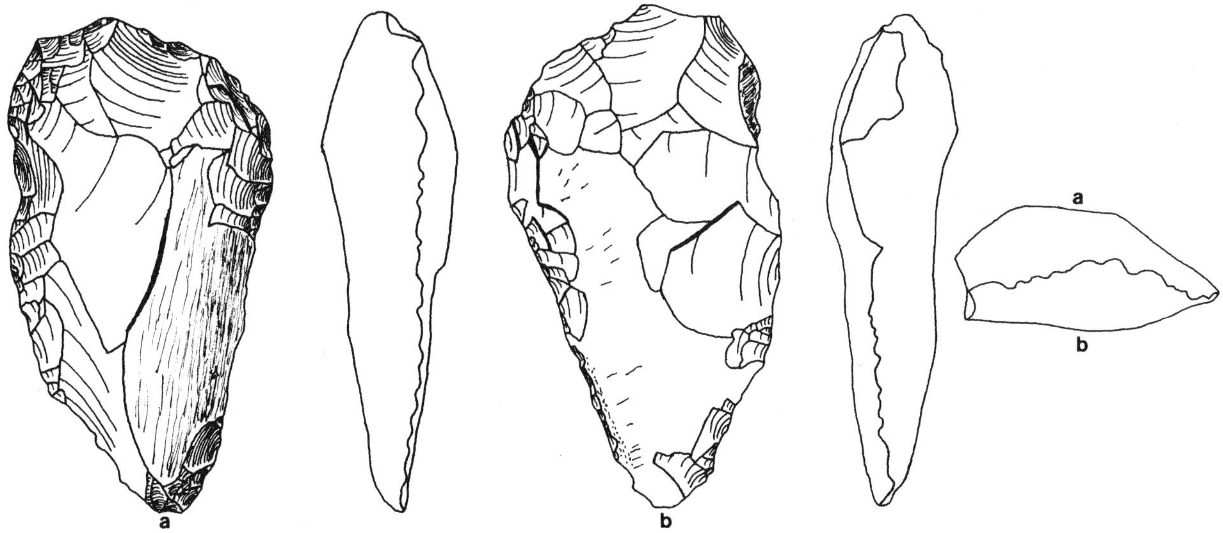

20-GR-33-135
Area I
Bayport

A

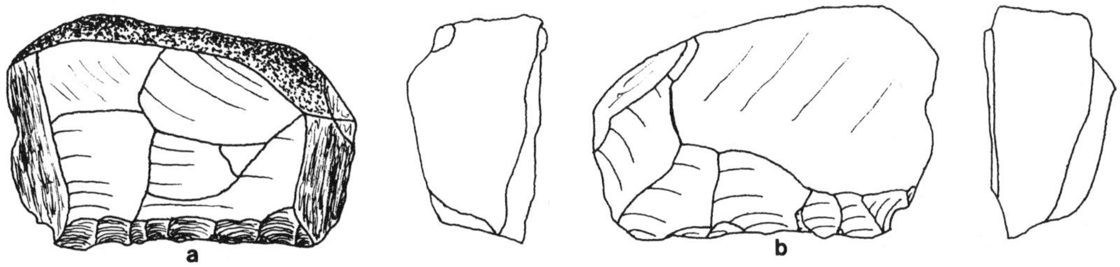

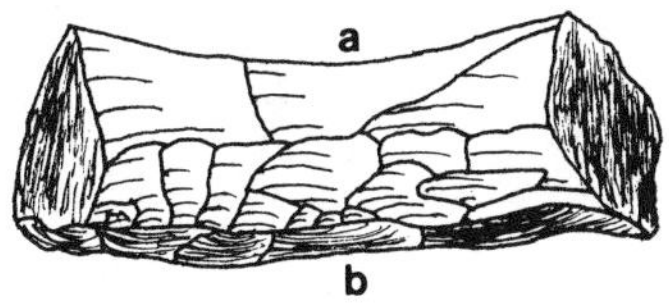

20-GR-33-159
Area I
Bayport

B

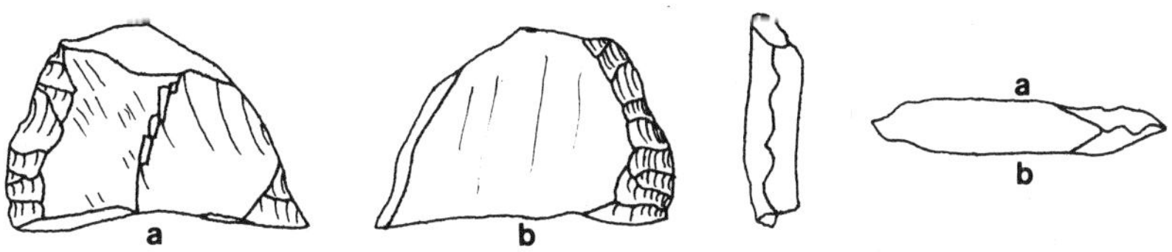

20-GR-33-203
Area I
Bayport

C

BIFACES

FIGURE 53

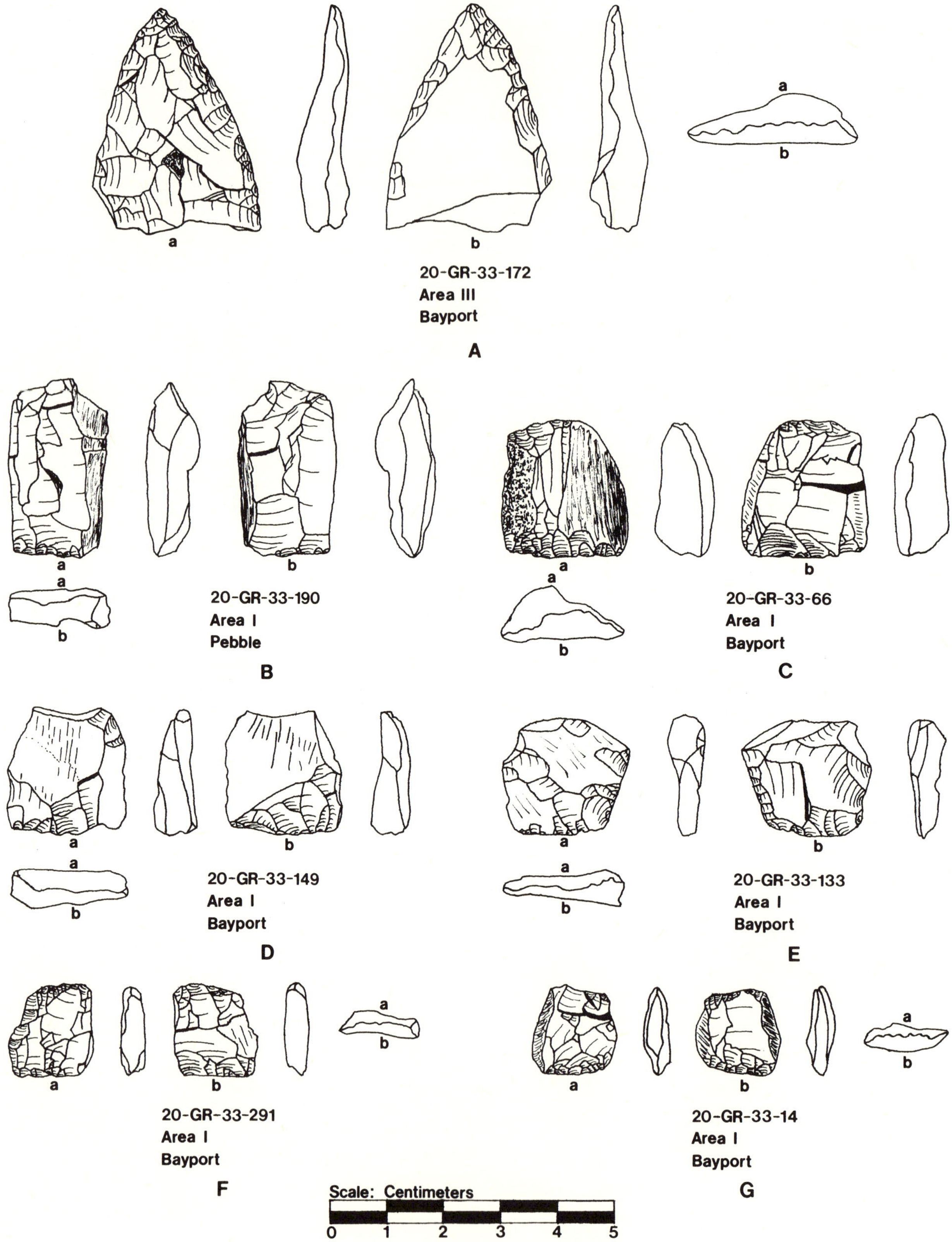

BIFACE and BIPOLAR CORES

FIGURE 54

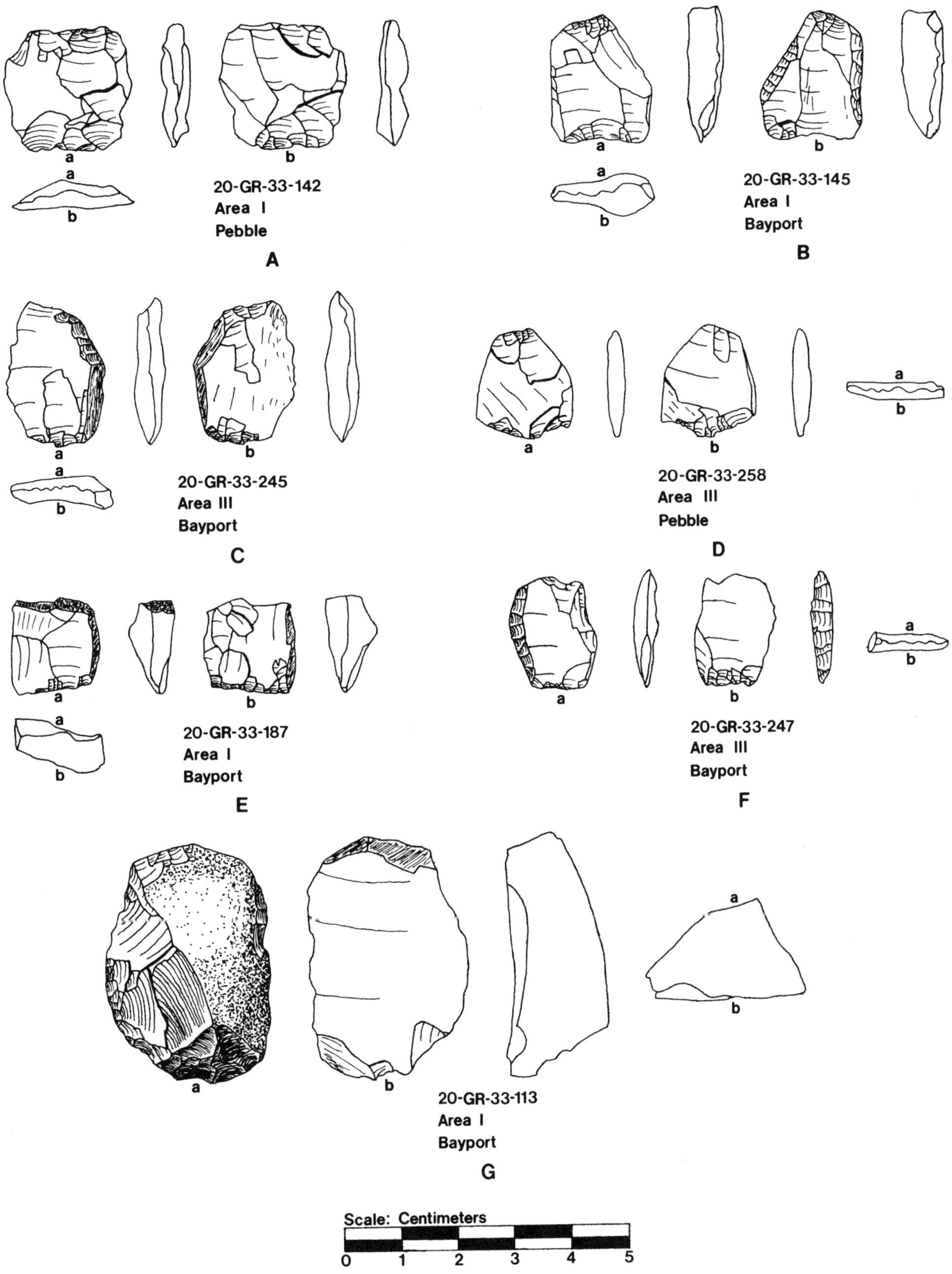

BIPOLAR CORES and UNIFACE

FIGURE 55

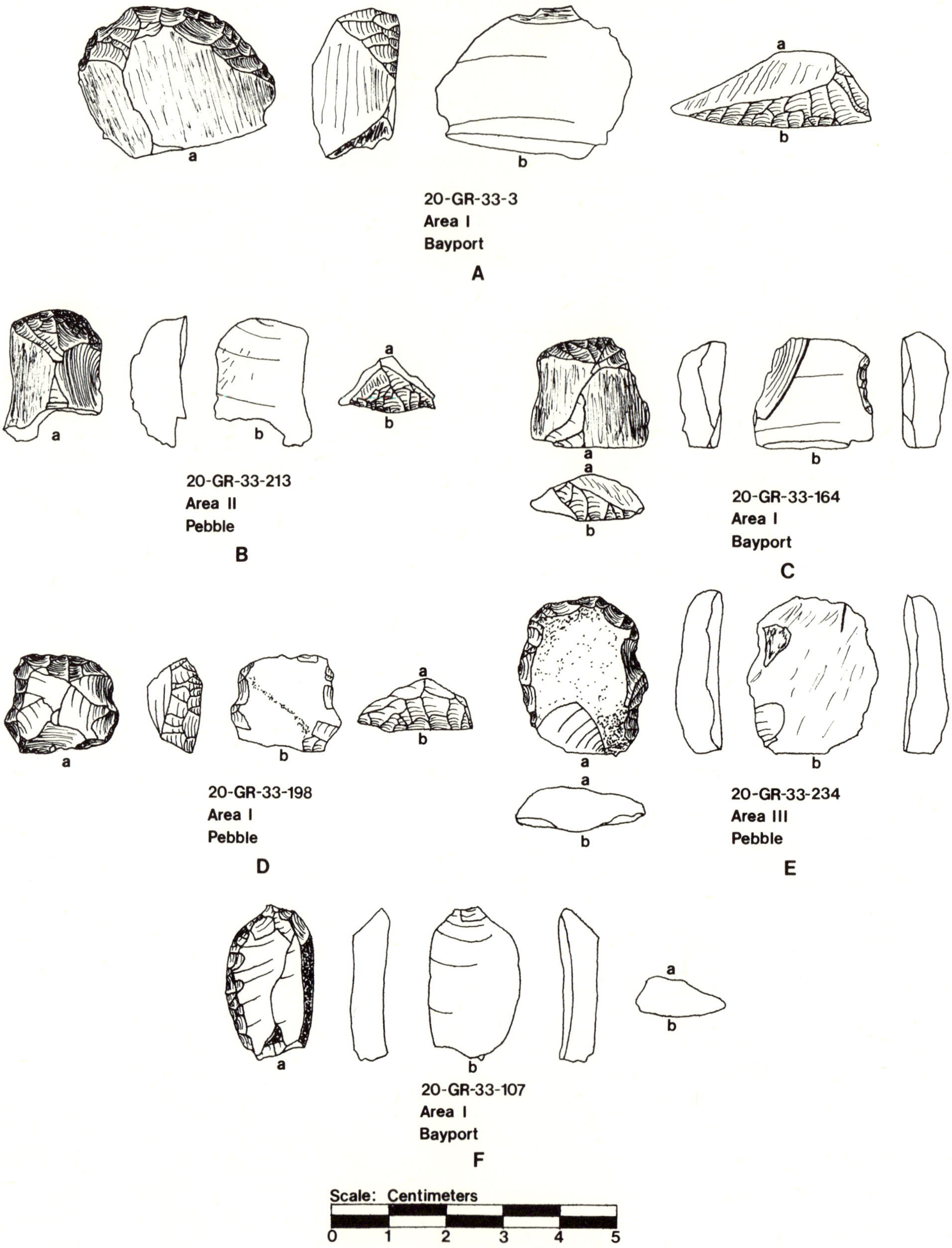

UNIFACES

FIGURE 56

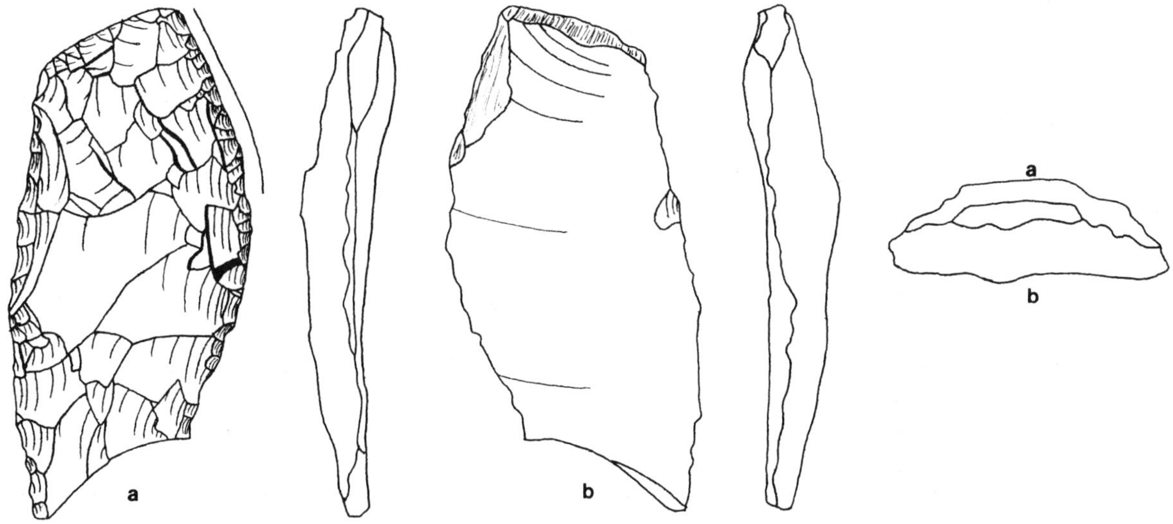

20-GR-33-167
Area II
Onodaga

A

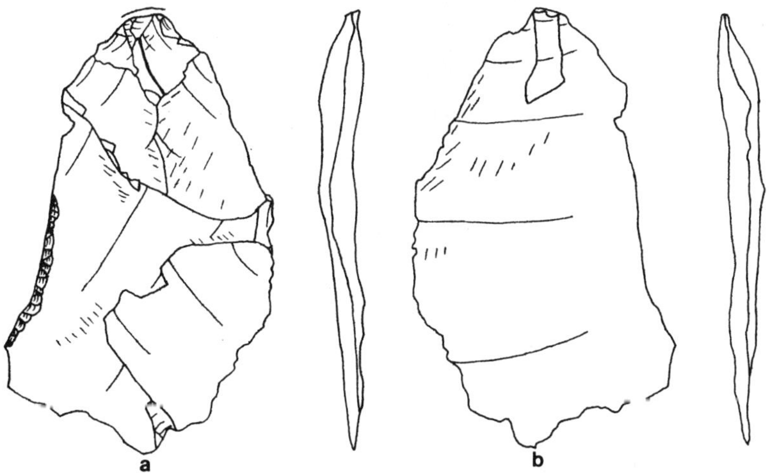

20-GR-33
Area I
Bayport

B

UNIFACIAL BLANK
and
UTILIZED FLAKE

FIGURE 57

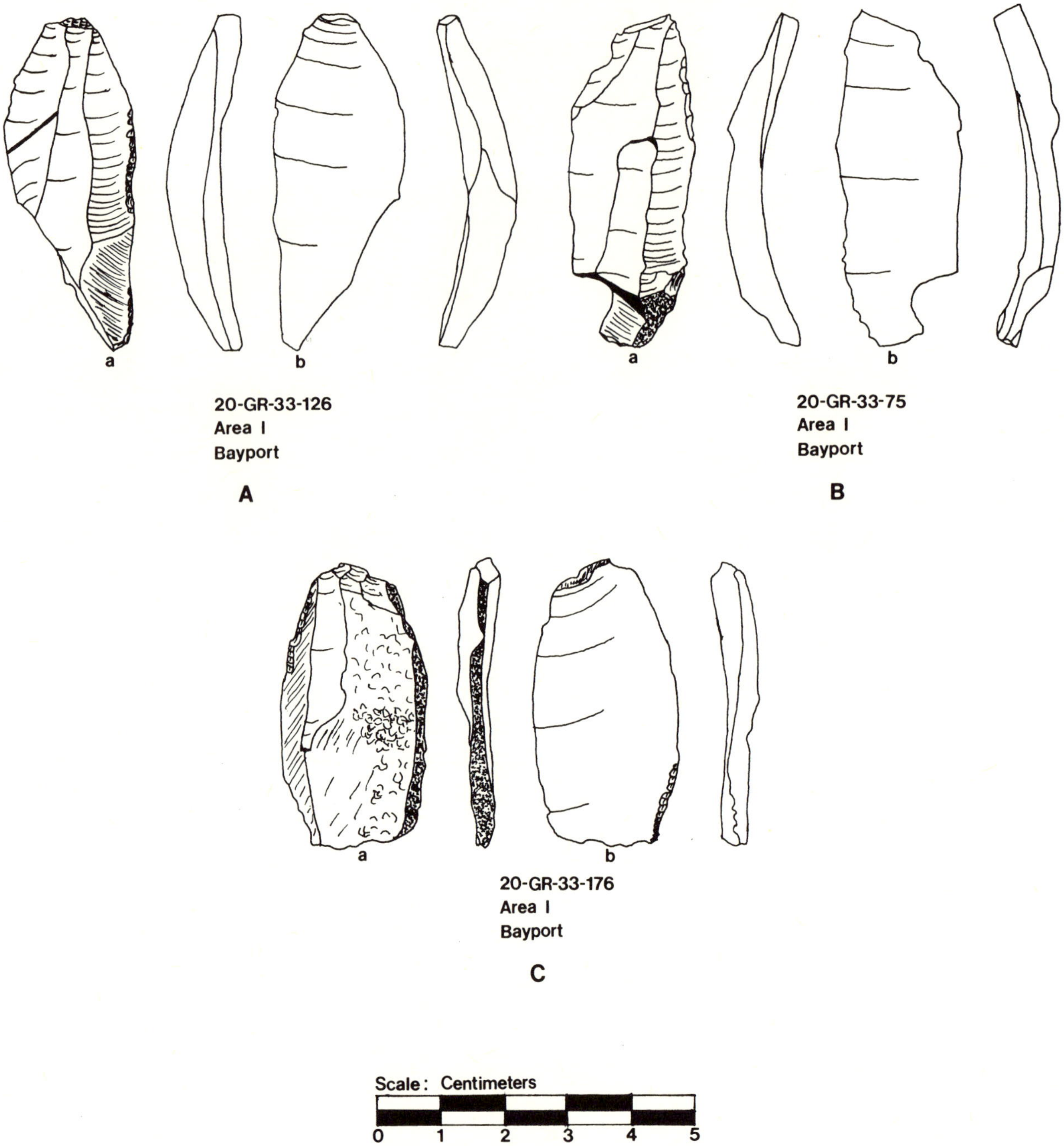

BLADES

FIGURE 58

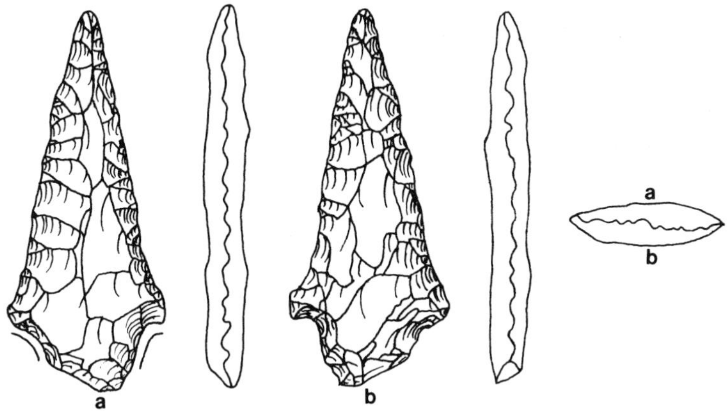

20-GR-45
Onondaga

A

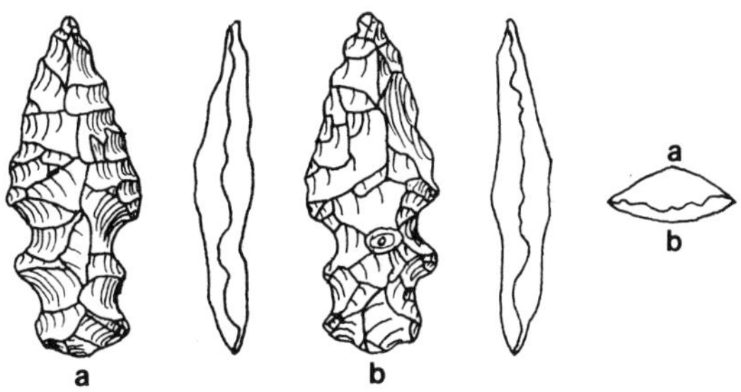

20-SA-371
Bayport

B

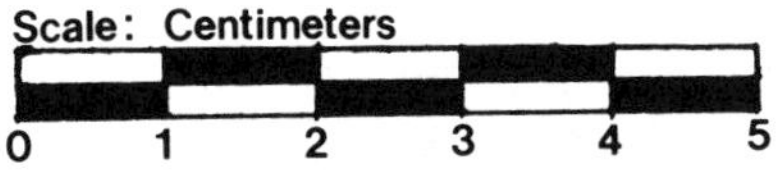

"STEMMED MEADOWOOD"

and

"DOUBLE-NOTCHED DUSTIN"

FIGURE 59

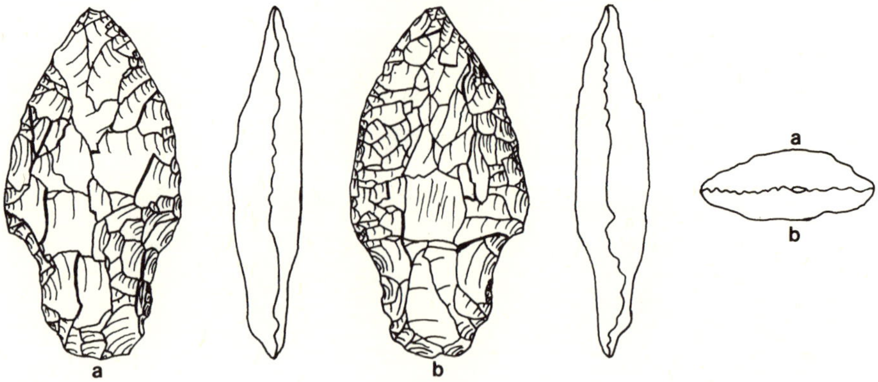

20-TU-149
Onondaga

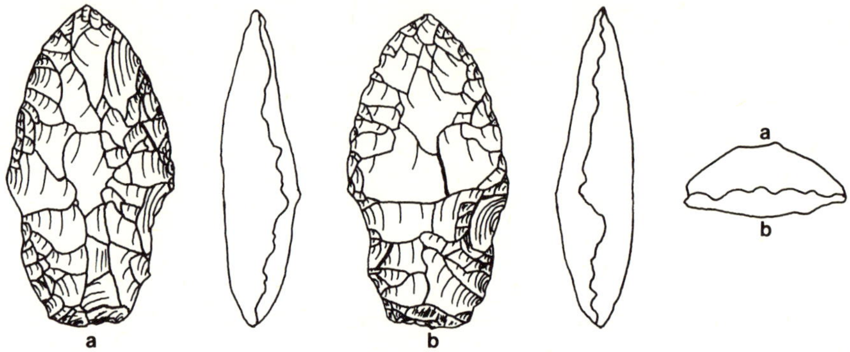

20-TU-149
Onondaga

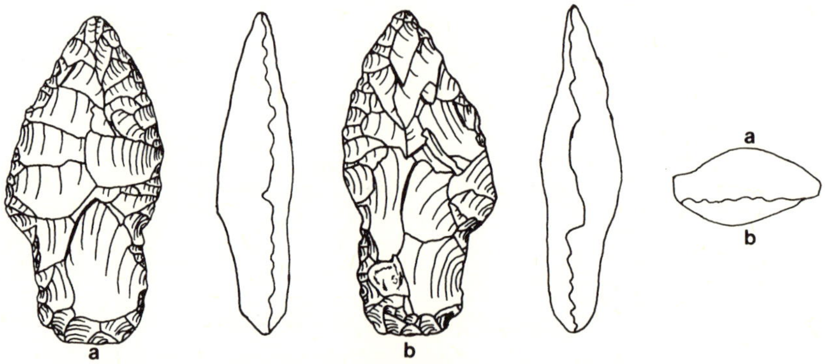

20-TU-149
Onondaga

FIGURE 60

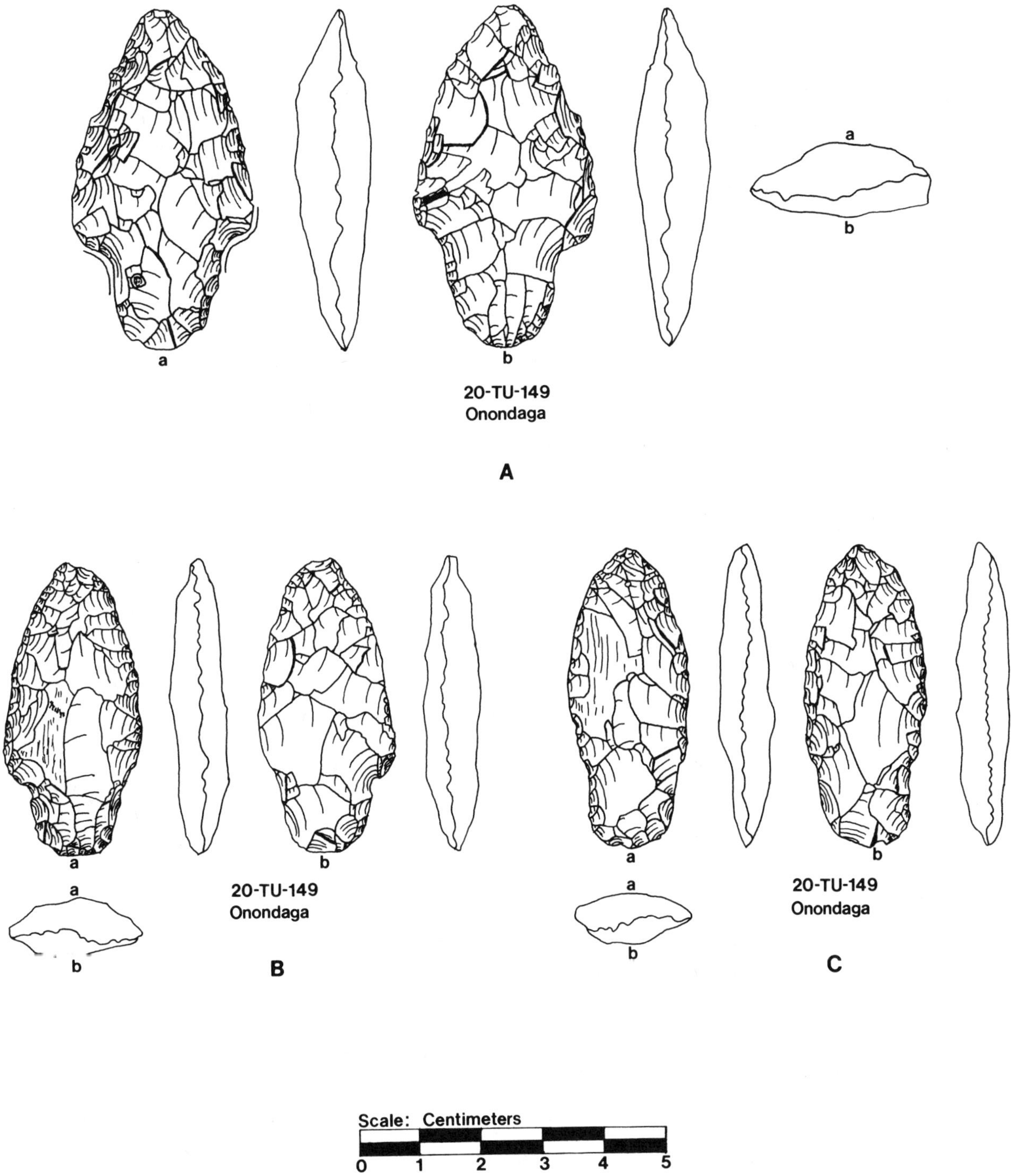

LOBATE STEM POINTS

FIGURE 61

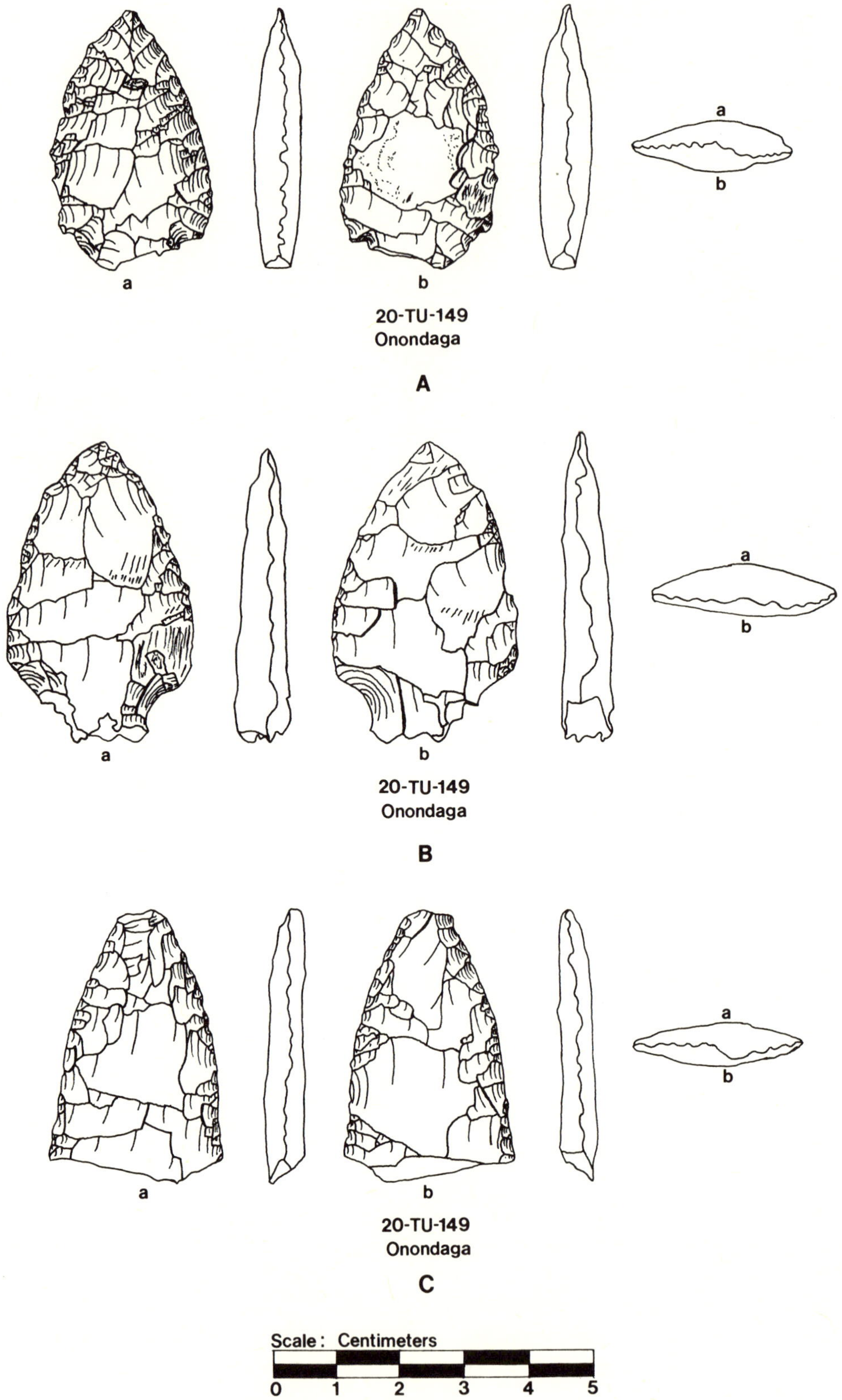
a
b
a
b
20-TU-149
Onondaga
A
a
b
a
b
20-TU-149
Onondaga
B
a
b
a
b
20-TU-149
Onondaga
C
Scale: Centimeters
0 1 2 3 4 5

FIGURE 62

REFERENCES CITED

Bamforth, Douglas B.
1986 Technological Efficiency and Tool Curation. *American Antiquity* 51:38-50.

Beld, Scott G.
1990 20GR91: A Late Woodland Site in Gratiot County, Michigan. *The Michigan Archaeologist* 36:57-77.

Binford, Lewis R.
1962 Archaeology as Anthropology. *American Antiquity* 28:217-225.

1963a The Hodges Site. A Late Archaic Burial Station. Pp. 124-147 in Anta M. White, Lewis R. Binford, and Mark L. Papworth, *Miscellaneous Studies in Typology and Classification.* University of Michigan, Museum of Anthropology, Anthropological Papers, No. 19.

1963b The Pomranky Site. A Late Archaic Burial Station. Pp. 149-192 in Anta M. White, Lewis R. Binford, and Mark L. Papworth, *Miscellaneous Studies in Typology and Classification.* University of Michigan, Museum of Anthropology, Anthropological Papers, No. 19.

1963c A Proposed Attribute List for the Description and Classification of Projectile Points. Pp. 193-221 in Anta M. White, Lewis R. Binford, and Mark L. Papworth, *Miscellaneous Studies in Typology and Classification.* University of Michigan, Museum of Anthropology, Anthropological Papers, No. 19.

1963d "Red Ochre" Caches from the Michigan Area: A Possible Case of Cultural Drift. *Southwestern Journal of Anthropology* 19:89-108.

1977 Forty-seven Trips. Pp. 24-36 in R. V. S. Wright, ed., *Stone Tools as Cultural Markers.* Canberra: Australian Institute of Aboriginal Studies.

1979 Organization and Formation Processes: Looking at Curated Technologies. *Journal of Anthropological Research* 35:255-273.

Binford, Lewis R., and Mark L. Papworth
1963 The Eastport Site, Antrim County, Michigan. Pp. 71-123 in Anta M. White, Lewis R. Binford, and Mark L. Papworth, *Miscellaneous Studies in Typology and Classification.* University of Michigan, Museum of Anthropology, Anthropological Papers, No. 19.

Brown, James A.
1985 Long-Term Trends to Sedentism and the

Emergence of Complexity in the American Midwest. Pp. 201-231 in T. Douglas Price and James A. Brown, eds., *Prehistoric Hunter-Gatherers: The Emergence of Cultural Complexity*. New York: Academic Press, Inc.

Brown, James A., and Robert K. Vierra
1983 What Happened in the Middle Archaic? Introduction to an Ecological Approach to Koster Site Archaeology. Pp. 165-195 in James L. Phillips and James A. Brown, eds., *Archaic Hunters and Gatherers in the American Midwest*. New York: Academic Press.

Conrad, Lawrence A., Susan L. Gardner, and J. Joe Alford
1986 A Note on the Late Archaic, Early Woodland and Early Middle Woodland Occupations of the Lima Lake Locality, Adams and Hancock Counties, Illinois. Pp. 191-206 in Kenneth B. Farnsworth and Thomas E. Emerson, eds., *Early Woodland Archaeology*. Kampsville: Center for American Archaeology.

Emerson, Thomas E., and Dale L. McElrath
1983 A Settlement-Subsistence Model of the Terminal Late Archaic Adaptation in the American Bottom, Illinois. Pp. 219-242 in James L. Phillips and James A. Brown, eds., *Archaic Hunter and Gatherers in the American Midwest*. New York: Acade-mic Press.

Farnsworth, Kenneth B., and David L. Asch
1986 Early Woodland Chronology, Artifact Styles, and Settlement Distribution in the Lower Illinois Valley Region. Pp. 326-457 in Kenneth B. Farnsworth and Thomas E. Emerson, eds., *Early Woodland Archaeology*. Kampsville: Center for American Archaeology.

Feenstra, James E.
1979 *Soil Survey of Gratiot County, Michigan*. United States Department of Agriculture Soil Conservation Service in cooperation with the Michigan Agriculture Experiment Station.

Fitting, James E.
1972 Lithic Industries of the Schultz Site. Pp. 191-224 in James E. Fitting, ed., *The Schultz Site at Green Point: A Stratified Occupation Area in the Saginaw Valley of Michigan*. University of Michigan, Museum of Anthropology, Memoirs No. 4.

1975 *The Archaeology of Michigan: A Guide to the Prehistory of the Great Lakes Region*. 2nd edition. Bloomfield Hills: Cranbrook Institute of Science.

Garland, Elizabeth B.
1986 Early Woodland Occupations in Michigan: A Lower St. Joseph Valley Perspective. Pp. 47-83 in Kenneth B. Farnsworth and Thomas E. Emerson, eds., *Early Woodland Archaeology*. Kampsville: Center for American Archeology Press.

Goodyear, Albert C.
1974 *The Brand Site: A Techno-Functional Study of a Dalton Site in Northeast Arkansas*. Arkansas Archeological Survey, Publications on Archeology, Research Series No. 7.

Granger, Joseph E.
1978 *Meadowood Phase Settlement Pattern in the Niagara Frontier Region of Western New York State*. University of Michigan, Museum of Anthropology, Anthropological Papers, No. 65.

1980 Cache Blades, Chert and Communication: A Reappraisal of Certain Aspects of Meadowood Phase and the Concept of a Burial Cult in the Northeast. Pp. 96-122 in William E. Engelbrecht and Donald K. Grayson, eds., *Essays in Northeastern Anthropology in Memory of Marian E. White*. Occasional Publications in Northeastern Anthropology, No. 5.

Green, Amos R., and James E. Fitting
1964 A Turkey Tail Cache from Southwestern Michigan. *The Michigan Archaeologist* 10:83-88.

Gregory, C. A.
1982 *Gifts and Commodities*. London: Academic Press.

Harrison, Sidney
1966 The Schmidt Site (20 SA 192), Saginaw County, Michigan. *The Michigan Archaeologist* 12:49-75.

Hill, Jane H.
1978 Language Contact Systems and Human Adaptations. *Journal of Anthropological Research* 34:1-26.

Jackson, L. J.
1980 Dawson Creek: An Early Woodland Site in South-Central Ontario. *Ontario Archaeology* 33:13-32.

1986 New Evidence for Early Woodland Seasonal Adaptation from Southern Ontario, Canada. *American Antiquity* 51:389-401.

Johnston, Richard B.
1984 *The McIntyre Site: Archaeology, Subsistence, and Environment*. National Museum of Man, Mercury Series, Archaeological Survey of Canada Paper No. 126.

Kapp, Ronald O.
1978 Presettlement Forests of the Pine River Watershed (Central Michigan) Based on Original Land Survey Records. *The Michigan Botanist* 17:3-15.

Keene, Arthur S.
1979 *Prehistoric Hunter-Gatherers of the Deciduous Forest: A Linear Programming Approach to Late Archaic Subsistence in the Saginaw Valley (Michigan)*. Ph.D. dissertation, University of Michigan.

1981 Optimal Foraging in a Nonmarginal Environment: A Model of Prehistoric Subsistence Strategies in Michigan. Pp. 171-193 in Bruce Winterhalder and Eric Alden Smith, eds., *Hunter-Gatherer Foraging Strategies: Ethnographic and Archaeological Analyses*. Chicago: University of Chicago Press.

Kenyon, Ian T.
1980 The Satchell Complex in Ontario: A Perspective from the Ausable Valley. *Ontario Archaeology* 34:17-43.

Krakker, James J.
1984 Investigation of a Small Late Prehistoric Site in St. Clair County, Michigan. *The Michigan Archaeologist* 30:89-123.

Lee, Richard B.
1976 !Kung Spatial Organization: An Ecological and Historical Perspective. Pp. 73-97 in Richard B. Lee and Irven DeVore, eds., *Kalahari Hunter-Gatherers: Studies of the !Kung San and their Neighbors*. Cambridge, Mass.: Harvard University Press.

Lovis, William A., and James A. Robertson
1989 Rethinking the Archaic Chronology of the Saginaw Valley, Michigan. *Midcontinental Journal of Archaeology* 14:226-260.

Lynott, Mark J., Thomas W. Boutton, James E. Price, and Dwight E. Nelson

1986 Stable Carbon Isotopic Evidence for Maize Agriculture in Southeast Missouri and Northeast Arkansas. *American Antiquity* 51:51-65.

Mauss, Marcel
1967 *The Gift: Forms and Functions of Exchange in Archaic Societies* (Translated by Ian Cunnison). New York: W. W. Norton & Company.

McElrath, Dale L. and Andrew C. Fortier
1983 *The Missouri Pacific #2 Site (11-S-46).* American Bottom Archaeology, FAI-270 Site Reports, Volume 3. Urbana: University of Illinois Press.

Ozker, Doreen
1976 A Descriptive Report of the Surface Collections from Site 20MD28, Chippewa Nature Center, Midland County, Michigan. *The Michigan Archaeologist* 22:1-100.

1977 The Naugle Site, 20MD30, Midland County, Michigan: Early Late Woodland and Late Archaic Components on a Pine River Site. *The Michigan Archaeologist* 22:315-355.

1982 *An Early Woodland Community at the Schultz Site 20SA2 in the Saginaw Valley and the Nature of the Early Woodland Adaptation in the Great Lakes Region.* University of Michigan, Museum of Anthropology, Anthropological Papers, No. 70.

Phillips, James L., and Bruce G. Gladfelter
1983 The Labras Lake Site and the Paleogeographic Setting of the Late Archaic in the American Bottom. Pp. 197-218 in James L. Phillips and James A. Brown, *Archaic Hunters and Gatherers in the American Midwest.* New York: Academic Press.

Ritchie, William A.
1971 *A Typology and Nomenclature for New York Projectile Points* (revised edition). New York State Museum and Science Service Bulletin No. 384.

Ritzenthaler, Robert E., and George I. Quimby
1962 The Red Ocher Culture of the Upper Great Lakes and Adjacent Areas. *Fieldiania: Anthropology* 36/11:243-275.

Robertson, James A.
1989 The Lithic Assemblage of 20SA581: Description and Analysis. Pp. 51-137 in William A. Lovis, editor, *Archaeological Investigations at the Weber I and Weber II Sites, Frankenmuth Township, Saginaw County, Michigan.* Lansing: State of Michigan.

Sahlins, Marshall
1972 *Stone Age Economics.* New York: Aldine Publishing Company.

Salkin, Philip H.
1986 The Lake Farms Phase: The Early Woodland Stage in South-Central Wisconsin as Seen from the Lake Farms Archeological District. Pp. 92-120 in Kenneth B. Farnsworth and Thomas E. Emerson, eds., *Early Woodland Archaeology.* Kampsville: Center for American Archaeology Press.

Service, Elman R.
1962 *Primitive Social Organization: An Evolutionary Perspective.* New York: Random House.

Simons, Donald B.
n.d. Michigan Pomranky Complex Exotic Chert Types and Habitation Sites. Unpublished manuscript.

Smart, Tristine Lee
n.d. Plant Remains from the Conservation

Park and Holiday Park Sites Gratiot County, Michigan. Pp. 265-277 in J. Tracy Luke, ed., *Radiocarbon Dating in Gratiot County - S84-194*. National Register Grant Program, Michigan History Division, Michigan Department of State, Archaeological Survey Completion Report by Alma College. March 1, 1985.

Spence, Michael W., and William A. Fox
1986 The Early Woodland Occupations of Southern Ontario. Pp. 4-46 in Kenneth B. Farnsworth and Thomas E. Emerson, eds., *Early Woodland Archaeology*. Kampsville: Center for American Archeology Press.

Speth, John D.
1972 Geology of the Schultz Site. Pp. 53-75 in James E. Fitting, ed., *The Schultz Site at Green Point: A Stratified Occupation Area in the Saginaw Valley of Michigan*. University of Michigan, Museum of Anthropology, Memoirs No. 4.

Stothers, David M.
1975 Evidence of An Archaic Time Period Habitation Structure in Northwestern Ohio and Inferences about the Settlement System of the Late Archaic - Early Woodland Time Period in Northwestern Ohio, Southeastern Michigan and Southwestern Ontario. *Toledo Area Aboriginal Research Club Bulletin*:1-18.

Stuiver, M. and B. Becker
1986 High Precision Decadal Calibration of the Radiocarbon Time Scale, A.D. 1950-2500 B.C. *Radiocarbon* 28:863-910.

Summerlee, Gregory W.
1981 Proton Magnetometer Surveying and Michigan Archaeology: The Conservation and Pine River Park Site Study. *Michigan Academician* 13:337-348.

Taggart, David W.
1967 Seasonal Patterns in Settlement, Subsistence, and Industries in the Saginaw Late Archaic. *The Michigan Archaeologist* 13:153-170.

Thompson, Harold W.
1982 A Turkey Tail from the Stroebel Site (20SA14). *The Michigan Archaeologist* 28:73-75.

Winters, Howard D.
1969 *The Riverton Culture: A Second Millennium Occupation in the Central Wabash Valley*. Springfield: The Illinois State Museum and the Illinois Archaeological Survey.

Wobst, H. Martin
1968 The Butterfield Site, 20 BY 29, Bay County, Michigan. Pp. 173-275 in James E. Fitting, John R. Halsey, and H. Martin Wobst, *Contributions to Michigan Archaeology*. University of Michigan, Museum of Anthropology, Anthropological Papers, No. 32.

1977 Stylistic Behavior and Information Exchange. Pp. 317-342 in Charles E. Cleland, ed., *For the Director: Research Essays in Honor of James B. Griffin*. University of Michigan, Museum of Anthropology, Anthropological Papers, No. 61.

Wright, Henry T.
1964 A Transitional Archaic Campsite at Green Point (20 SA 1). *The Michigan Archaeologist* 10:17-22.

Wright, Henry T., and Richard E. Morlan
1964 The Hart Site: A Dustin Complex Fishing Camp on the Shiawassee Embayment. *The Michigan Archaeologist* 10:49-53.

UMMA Backlist

Four series of publications are available from the Publications Office of the University of Michigan Museum of Anthropology. The Occasional Contributions, published from 1932 through 1956, and the Anthropological Papers, begun in 1949, are two series of short monographs, while the Memoirs, first published in 1970, are longer, more detailed studies. The fourth series, Technical Reports, begun in 1971, are brief, highly technical discussions of recent advances in several areas of anthropological study. New subseries will be added to the Technical Reports from time to time. Contributions to all of the series are prepared by staff members, associates, and friends of the Museum and include descriptions of museum collections and field work, results of research in various anthropological fields, and discussions of field and museum techniques.

Henry T. Wright, Director
Museum of Anthropology

The books below may be ordered from the Museum of Anthropology, 4009 Museums, University of Michigan, Ann Arbor, MI 48109. Libraries and members of the Michigan Archaeological Society receive a 20% discount. Checks must be in U.S. funds drawn on a U.S. bank. Please include $2 postage for all orders less than $10, $4 postage for orders over $10. Prepayment is required.

Occasional Contributions

6. The Younge Site: An Archaeological Record from Michigan, by Emerson F. Greenman. 1937. Reprinted 1967. Pages 172, 33 plates, 9 figures, 10 maps. Price $3.
15. Araucanian Culture in Transition, by Mischa Titiev. 1951. Pages 164, 17 plates, 9 figures, 2 maps. Price $2.50.

Anthropological Papers

13. The Puerto Rican Population: A Study of Human Biology, by Frederick P. Thieme. 1959. Pages 156, 4 figures, 2 maps. Price $2.50.
14. Tell Toqaan: A Syrian Village, by Louise E. Sweet. 1960. Pages 280, 54 figures. Price $2.50.
39. Rules of Descent: Studies in the Sociology of Parentage, by Guy E. Swanson. 1969. Pages 108. 4 figures, 7 tables. Price $2.
41. The Archaeology of Summer Island: Changing Settlement Systems in Northern Lake Michigan, by David S. Brose. 1970. Pages 236, 31 tables, 17 figures, 35 plates. Price $3.
42. The Occupations of Migrants in Ghana, by Polly Hill. 1970. Pages 84, 11 tables. Price $2.
44. Property Control and Social Strategies: Settlers on a Middle Eastern Plain, by Barbara C. Aswad. 1971. Pages 180, 16 tables, 33 figures, 2 plates. Price $3.50.
48. The Wardell Buffalo Trap 48 SU 301: Communal Procurement in the Upper Green River Basin, Wyoming, by George C. Frison. 1973. Pages 111, 29 figures, 6 tables, 14 plates. Price $3.
50. Faction and Conversion in a Plural Society: Religious Alignments in the Hindu Kush, by Robert Leroy Canfield. 1973. Pages 142, 11 figures, 4 tables, 1 appendix. Pricce $3.
55. The Ait Ndhir of Morocco: A Study of the Social Transformation of a Berber Tribe, by Amal Rassam Vinogradov. 1974. Pages 128, 11 figures, 13 plates. Price $4.
59. An Analysis of Effigy Mound Complexes in Wisconsin, by William M. Hurley. 1975. Pages 466, 63 figures, 48 tables, 45 plates. Price $8.
62. The Demography of the Semai Senoi, by Alan G. Fix. 1977. Pages 123, 17 figures, 38 tables. Price $5.
63. Economic and Social Organization of a Complex Chiefdom: The Halelea District, Kauai, Hawaii, by Timothy Earle. 1978. Pages 205, 27 figure, 7 tables, 6 plates. Price $6.
64. Wāsita in a Lebanese Context: Social Exchange Among Villagers and Outsiders, by Frederick Charles Huxley. 1978. Pages 174, 6 figures, 47 tables, 5 plates. Price $6.
65. Meadowood Phase Settlement Patterns in the Niagara Frontier Region of Western New York State, by Joseph E. Granger, Jr. 1978. Pages 403, 73 figures, 113 tables, 35 plates. Price $8.
66. The Snodgrass Site of the Powers Phase of Southeast Missouri, by James E. Price and James B. Griffin. 1979. Pages 189, 80 figures, 2 tables, 17 plates. Price $6.

67. The Nature and Status of Ethnobotany, edited by Richard I. Ford. 1978. Pages 428, 33 figures, 28 tables, 24 plates. Price $10.
68. The Biological and Social Analyses of a Mississippian Cemetery from Southeast Missouri: The Turner Site, 23BU21A, by Thomas K. Black III. 1979. Pages 170, 7 figures, 69 tables, 10 plates. Price $6.
69. The Ait Ayash of the High Molouuya Plain: Rural Social Organization in Moroco, by John Chiapuris. 1980. Pages 186, 15 figures 9 maps, 12 plates. Price $6.
70. An Early Woodland Community at the Schultz Site 20SA2 in the Saginaw Valley and the Nature of Early Woodland Adaptation in the Great Lakes Region, by Doreen Ozker. 1982. Pages 273, 27 tables, 33 figures, 15 plates. Price $10.
71. Persian Diary, 1939–1941, by Walter N. Koelz. 1983. Pages 227, 2 maps, 68 photos. Price $10.
72. Lulu Linear Punctated: Essays in Honor of George Irving Quimby, edited by Robert C. Dunnell and Donald K. Grayson. 1983. Pages 354, 39 figures, 19 plates, 20 tables. Price $12.
73. Paleoethnobotany of the Kameda Peninsula Jomon, by Gary W. Crawford. 1983. Pages 200, 27 figures, 12 tables, 23 plates. Price 48.
74. The Archaeology of the Sierra Blanca Region of Southeastern New Mexico, by Jane Holden Kelley. 1983. Pages 527, 85 figures, 10 maps, 41 tables, 87 plates. Price $15.
75. Prehistoric Food Production in North America, edited by Richard I. Ford. 1985. Pages 411, 39 figures, 22 tables. Price $15.
76. Primitive Polluters: Semang Impact on the Malaysian Tropical Rain Forest Ecosystem, by A. Terry Rambo. 1985. Pages 104, 5 figures, 5 tables, 16 plates. Price $8.
77. Jumano and Patarabueye: Relations at La Junta de los Rios, by J. Charles Kelley. 1986. Pages 180, 14 figures, 9 plates. Price $10.
78. Protohistoric Yamato: Archaeology of the First Japanese State, by Gina L. Barnes. 1988. Pages 473, 94 figures, 17 tables. Price $15.
79. The Foxie Otter Site: A Multicomponent Occupation North of Lake Huron, by Christopher C. Hanks. 1988. Pages 203, 21 figures, 14 tables. Price $12.
80. Living in a Lean-to: Philippine Negrito Foragers in Transition, by Navin K. Rai. 1990. Pages 184, 4 figures, 10 plates, 12 appendices. Price $12.
81. The Bridgeport Township Site: Archaeological Investigation at 20SA620, Saginaw County, Michigan, edited by John O'Shea and Michael Shott. 1990. Pages 326, 50 figures, 68 tables, 1 appendix. Price $15.00
82. Maguey Utilization in Highland Central Mexico: An Archaeological Ethnography, by Jeffrey R. Parsons and Mary H. Parsons. 1990. Pages 388, 46 figures, 172 plates, 26 tables, appendix. Price $22.
83. Vertebrate Faunal Remains from Grasshopper Pueblo, Arizona, by John W. Olsen. 1990. Pages 200, 17 figures, 6 tables, appendix. Price $15.
84. Debating Oaxaca Archaeology, edited by Joyce Marcus. 1990. Pages 270, 79 illustrations, 11 tables. Price $18.
85. Profiles in Cultural Evolution: Papers from a Conference in Honor of Elman R. Service, edited by A. Terry Rambo and Kathleen Gillogly. 1991. Pages 450, 33 figures, 11 tables. Price $20.

Memoirs

2. The Burial Complexes of the Knight and Norton Mounds in Illinois and Michigan, by James B. Griffin, Richard E. Flanders and Paul F. Titterington. 1970. Pages 216, 177 plates. Price $7.
3. Prehistoric Settlement Patterns in the Texcoco Region, Mexico, by Jeffrey R. Parsons. 1971. Pages 447, 8 tables, 14 maps, 88 figures, 57 plates. Price $8.
4. The Schultz Site at Green Point: A Stratified Occupation Area in the Saginaw Valley of Michigan, edited by James E. Fitting. 1972. Pages 317, 84 figures, 70 tables, 2 appendixes. Price $8.
7. Formative Mesoamerican Exchange Networks with Special Reference to the Valley of Oaxaca, by Jane W. Pires-Ferreira. Prehistory and Human Ecology of the Valley of Oaxaca, Vol. 3. Pages 111, 44 figures, 27 tables, 4 plates. Price $6.
8. Fábrica San José and Middle Formative Society in the Valley of Oaxaca, by Robert D. Drennan. Prehistory and Human Ecology of the Valley of Oaxaca, Vol. 4. 1975. Pages 300, 10 tables, 2 maps, 75 figures, 29 plates. Price $8.
9. Studies in the Archaeological History of the Deh Luran Plain, by Frank Hole. 1977. Pages 369, 94 tables, 119 illustrations, 55 plates. $10.
10. Part 1. The Vegetational History of the Oaxaca Valley, by C. Earle Smith, Jr. Pages 39, 1 table, 2 maps, 10 plates. Part 2. Zapotec Plant Knowledge: Classification, Uses, and Communication About Plants in Mitla,

Oaxaca, Mexico, by Ellen Messer. Pages 149, 29 figures, 1 map, 10 plates. Prehistory and Human Ecology of the Valley of Oaxaca, Vol. 5. 1978. Price $8.

11. An Archaeological Survey of the Keban Reservoir Area of East-Central Turkey, by Robert E. Whallon. 1979. Pages 309, 211 figures, 20 tables, 2 plates. Price $10.
12. Excavations at Santo Domingo Tomaltepec: Evolution of a Formative Community in the Valley of Oaxaca, Mexico, by Michael E. Whalen. Prehistory and Human Ecology of the Valley of Oaxaca, Vol. 6. 1981. Pages 225, 38 tables, 58 figures, 73 plates. Price $13.
13. An Early Town on the Deh Luran Plain: Excavations at Tepe Farukhabad, edited by Henry T. Wright. 1981. Pages 462, 99 figures, 96 tables, 21 plates. Price $15.
14. Prehispanic Settlement Patterns in the Southern Valley of Mexico: The Chalco-Xochimilco Region, by Jeffrey R. Parsons, Elizabeth Brumfiel, Mary H. Parsons, and David J. Wilson. 1982. Pages 504, 128 figures, 115 tables, 40 maps, 31 plates. Price $16.
15. Monte Albán's Hinterland, Part 1: The Prehispanic Settlement Patterns of the Central and Southern Parts of the Valley of Oaxaca, Mexico, by Richard E. Blanton, Stephen Kowalewski, Gary Feinman, and Jill Appel. Prehistory and Human Ecology of the Valley of Oaxaca, Vol. 7. 1982. Pages 506, 43 tables, 139 figures. Price $20.
16. A Fuego y Sangre: Early Zapotec Imperialism in the Cuicatlán Cañada, Oaxaca, by Elsa M. Redmond. Studies in Latin American Ethnohistory & Archaeology, Vol 1. 1983. Pages 216, 75 figures, 46 tables, 42 plates. Price $15.
17. Irrigation and the Cuicatec Ecosystem: A Study of Agriculture and Civilization in North Central Oaxaca, by Joseph W. Hopkins, III. Studies in Latin American Ethnohistory & Archaeology, Vol. 2. 1984. Pages 148, 13 figures, 3 tables, 16 plates. Price $15.
18. Aztec City-States, by Mary G. Hodge. Studies in Latin American Ethnohistory & Archaeology, Vol. 3. 1984. Pages 166, 64 figures, 30 tables. Price $15.
19. Early Neolithic Settlement and Society at Olszanica, by Sarunas Milisauskas. 1986. Pages 319, 160 figures, 153 tables, 51 plates. Price $20.
20. Chipped Stone Tools in Formative Oaxaca, Mexico: Their Procurement, Production and Use, by William J. Parry. Prehistory and Human Ecology of the Valley of Oaxaca, Vol. 8. 1987. Pages 178, 42 tables, 52 figures, 20 plates. Price $18.
21. Conflicts Over Coca Fields in XVIth-Century Perú, by María Rostworowski de Diez Canseco. Studies in Latin American Ethnohistory & Archaeology, Vol. 4. 1988. Pages 314, 21 figures, 2 tables. Price $19.50.
22. Agricultural Intensification and Prehistoric Health in the Valley of Oaxaca, Mexico, by Denise C. Hodges. Prehistory and Human Ecology of the Valley of Oaxaca, Vol. 9. 1989. Pages 146, 6 figures, 42 tables, 4 appendices. Price $16.
23. Monte Albán's Hinterland, Part II: Prehispanic Settlement Patterns in Tlacolula, Etla and Ocotlán, the Valley of Oaxaca, Mexico, by Stephen Kowalewski, Gary Feinman, Laura Finsten, Richard Blanton and Linda Nicholas. 1989. Pages 1146 (in 2 vols.), 141 figures, 116 tables, 8 plates, 9 appendices. Price $40.

Technical Reports

2. LONGTERM and PEAKSCAN: Neutron Activation Analysis Computer Programs, by Thomas Meyers and Mark Denies. Contributions in Computer Applications to Archaeology, No. 2. 1972. Pages 76, 43 pages computer output, 2 figures. Price $1.
3. Data on the Abnormal Hemoglobins and Glucose-6-Phosphate Dehydrogenase Deficiency in Human Populations, by Frank B. Livingstone. Contributions in Human Biology, No. 1. 1973. Pages 289. Price $2.50.
4. An Archaeological Investigation on the Loboi Plain, Baringo District, Kenya, by William R. Farrand, Richard W. Redding, Milford H. Wolpoff, and Henry T. Wright. Research Reports in Archaeology, No. 1. 1976. Pages 59, 10 figures. Price $3.50.
5. Digging for Gold: Papers on Archaeology for Profit, edited by William K. Macdonald. Research Reports in Archaeology, No. 2. 1976. Pages 86. Price $3.50.
6. An Investigation of Ethnographic and Archaeological Specimens of Mescalbeans (*Sophora seconiflora)* in American Museums, by William L. Merrill. Research Reports in Ethnobotany, No. 1. 1977. Pages 167, 3 figures, 3 tables, 25 plates. Price $5.
7. Excavations at Quachilco: A Report on the 1977 Season of the Palo Blanco Project, by Robert D. Drennan. Research Reports in Archaeology, No. 3. Pages 81, 18 figures. Price $4.
10. Archaeological Investigations in Northeastern Xuzestan, 1976, edited by Henry T. Wright. Research Reports in Archaeology, No. 5. 1979. Pages 140, 52 figures, 20 tables. Price $6.

11. Prehistoric Social, Political, and Economic Development in the Area of the Tehuacan Valley: Some Results of the Palo Blanco Project, edited by Robert D. Drennan. Research Reports in Archaeology, No. 6. 1979. Pages 260, 46 figures, 26 tables. Price $6.50.
12. Late Prehistoric Bison Procurement in Southeastern New Mexico: The 1978 Season at the Garnsey Site, by John D. Speth and William J. Parry. Research Reports in Archaeology, No. 7. 1980. Pages 384, 39 figures, 32 tables, 34 plates. Price $9.
14. Archaeological Settlement Pattern Data from the Chalco, Xochimilco, Ixtapalapa, Texcoco and Zumpango Regions, Mexico, by Jeffrey R. Parsons, Keith W. Kintigh, and Susan Gregg. Research Reports in Archaeology, No. 9. Pages 222. Price $8.
15. The Garnsey Spring Campsite: Late Prehistoric Occupation in Southeastern New Mexico, by William J. Parry and John D. Speth. Research Reports in Archaeology, No. 10. Pages 228, 24 figures, 27 tables, 24 photos. Price $8.
16. Regional Archaeology in the Valle de la Plata, Colombia: A Preliminary Report on the 1984 Season of the Proyecto Arqueológico Valle de la Plata, edited by Robert D. Drennan. Research Reports in Archaeology, No. 11. 1985. Pages 195 (including complete Spanish translation), 43 figures, 16 tables. Price $8.
17. Zooarchaeology of Six Prehistoric Sites in the Sierra Blanca Region, New Mexico, by Jonathan C. Driver. Research Reports in Archaeology, No. 12. 1985. Pages 103, 29 tables, 8 figures, 1 appendix. Price $5.
18. The Henderson Site Burials: Glimpses of a Late Prehistoric Population in the Pecos Valley, by Thomas R. Rocek and John D. Speth. Research Reports in Archaeology, No. 13. 1986. Pages 348, 118 figures, 63 tables. Price $13.
19. Medicinal Plants of Native America, by Daniel E. Moerman. 1987. Pages 912 (in 2 vols.). Price $30.
20. Late Intermediate Occupation at Cerro Azul, Peru, by Joyce Marcus. 1987. Pages 112, 70 figures. Price $8.
21. The Inscriptions of Calakmul: Royal Marriage at a Maya City in Campeche, Mexico, by Joyce Marcus. 1987. Pages 205, 65 figures, 7 tables. Price $8.

Special Publications

The Williams Collection of Far Eastern Ceramics, Chinese, Siamese, and Annamese Ceramic Wares Selected from the Collection of Justice and Mrs. G. Mennen Williams in the University of Michigan Museum of Anthropology, by Kamer Aga-Oglu. 1972. Pages 73, 85 black and white photographs. Price $4.

The Williams Collection of Far Eastern Ceramics—Tonnancour Section, by Kamer Aga-Oglu. 1975. Pages 185, 183 black and white photographs, 18 color photographs. Price $8.